D0931474

GROWING OLD IN AMERICA

GROWING OLD IN AMERICA

THE BLAND-LEE LECTURES
DELIVERED AT CLARK UNIVERSITY

BY
DAVID HACKETT FISCHER

NEW YORK
OXFORD UNIVERSITY PRESS
1977

Acknowledgment is made for permission to reprint the following materials:

Excerpt from *Aging in America* by Bert K. Smith. Copyright © 1973 by The Beacon Press.

Lyrics from "Methus'lah Lived . . . What's 900 Years" from *Porgy and Bess* (lyrics: Ira Gershwin). Copyright © 1935 Gershwin Publishing Corporation. Copyright Renewed, assigned to Chappell & Co., Inc. Used by permission.

Excerpts from *The Grapes of Wrath* by John Steinbeck. Copyright © 1939 by The Viking Press, Inc.

FOR MARY AND MILES

FOREWORD

G ROWING OLD is a subject we all know more about every day. In that sense, perhaps, the author may qualify as an expert, but not in any other. This is not a book by a specialist in geriatrics or gerontology. Rather, it is the work of a social historian who was impressed both by the importance of the subject and by the astonishing fact that nearly nothing had been written of its history.

Old age is a topic that has been almost totally ignored by historians. That condition of neglect will not long continue. Old age is likely to become a subject of much interest to the "new" social historians—partly because they are themselves beginning to grow old, but mostly because it lies at the intersection of many major questions, about demography, the family, the life cycle, stratification, welfare, and many other things. The history of old age is related to all of these important subjects.

But at the same time, old age is an important subject in its own right. That is the way in which it will be discussed here. A society may be studied from many different perspectives. From one point of view it is a demographer's "population." From another, it becomes an economy—a web of wealth relations. From a third, it is a polity—a system of power relationships. There are many such perspectives. One of them, which is only beginning to be exploited, shows society to be a system of age relations which embraces everyone according to his chronological condition. This, I think, is the context within which the history of old age may be fruitfully studied.

A system of age relations is something which has a history

—its own special pattern of change through time, which is the business of this book. In the absence of much prior attention to the history of the subject, the first order of business is to establish the main lines of change—its pattern, pace, and timing.

Second, we must confront the problem of source material. One of the major difficulties of the new social history is the location of primary evidence. The major historical records of American society, and most others, have been collected and arranged by scholars who believed that history was primarily the study of past politics. The archives were organized around that idea, and they are slow to surrender their secrets to a social historian. Our task in this inquiry is to locate some of the many pieces of evidence which bear upon the subject.

Our third purpose is to put the pieces together in a coherent way. The subject is complex—so much so that it cannot be reduced to a simple story line. But still it may be organized within a narrative framework which helps to clarify the processes of social change. That framework may also help us to understand something of the intimate relationship between the past and the present. History is not about the past alone. It is about change, with past and present in a mutual perspective. It clarifies the temporal context within which all of us must live, and helps us to understand the conditions of our own existence. That is the most important purpose of all.

Wayland, Mass.   D.H.F.
December 1976

CONTENTS

GROWING OLD IN AMERICA

INTRODUCTION

IN 1975, an American woman was preparing to attend her fifty-fifth college reunion when she discovered to her surprise that she had driven more than 21,000 miles during the previous year. She turned to her daughter and said, "I suppose I should start acting like an old lady."

"Why?" her daughter replied. "You aren't *really* old."

But in fact she was seventy-seven. And her daughter was forty-five—middle-aged according to Webster's Dictionary ("between forty and sixty")—but still young in her own mind.

That sort of confusion is common in our society. We all grow older faster than we think. Old age, when it comes, is apt to take us by surprise. Nothing in life is so inevitable, and yet so unexpected, as the end of it. The seasons of life have a way of changing more swiftly than our sense of them.

At the same time, the experience of aging itself has changed faster than our understanding of it. Growing old in America (and increasingly throughout the world) is an experience profoundly different today from what it was two or three centuries ago. In the seventeenth century, only a small minority of Americans lived long enough even to reach old age. As late as 1790, when the first federal census was taken, less than 20 per cent of the American population survived from birth to the age of seventy. Today, more than 80 per cent can expect to do so. The proportion of elderly people, sixty-five and older, in the population has also changed remarkably—from less than 2 per cent in 1790 to more than 10 per cent in the 1970's. If birth and death rates remain at their present level, then that proportion will continue to rise, to 17 per cent.

Other changes are more difficult to measure, but no less important in their human implications. Two hundred years ago, scarcely anyone "retired" in the full modern sense of the word. Most men worked until they wore out. So also did many women, whose maternal tasks normally continued to the end of life. Today, the majority of men cease working before they are sixty-five, and women commonly see their last child leave home before they are forty-five or fifty. The life cycle has been radically transformed.

These great demographic and economic changes have had a major impact upon our individual lives. But another revolution in cultural values may have been even more profound. Both young and old have greatly changed their attitudes toward one another, and their expectations for themselves as well. The people of early America exalted old age; their descendents have made a cult of youth. In the Constitutional Convention of 1787, Benjamin Franklin had enormous influence, partly because his fellow delegates knew him to be shrewd and wise, but also because he was very old—an octogenarian—and old men were held in high esteem. In the twentieth century, the prevailing attitude is the reverse. In one of the most popular motion pictures of the 1960's—the Beatles' *A Hard Day's Night*—an old man is treated throughout the film with sovereign contempt, punctuated only by occasional expressions of pity. "Poor thing," one Beatle says to another. "He can't help being old." That film was made as recently as 1964, and yet the Beatles themselves have already become faded historical figures. A new set of attitudes toward old age is presently in the making.

These many changes—demographic, economic, social, cultural—are full of difficulty for young and old alike. The circumstances which surround old age in the modern world are totally without precedent in history. They have spawned monumental economic problems which still remain unsolved, despite many serious efforts to deal with them. They have created dangerous new forms of age discrimination. And most dangerous of all, they have caused a great deal of confusion in the way that we think about ourselves, and organize our lives, and exercise our ethical choices in the world.

All of these things have happened because the world has changed faster than our thoughts about it. If we really wish to confront the social problems of aging in our own time, we must begin by understanding them. And if we want to understand them, we must know something of their history. We must know how the experience of growing old and attitudes toward aging have changed through time.

ᵯ᷍

Not everything about the subject has changed, of course. Some things stay the same. One of them is the existence of old age itself, both as an idea and as a social institution. Every human society, without exception, has divided its people into categories according to age. Sometimes those categories remain purely abstract; occasionally they become as formal and rigid as the "age regiments" of black Africa. But always they exist. At least one of them is assigned to old age, and its assignment entails a set of social roles imposed upon the aged. Every society expects its elders to "act their age," in some way or another, but the nature of those expectations has changed remarkably through time. Our historical problem is to find the pattern of change, and its probable cause.

The condition of old age in primitive and prehistoric societies has been described in the writings of both ancient historians and modern anthropologists. Their work, taken altogether, appears at first sight to describe an astonishing diversity. The range of practice seems to have been as broad as the limits of possibility. Herodotus tells us of some tribes who worshipped their elders as gods and of others who ate them. At one extreme were the Issedones, who gilded the heads of their aged parents and offered sacrifices before them.[1] At the other were the people of Bactria, who disposed of their old folk by feeding them to flesh-eating dogs; or the ancient Sardinians, who hurled their elders from a high cliff and shouted with laughter as they fell on the rocks below.[2]

So many different customs have been described that almost any imaginable generalization seems to be true of one tribe and not true of another. But as we study the evidence, a single, consistent pattern slowly emerges from the cloud of contradictory detail—a pattern that fits most prehistoric cultures and the majority of primitive societies visited by modern anthropologists. It might be summarized in five general statements:

First, people of advanced age were very rare. The extreme limit of life was much the same as in the modern world, but few people lived to reach it. We think of a "normal" life as seventy years' long. But most lives in history have been pathetically short—probably less than twenty-five years on the average. Only in the past two hundred years has a life span that is normal in a biological sense also become normal in a statistical sense. An archeologist who has studied age at death in prehistoric skeletons has found that 95 per cent died before they reached the age of forty; 75 per cent

---

[1] Herodotus, iv, 26, 1-9.
[2] Strabo, xi, 11, 8, 3; Aelian, *Varia Historia,* iv, 1.

failed even to reach thirty.[3] That conclusion rests upon a small number of cases—less than a hundred—but it has been impressively confirmed by other investigations. A distinguished scholar who has examined the evidence has concluded that "before the rise of the Mesopotamian and Egyptian civilizations, aging as we now know it simply did not exist."[4]

Second, although only a few reached the age of fifty in those societies, there were always people who were perceived to be old. Maturity and decay came quickly in primitive settings. Among the Igorot a person was thought to be in his prime at twenty-three, "getting old" by thirty, "old" at forty-five, and "superannuated" at fifty. Mongol women were described as decrepit at forty. One anthropologist in South Africa observed that "almost every Bushman presented to me as being exceptionally old proved on investigation to be twenty or thirty years younger than supposed."[5]

[3] The length of life in prehistoric populations has been calculated:

	% Dead by Age		
Population	30	40	50
Neanderthal	80.0	95.0	100.0
Cro-Magnon	61.7	88.2	90.0
Mesolithic	86.3	95.5	97.0

See Sherburne Cook, "Aging of and in Populations," P. S. Timiras (ed.), *Developmental Physiology and Aging* (New York, 1972), p. 595.

[4] In another group of 122 Paleolithic skeletons, none survived to age 60. And still another 187 skeletons contained only 3 who had passed 50. Cook, "Aging of and in Populations." See also Calvin Wells, *Bones, Bodies and Disease* (London, 1964), and Edward Rosset, *Aging Process of Population* (Oxford, 1964).

[5] See Leo Simmons, *The Role of the Aged in Primitive Society* (New Haven, 1945), p. 17. This excellent study summarizes the experience of aging in 71 primitive societies throughout the world. See also Simmons, "Attitudes Toward Aging and the Aged: Primitive Society," *Journal of Gerontology*, I (1946), 72-95.

Has the physiology of aging changed through historical time? I put that question to a leading pathologist, Professor Robert Kohn, author of *Aging* (1973) and *Principles of Mammalian Aging* (1971). He thought not, but was

Third, these "old" people were treated in ways which were invested with the authority of sacred obligation. Customs concerning elders and ancestors were often very different from one society to another, but they were always more than merely a matter of habit or utility. They were moral, even religious, in their nature. Herodotus tells a tale about King Darius of Persia, who asked the Greeks in his court how much money they would take to eat their parents' bodies instead of burning them. The Greeks replied in horror that there was not money enough in all the world to make them do it. Then Darius asked the Callatiae, who ate their dead parents, how much they would take to burn them instead. The Callatiae were as shocked as the Greeks had been, and begged Darius not even to speak of such a thing. Herodotus concluded that "not Darius, but custom was the king of all."

Those customs almost invariably included high respect for elders. There were many differences of degree, of course. Elders had more prestige in some societies than others; and in every society, all elders were not equally prestigious. But respect for age was very common. The leading authority writes: "The most striking fact about respect for old age is its widespread occurrence [in primitive societies]. Some de-

quick to add that very little evidence exists on the subject and that nobody to his knowledge has made an extended effort to answer the question.

Certainly there have been superficial changes. The physical appearance of people in primitive societies could probably fool any number of professional age-guessers. People in what we would call middle age often had wrinkled faces, parchment skin, knotted muscles, and twisted frames, out of all proportion to the appearance of men and women of the same number of years in modern societies. But all of those differences can be explained in ways which would not require us to believe that the physical process of aging has itself changed in a fundamental way. Wrinkled faces, for example, tend to appear early in people who smile and frown a great deal. In an oral culture, facial features become organs of communication. In our own world of literacy and electronics, people remain comparatively wrinkle-free. Parchment skin can be caused by exposure to sunlight, knotted muscles by hard physical labor, and twisted bodies by dietary deficiencies.

gree of prestige for the aged seems to have been practically universal."[6]

Prestige for the aged appeared in many different forms. On ceremonial occasions elders occupied places of high honor. In some societies—the Maya, for example—we are informed that elders had the right to demand absolute obedience. Conversations in large groups were dominated by them, while the rest of the people maintained a respectful silence. Visitors were honored in the order of their age.[7] Similar practices have been observed among the Aztec, the Inca, most of the major North American tribes, the aborigines of Australia, the Ainu of Japan, the major African tribes, and the peoples of Oceania.[8]

But, fourth, there was another stage of life beyond that of "elder." That final period was called by many different names: it was the stage of the "overaged," or the "sleeping period," or the age of the "already dead," or the "age grade of the dying."[9] Those few persons who were so unfortunate as to reach it were sometimes treated with great brutality. Even as most primitive societies honored their elders, many societies (though not all) showed little mercy toward senility or decrepitude. When the old were no longer able to contribute to the common welfare, and no longer able to look after themselves, they were often destroyed. A minority of

[6] Simmons, *Role of the Aged*, p. 79.

[7] J. E. S. Thompson, *The Rise and Fall of Maya Civilization* (Norman, Okla., 1967), p. 135.

[8] In some primitive societies the privileges of eldership belonged only to males, but in others older women fully shared the honor, authority, and perquisites of age. It is perhaps significant that in prehistoric Danish burial mounds described by P. V. Glob the most richly furnished remains were those of a middle-aged man and an "old woman" in her fifties. Those of young adults were less ornate. It would be interesting to know if that pattern is general in prehistoric archaeology. See P. V. Glob, *Hojfolket: Bronzealderens Minnesker bevaret i 3000 AR.* (Copenhagen, 1970).

[9] Ethel Shanas et al., *Old People in Three Industrial Societies* (New York, 1968), p. 4.

primitive tribes killed their aged members outright, sometimes in horrible ways, and with the active collaboration
of the victim. The people of Samoa, for example, buried
their elders alive, and the victim even helped to organize
the elaborate ceremony. Those bizarre rites were uncom-
mon; more typical were tribes which disposed of the aged
by abandonment or deliberate neglect. Some encouraged
suicide among the aged; in eleven of seventeen tribes for
which evidence is available, suicide was a "frequent" or
"customary" practice in the last stage of life. In any case,
senecide was widely practiced.[10]

In short, the plurality of age customs in primitive and
prehistoric societies fits a single pattern. It was normal for
a tribe to show great respect for elders until they had outlived their social usefulness, then to slay them in some
bloody ritual, and finally to convert the mangled corpse
into a sort of shrine. The functional role of those customs
is clear. A primitive tribe had no way of transmitting the
wisdom of experience from one generation to the next except through the memory of its oldest members. As long as
an elder was able to contribute to his society in that way, his
contributions were important and even vital to its success.
Authority was given to the aged because only they could
transmit knowledge from one generation to another. But
in a society which lived close to the edge of subsistence, old
people who had outlived their usefulness became a heavy
burden. Worse, senility was deeply threatening to a society
which was so dependent upon the wisdom of its elders. Its
immediate destruction became a cultural imperative.[11]

[10] Senecide received much scholarly attention in Germany after 1933. See
John Koty, *Die Behandlung der Alten und Kranken bei den Naturvolken*
(Stuttgart, 1934); also Fritz Paudler, "Alten- und Krankentötung als Sitte bei
in dogermanischen Völkern," *Worter und Sachen,* 17 (1936), 1-57.

[11] This is to dissent from the conventional wisdom of cultural anthropology
in an important matter. Simmons argues that elders were more likely to be

With the development of more advanced forms of civilization, the condition of old age was transformed in many ways at once. In China and India, Mesopotamia and the Mediterranean, the length of life rose far above its prehistoric limits. In the late Roman Empire, about a fifth of the population survived to the age of fifty-five. The other great ancient civilizations were probably similar. Still, life was very short by modern standards; four-fifths perished before reaching what we call middle age. But the aging process as we know it may be said to have begun.[12] So also did our chronological

---

cared for in societies with the strongest collectivist traditions. In one sense that is certainly true; it is impossible for a person to be cared for in a society which does not have some sense of collective responsibility. But philanthropy for individuals cannot exist without some sense of individuation, which did not flourish in primitive environments. The brutality with which primitive tribes so often treated their members was partly a consequence of their collectivism.

[12] Survival in the late Roman Empire has been estimated as follows:

| Population | % Population dead by age | | | | |
	30	40	50	60	70
Asia, Greece	61.1	66.0	70.5	77.3	79.2
Cisalpine Gaul	70.0	73.5	77.6	81.6	84.2
Rome (males)	65.8	70.7	75.6	80.2	82.9
Italy	62.9	67.1	71.7	78.2	82.3

Calculated from data in Cook, "Primitive and Ancient Populations," p. 599, and J. C. Russell, "Late Ancient and Medieval Populations," *Trans. Am. Phil. Soc.*, 48 (1958), 1-152.
    Those estimates were obtained by a method roughly comparable to the best available evidence for prehistoric populations. More recent scholarship suggests that life was shorter in the city of Rome itself, but nearly the same in healthier parts of the Empire. In any case, the main point remains. K. Hopkins, "On the Probable Age Structure of the Roman Population," *Population Studies,* 20 (1966), 245-64; see also A. R. Burn, "Hic Breve Vivetur," *Past and Present,* 4 (1953), 2-15; A. Mocsy, "Die Unkenntnis des Lebensalters in Römischen Reich," *Acta Antiqua Academiae Scientiarum Hungariae,* 14 (1966), 387-421; M. Clauss, "Probleme der Lebensalterstatiken auf Grund romischer Grabinschriften," *Chiron,* 3 (1973), 395-417.

conception of old age, which Greeks and Romans commonly defined as life after the age of sixty. Sometimes it was said to begin in the fifties, occasionally at seventy. But from the great classical cultures to our own time, the definition of old age in terms of a number of years has remained more or less the same.[13]

The cause of those innovations was at once material and spiritual. A higher level of economic organization produced a more abundant supply of life's necessities—of food, shelter, and security. At the same time, social ethics changed, perhaps in part as a consequence of the development of literacy. The invention of writing meant that a society was no longer solely dependent upon the memory of its elders for the transmission of its culture. As a result, senility was no longer dangerous to society. The deliberate destruction of the aged was not sanctioned by any major ancient civilization. Infanticide was widely practiced, but senecide was generally condemned.[14] The Romans even established a system of old age homes for the elderly—the *gerocomeia* of the eastern Empire. The first of them in Constantinople, is said to have been founded by Helen, mother of Constantine the Great. They appeared throughout the Mediterranean, were sustained by private gifts, and were encouraged by both the

---

[13] This point requires emphasis, all the more because historians have made much of the "discovery" of childhood and adolescence in the modern world. There was no comparable "discovery" of old age, at least not more recently than 44 B.C., when Cicero composed his *Cato Maior*. Nor is it correct (as I had first thought) to draw an historical distinction between a traditional world in which old age was conceived as part of a "continuum" and a modern world in which it is thought of as a "stage of life," or between "existential" and "chronological" conceptions of aging. The Ciceronian conception of old age was in those respects much the same as that of the 20th century—a stage within a life continuum, an existential phenomenon with chronological boundaries.

[14] That was not the case in the prehistoric societies from whence the great civilizations arose. When the ancient Romans were still a primitive tribe they probably disposed of their decrepit elders by drowning them in the Tiber. Thus the expression *sexagenarius de ponte*.

Church and the Emperor, who made it a custom to visit all the *gerocomeia* in Constantinople on Holy Thursday or Good Friday.[15]

Only a small minority of the population benefited from those institutions. For the poor—for the vast and wretched majority of every ancient civilization—nothing had changed but the name of their misfortune. For the slaves and servants of Athens and Rome, old age was probably so cruel that an early death was a kind of blessing. But for the elites of the great civilizations, old age acquired the protection of power and property. And it was primarily for the elites that ethical structures of those societies were invented and institutionalized.

Age was power in ancient polities, which were ruled by councils of elders who took the nature of their authority from the number of their years. The actual age of those "elders" was younger than that of modern leaders, because life was so much shorter. But it was sufficient to sustain a sense of eldership, in a relative sense. So important were old men in the government of Rome that Cicero could argue that they were indispensable to its operation. "If there were no old men," he wrote, "there would be no civilized states at all."[16] The Roman Senate (from *senex,* aged) and the Spartan *Gerusia* (from *gera,* old) were only two of many institutions in which elders governed by virtue of their age.

The family was also organized as a gerontocracy, in which the eldest male's authority was nearly absolute. He could put his children to death, if he wished. The classic model of a Roman patriarch was Appius, who, "though he was both old and blind, governed four sturdy sons, five daughters, a great household, and many dependents." According to Cic-

15 D. J. Constantelos, *Byzantine Philanthropy and Social Welfare* (New Brunswick, N.J., 1968), Chap. 13, pp. 222-40.

16 "Mens enim et ratio et consilium in senibus est, qui si nulli fuissent, nullae omnio civitates fuissent." *De Senectute,* xix, 67.

ero, "he did not languidly succumb to old age, but kept his mind ever taut, like a well-strung bow. Over his household he maintained not mere authority, but absolute command. His slaves feared him, his children revered him, everyone loved him, and the customs and discipline of his ancestors flourished beneath his roof."[17] In Confucian China, age groups were also arranged in a hierarchy. At the bottom were the very young, called *tao,* a word which also meant "pitiful." The younger son was expected to obey his older brother; both owed strict obedience to their father; and all of the family together owed that same obedience to the eldest male, from whom there was no appeal.[18]

Most ancient civilizations were more or less the same in that respect. Cicero observed that "old age is honored only on condition that it defends itself, maintains its rights, is subservient to no one, and to the last breath rules over its own domain." But honored it was. So much so that he

[17] *De Senectute,* xi, 37-38.

[18] The extreme to which age deference was carried in ancient China appears in the horrors which were visited upon its transgressors: "A Chinese aided by his wife flogged his mother. The imperial order not only commanded that the criminals should be put to death; it further directed that the head of the clan should be put to death, that the immediate neighbors each receive eighty blows and be sent into exile; that the head or representatives of the graduates of the first degree (or B.A.) among whom the male offender ranked should be flogged and exiled; that the granduncle, the uncle, and two elder brothers should be put to death; that the prefect and rulers should for a time be deprived of their rank; that on the face of the mother of the female offender four Chinese characters expressive of neglect of duty should be tattooed, and that she be exiled to a distant province; that the father of the female offender, a bachelor of arts, should not be allowed to take any higher literary degrees, and that he be flogged and exiled; that the son of the offenders should receive another name, and that the lands of the offenders for a time remain fallow." J. Dewey and J. H. Tufts, *Ethics* (New York, 1913), pp. 17-18. See also C. K. Yang, "The Crumbling of the Age Hierarchy," in Yang, *The Chinese Family in the Communist Revolution* (Cambridge, Mass., 1959), pp. 86-104; Han-yi Feng, "The Chinese Kinship System," *Harvard Journal of Asiatic Studies,* II (1937), 141-275; Marion J. Levy, *The Family Revolution in Modern China* (Cambridge, Mass., 1949); Albert Chandler, "The Traditional Chinese Attitude Towards Old Age," *Journal of Gerontology,* IV (1949), 239-47.

could argue that "The crowning glory of old age" was "its power, authority, and influence ("auctoritas")."[19] The classical literature of Greece is full of the same spirit. Elders were to be treated with deference and deep respect. Seniority was honored even among the gods. When they came together in Lucian's convention they were made to speak in order of their age. The great Homeric heroes distinguished themselves not merely by their valor, but also by their deference to elders.[20] In the public councils of Athens, Sparta, and Rome men spoke in order of age. In the College of Augurs, Cicero wrote, "each has precedence in debate according to his age, and the oldest is preferred, not only to those of higher official rank, but even to those having imperium."[21]

Where respect for age was not freely given, it was made compulsory. The young remained dependent upon the old in custom and in law long after the old had become dependent upon the young in every other way. Occasionally we learn of intense struggles over the control of property between the generations in Greece and Rome. Cicero tells a story about Sophocles, who kept writing plays in his old age with such dedication that he was thought to be neglecting his property. His sons brought suit against him, seeking to take over the family estate on the ground that their father's behavior showed imbecility. Sophocles responded by reading to the jury *Oedipus at Colonus,* the play he had just written, and when he finished he asked, "Does that poem seem to you to be the work of an imbecile?" He won his case.[22]

19 *De Senectute,* xi, 37-38; xvii, 61.
20 Bessie Richardson, *Old Age Among the Ancient Greeks* (Baltimore, 1933), Chap. 4: Louis J. Berelson, "Old Age in Ancient Rome," unpubl. Ph.D. thesis, Univ. of Virginia, 1934. Similar attitudes existed in ancient Israel; see L. Löw, *Des Lebensalters in der Jüdischen Literatur* (1875).
21 *De Senectute,* xviii, 64-65.
22 *De Senectute,* vii, 21-23.

The existence of generational conflict explains how it could have happened that ancient societies were so often organized upon the principle of respect for age while at the same time their literature was filled with intense and bitter satire against the aged. The comic art of Aristophanes and Plautus contains much biting satire aimed at old men, who appear not merely as amiable incompetents, but vicious tyrants.[23] The vices of age were the vices of power—the greed and covetousness of economic power, the bullying and hectoring of political power, the lust and lechery of sexual power, the arrogance of social power. Satire is rarely used against the weak; its power is drawn from the eminence of its object.[24]

The tension between the generations may also help to explain why the ethics of many ancient societies encouraged the elderly to lay down their authority in their final years. In ancient India, the highest stage of life was the last—the stage of *vanaprastha,* or forest hermit. When a man had survived to see the sons of his sons and his hair had turned white, it was time to leave his property and move to a hut in the forest where he could perform his religious rites and read the Upanishads. He was instructed to increase his physical hardships by self-mortification, so that he would be prepared for a higher and even more ascetic stage. And in time he would leave even the small comfort of his forest

[23] See Victor Ehrenberg, *The People of Aristophanes: The Sociology of Old Attic Comedy* (Cambridge, Mass., 1951).

[24] A slightly different note was struck by Horace in his *Ars Poetica* (169-74), which might be freely translated:

> Many are the miseries of an old man
> Who seeks a fortune and fears to use it,
> Who seeks the future and fears to lose it,
> Who lacks courage, spirit, fire.
> He is slow, inert, quarrelsome, querulous,
> He celebrates the days of his youth
> And condemns the youth of others.

shelter and take up the life of a wandering beggar, dressing in rags, living upon alms, and cultivating an attitude of ascetic detachment from everything, with no worldly possessions but his staff and his begging bowl.[25]

A similar attitude existed in China, where Taoism taught that old age was a virtue in itself, for it promised to take a man out of the confining shell of his own sensuality, to set him free from the material prison of his own possessions, and to promote him to the rank of a living spirit. The Stoic and Epicurean ethics of the Mediterranean world were also much the same. The advice which Epicurus had for the aged may be summarized in his single famous phrase, "Live unknown."

Those cultural attitudes, which were remarkably similar in all of the great ancient civilizations, also appeared in medieval Europe. The experience of old age might have been a little different, but life expectancy did not increase in the Middle Ages, and may even have fallen a little. Not until the eighteenth century was length of life in the West significantly greater than it had been in the late Roman Empire. The result was a world in which people were very young on the average, and yet one in which they aged very quickly. Marc Bloch, in his discussion of health in that period, wrote that "old age seemed to begin very early, as early as mature adult life with us. This world which . . . considered itself very old, was in fact governed by young men."[26]

So it was, and yet those young men governed by the authority of age. The idea of eldership was incorporated into the affairs of both Church and State. The Christian Church began as a commune of the young; it became a gerontocracy of "popes" (from the Greek word for father) and "presby-

[25] A. L. Basham, *The Wonder That Was India* (London, 1954), p. 177; see also Rudyard Kipling, "The Miracle of Purun Bhagat," in *The Second Jungle Book* (Garden City, N.Y., 1921).

[26] Bloch, *Feudal Society* (2 vols., Chicago, 1964), I, pp. 72-73.

ters" (from the Greek for elder). The towns were run by "aldermen" (from the Middle English *eald,* old), the countryside by feudal *seigneurs* (from the Old French word for seniority). Dante celebrated a world in which "every house was ruled by its eldest member, on the sole authority of his age."[27] The ideal of family government in medieval Europe was not very different from that of ancient Rome. Age—among the elite—brought power and authority.

But again we find the same expressions of resentment against the elderly.[28] Medieval literature is filled with the satirical themes that had appeared in Greek and Roman comedy—the powerful but absurd cuckolds of Boccaccio and Chaucer,[29] the hideous old men of Villon, the senile fools of the *commedia dell'arte.*[30] And once again, we find that old age was honored only among the elite. Attitudes toward the elderly poor were no different from those of ancient civilizations.[31]

In short, medieval writing on old age was full of the same ambivalence which appeared in ancient writings. In the thirteenth century, that ambivalent spirit was nicely cap-

[27] It is interesting to observe the disparity in age between husbands and wives in early modern Europe. In 15th-century Florence husbands were on the average 13 years older than their wives. In only 1 per cent of marriages were both the same age, and in many the difference in age between husband and wife equaled that between mother and child. It was not merely a matter of demographic circumstances; a differential of roughly that size was recommended by moralists. David Herlihy, "Vieillir à Florence au Quattrocento," *Annales,* 27 (1969), 1341-42.

[28] The strong continuity in poetical ideas about old age from the 1st century B.C. to the 14th century A.D. is the thesis of George R. Coffman, "Old Age from Horace to Chaucer; Some Literary Affinities and Adventures of an Idea," *Speculum,* IX (1934), 249-77.

[29] Maria S. Haynes, "The Concept of Old Age in the Late Middle Ages with Special Reference to Chaucer," unpubl. Ph.D. thesis, U.C.L.A., 1956.

[30] Another popular expression of hostility toward old age were Italian carnival songs of the Renaissance. See Charles S. Singleton (ed.), *Canti Carnascialeschi del Rinascimento* (Bari, 1936).

[31] Robert S. Haller, "The Old Whore and Medieval Thought," unpubl. Ph.D. thesis (literature), Princeton, 1960.

tured in an oxymoron by a Dominican friar, Vincent of Beauvais—"What is old age? A desirable evil, a living death, a strong weakness."[32]

♫♫ ♫♫

In the modern era, the history of old age becomes obscure—partly because of the lack of perspective upon the subject, but mostly because of the absence of sustained attention to it. Careful studies were published many years ago on old age in primitive society and in the ancient world. But at the date of this writing, no modern history of old age has been published in any western language. The subject has suffered almost total neglect at the hands of historians.

It is an astonishing omission—and one which cannot long continue. Historians today are painfully aware that for generations history was something which happened primarily to prosperous males in the middle years of life. Scholars who have recently "discovered" the history of childhood and adolescence must soon discover the history of old age as well. But it has not happened yet. Old age is a subject on which the second sight of history is not merely blurred, but blind.

Other academic disciplines have been more attentive to the question. During the past generation, a large and lively literature on aging has been produced by all the major social sciences.[33] At the same time, two dynamic new disci-

[32] "Quid est senectus? Optatum malum, mors viventium, incolumnis langour." Coffman, "Old Age from Horace to Chaucer," p. 260.

[33] On the politics of old age, see F. R. Eisele (ed.), "Political Consequences of Aging," *Annals of the American Academy of Political and Social Science,* special issue, 415 (1974). As to demography, Henry D. Sheldon, *The Older Population of the United States* (New York, 1958), has been followed by much recent work. There is also a very large literature on the economics of old age; e.g. see Michael Brennan *et al., The Economics of Age* (New York, 1967). For the sociology of old age, see Zena Blau, *Old Age in a*

plines called geriatrics and gerontology have been invented
to study the subject in a central way. Commercial publishers have also issued a large polemical literature, of which
the best is surely Simone de Beauvoir's *La Veillesse,* an
enormous encyclopaedia on the subject of old age, and a
learned, graceful, and intelligent work.[34]

Most of those writings are heavily present-minded. Their
subject is old age today; their aim is its improvement in the
future. With the sole exception of Simone de Beauvoir, its
authors are not much interested in its history. But it is impossible to discuss old age in the present without describing
its past. And in those descriptions, there is a body of beliefs,
often implicit, which comprises a coherent idea of the modern history of old age. The details are apt to differ from one
work to another: the ideological framework may be Marxian, Freudian, or Jeffersonian. But the main lines of the
story are more or less the same. They run as follows.

Nearly to our own time, the story goes, western society
remained nonliterate in its culture, agrarian in its economy,
extended in its family structure, and rural in its residence.
The old were few in number, but their authority was very
great. Within the extended family the aged monopolized
power; within an agrarian economy they controlled the
land. A traditional culture surrounded them with an almost magical mystique of knowledge and authority.

But since 1900 (or 1850) a revolutionary process called
"modernization" shattered this "traditional" society, and
transformed the status of the aged in four ways at once.
First, the development of "modern health technology" multiplied the numbers of the elderly, and contributed to "the

---

Changing Society (New York, 1973); J. Tunstall, *Old and Alone: A Sociological Study of Old Age* (London, 1966); and Ethel Shanas *et al., Old
People in Three Industrial Societies* (New York, 1968).

[34] Published in English as *The Coming of Age* (New York, 1972).

aging of the population and its work force." That situation, in turn, "created pressures toward retirement, forced people out of the most valued and highly regarded roles, deprived them of utility, curtailed their income, and lowered their status." Second, "modern economic technology" "created new occupations and transformed most of the old ones," which also meant loss of jobs, incomes, and status by the aged. Third, urbanization attracted the young to the cities, "thus breaking down the extended family in favor of the nuclear conjugal unit." Finally, the growth of mass education and literacy meant that "there can be no mystique of age" and no reverence for the aged on account of their superiority of knowledge and wisdom.

That summary is drawn from a single work, written by Professor Donald Cowgill. The literature of social science is filled with many similar interpretations.[35] The dating of the modernization process is imprecise in much of the lit-

[35] Cowgill, "The Aging of Populations and Societies," *Annals of the American Academy of Political and Social Science*, 415 (1974), 1-18; see also Cowgill and L. D. Holmes, *Aging and Modernization* (New York, 1972).

In much the same way, Ernest Burgess argued for "the similarity of gross changes in family relationships in all countries, according to their stages of industrialization and urbanization. In Europe, Great Britain and Sweden seem to be farthest along this course, with the United States the most advanced in the world." E. W. Burgess (ed.), *Aging in Western Societies* (Chicago, 1960); and Burgess, "The Transition from Extended Families to Nuclear Families," in R. H. Williams *et al.* (eds.), *The Process of Aging; Social and Psychological Perspectives* (2 vols., New York, 1963), II, 277-82. See also W. W. Rostow, *The Stages of Economic Growth* (Cambridge, Mass., 1960); and Daniel Lerner, *The Passing of Traditional Society* (New York, 1958), p. viii.

"Modernization" is increasingly understood in another way: scholars have begun to define it as a psychological and social phenomenon and to separate it from industrialization and urbanization. See Richard D. Brown, *Modernization, The Transformation of American Life* (New York, 1976); Robert Wells, "Family History and Demographic Transition," *Journal of Social History* (Sept. 1975); and E. A. Wrigley, "The Process of Modernization and the Industrial Revolution in England," *Journal of Interdisciplinary History*, III (1972), 225-29. These scholars are moderate revisionists. Others have made radical and sweeping attacks on the idea; see esp. Christopher Lasch, "The Family and History," *New York Review of Books*, Nov. 13, 1975.

erature. Professor Cowgill locates the change in America within "the last 120 years"—between 1850 and 1970. More often, modernization is regarded as a phenomenon of the twentieth century.[36]

Some social scientists stress one part of the process more than another. Those trained in Parsonian sociology, for instance, stress the changes in family structure, as did Talcott Parsons himself, who wrote that "By comparison with other societies the United States assumes an extreme position in the isolation of old age from participation in the most important social structures and interests. Structurally speaking there seem to be two primary bases of this situation. In the first place, the most important single distinctive feature of our family structure is the isolation of the individual conjugal family. . . . The second basis of the situation lies in the occupational structure."[37]

Others, principally economists, prefer to stress the importance of occupational change, the increasing numbers of the elderly, the shift from agriculture to industrial employment, technological developments, and the growth of retirement systems.[38] But all of those differences are variations

[36] Cowgill, *Aging of Populations*, p. 2; another scholar writes: "In 1900, in an era still agricultural, the aged were generally persons of considerable power in the family because they controlled property and occupations, and they were greatly respected for their knowledge and ability. Since then, with the growth of our industrial society, property and jobs have moved away from family control." N. F. Nimkoff, "Changing Family Relationships of Older People in the United States during the Past Fifty Years," in Clark Tibbetts and Wilma Donahue (eds.), *Social and Psychological Aspects of Aging* (New York, 1962), pp. 405-14. The economists date the change from the period 1890-1900; see Brennan *et al.*, *Economics of Age*, pp. 17-20.

[37] Talcott Parsons, "Age and Sex in the Social Structure," *American Sociological Review*, VII (1942), 604-16; see also Parsons, *Essays in Sociological Theory* (New York, 1949), p. 231.

[38] See, generally, Brennan *et al.*, "The Aging Problem in Historical Perspective," *Economics of Age*, Chap. II. Another disagreement concerns the linearity of the relationship between modernization and the status of the aged. The mass of the literature suggests that the more modern a society becomes, the more isolated are the aged. But the most recent writing also

upon a single theme. In studies of aging, as in the social sciences generally, the idea of modernization dominates the subject. A rising chorus of criticism is heard today, but even so, modernization has become an academic orthodoxy.

It is an historian's task to test the truth of those beliefs. We shall ask if the idea of modernization accurately fits the recent history of old age. At the outset we find there are several reasons for thinking that it does not. Recent work on the history of the family has called into question one of its major components, for it has been shown that most families in western Europe and America were nuclear long before urbanization and industrialization took place—a highly subversive fact for the modernization theory in its usual form. As Ethel Shanas has written, "Really good information on the family life of older people in the past is lacking. What information is available does not, in general, support the theories that suggest that old people in the family have been isolated as a result of industrialization."[39]

Still another reason to suspect the accuracy of the modernization model may be found in the history of Japan. In

---

suggests another model, with a reversal in the tendency coming with the most highly modernized nations. See e.g. E. B. Palmore and Kenneth Manton, "Modernization and the Status of the Aged: International Correlations," *Journal of Gerontology,* 29 (1974), 205-10.

Still another concerns the difference that modernization has actually made in the status of the aged. "Activity theorists" hold that a healthy old age requires a high level of physical, social and cerebral activity. They believe that people naturally wish to be active, but that the changes wrought by modernization have imposed an unnatural retirement from work and separation from community functions, and that the results have been alienation, apathy, and anomie. On the other side, "disengagement theorists" hold that normal aging is a process of natural withdrawal or "disengagement" or "desocialization." An enormous literature exists upon this question. Two good starting points are Robert Kastenbaum (ed.), *Contributions to the Psychobiology of Aging* (New York, 1965); and M. Elaine Cumming and William E. Henry, *Growing Old: The Process of Disengagement* (New York, 1961). An increasing number of gerontologists have expressed dissatisfaction with both these ideas; see Shanas *et al., Old People in Three Industrial Societies.*

[39] Shanas *et al., Old People,* p. 4.

that society, which industrialized more rapidly than any other in the world, the status of old men and women has remained very high. The ancient principle of *oya-kōko*, filial piety, still finds expression in many social customs—in the "silver seats" which are specially reserved for elderly railroad passengers; in the custom of celebrating the sixty-first birthday, much as the twenty-first is observed in America; in the domestic ceremonies, which make a ritual of respect for age; in the tendency of the elderly not to disguise their age with cosmetics and clothing, but actually to emphasize it.[40] The modern history of Japan demonstrates that industrialization does not necessarily drive down the status of the aged.

Still another cautionary hint appears in a recent attempt to establish a statistical correlation between "modernization"—defined in terms of national income, shifts out of agriculture, and levels of education—and the "status of the aged"—specified as the amount of economic and educational inequality between people over and under sixty-five. The attempt was unsuccessful.[41]

---

[40] Erdman Palmore, *The Honorable Elders: A Cross-Cultural Analysis of Aging in Japan* (Durham, N.C., 1975), pp. 21-25, 192, *passim*. Palmore concludes that "the theory of marked decline in the status of the aged as a necessary result of industrialization is false." See also R. Smith, "Japan, the Later Years of Life and the Concept of Time," in R. Kleemeier (ed.), *Aging and Leisure: A Research Perspective into the Meaningful Use of Time* (New York, 1961), pp. 95-99.

[41] Palmore and Manton, "Modernization and Status of the Aged." The authors claim the opposite—that high coefficients of correlation exist between "modernization" and the "status of the aged." But on close inspection we find that they omitted deviant cases which would have lowered the correlation substantially. Even so, strong correlations appeared in only 5 cases out of 18. The 13 tests that failed were dismissed as irrelevant. And the only strong correlations are largely tautological. They show that societies where educational levels have risen recently are also societies where educational inequality between age groups is highest—which merely "proves" that where education has improved, education has improved. All red wagons are red. They obtain an inverse correlation of .91 between the percentage of the population in farm work and the percentage of unemployment among the

In short, when we approach the history of old age in the modern world, we discover that the conventional interpretation is doubtful at best. But if it is mistaken in its usual form, we have nothing with which to replace it. The subject is enormous, and since we lack secondary materials, it must be studied almost entirely through primary sources. And those sources were originally arranged and indexed by archivists whose minds were on other things. Given such difficulties, one historian can only hope to study the modern history of old age in a single society. Here we shall examine the American history of old age—as a clue to the larger configurations of the subject.

---

elderly. But the only employment easily measured throughout the world is nonagricultural in nature. The result is another tautology. All red wagons are wagons.

Two findings are not tautological. The authors successfully correlate both literacy and mass education with retirement—but here they omit from their calculations two nations which lie more than 4 standard deviations away from the pattern they had hoped to find. We may establish many "laws" of social science if our rules of inference allow us to throw out the major exceptions! But this is to establish a double standard for our evidence: one for confirmation; another for contradiction.

I. THE EXALTATION OF AGE
IN EARLY AMERICA
1607-1820

*One is sometimes ready to wish that the aged who
have the most wisdom and experience, had most
strength; but while we have old heads to contrive and
advise, and young hands to work, it comes to much
the same. Besides, had the aged the strength of youth
they would be more ready to despise the young than
they now are.*

Job Orton (1717-83)

WE often imagine that our ancestors were older than
ourselves, for so they are whenever we actually meet
them. We know the past through its survivors, and easily
forget the flight of time. An example of this curious habit
of thought appears in the writings of Oliver Wendell
Holmes, Jr.: "When I went to the [Civil] War," he wrote, "I
thought that soldiers were old men. I remembered a picture
of the revolutionary soldier which some of you may have
seen, representing a white-haired man with his flint-lock
slung across his back. I remembered one or two living examples of revolutionary soldiers whom I had met, and I
took no account of the lapse of time."[1]

That common illusion is, of course, mistaken. Two hundred years ago the population of America was actually
younger than it is today. The median age of Americans in

[1] Oliver Wendell Holmes, Jr., *Speeches* (Boston, 1934), p. 61.

26

1976 was nearly thirty. In 1790 it was barely sixteen. Sixteen! Half the population was below that age. Few people were very old; less than 2 per cent were sixty-five or older, compared with 10 per cent today.[2] That distribution of ages changed scarcely at all during the first two hundred years of American history. From 1625 to 1810, the median age was much the same whenever it was measured, and the relative proportion of the elderly also remained remarkably stable.[3]

The astonishing youthfulness of the American popula-

[2] See Appendix. In New England "old age" was defined in chronological terms, starting at about 60. Cotton Mather wrote of a friend who had crossed the "borders . . . of old age" by the "out-living of three-score winters." *The Old Man's Honour* (Boston, 1691), p. 2. Compulsory military service ended at 60; many census tracts in early America used that age to subdivide the male population. For a more extended discussion see John Demos, "Aging in Pre-Modern Society: The Case of Early New England" (unpubl., 1975). In the southern colonies, on the other hand, old age may have been understood a little differently. Certainly, men and women aged more quickly in the Carolinas, where it was said that there "are few old men or women to be found in the province . . . we cannot say that there are many in the country who arrive at their sixtieth year, and several at thirty bear the wrinkles, bald head and grey hairs of old age." Alexander Hewatt, *An Historical Account of the Rise and Progress of the Colonies of South Carolina and Georgia* (2 vols., London, 1779), II, p. 294.

[3] There were many local variations. The median age was higher in the East than the West. Few elderly people were to be found on the frontiers, and were explicitly warned away. "I am not sure that English elderly people would do right to pass the mountains," one traveler wrote. "For young men, everybody agrees that the western territory will be best to settle in. But, alas, it is another world." Elias P. Fordham, *Personal Narrative of Travels in Virginia . . .* (Cleveland, 1906), pp. 152-53. A 1773 New Hampshire census shows these percentages of men aged 60 plus.

County	%
Rockingham	5.5
Strafford	4.1
Hillsborough	3.0
Cheshire	2.5
Grafton	2.0

Rockingham, on the coast, was first to be filled up; Cheshire and Grafton were the last. A similar pattern appears in all other colonies for which we have evidence. See Robert V. Wells, *The Population of the British Colonies in North America before 1776* (Princeton, 1975), p. 72.

tion was caused more by high fertility than by high mortality. The families of early America produced great swarms of children; the median age was low primarily on that account.[4] But high mortality also had an important effect. Two hundred years ago the length of human life in America was only a third of what it is today. In the Chesapeake colonies during the seventeenth century life expectancy at birth was below twenty—for both black slaves and their white masters. New England was much healthier. But even in Massachusetts, where life expectancy was highest, it was only about thirty. Few seventeenth-century Americans survived to an advanced age. As late as 1726 Cotton Mather guessed that "scarce three in a hundred live to three-score and ten."[5] The evidence of modern historical demography suggests that he was not far off the mark. In Charles County, Maryland, during the seventeenth century only 3.6 per cent of white male children survived from birth to the age of seventy.[6] Life chances were much better in New England, where perhaps 20 per cent reached Mather's biblical span. But even there mortality was much greater than it is today.[7]

---

[4] Ansley J. Coale, "The Effects of Changes in Mortality and Fertility on Age Composition," *Milbank Memorial Fund Quarterly,* 34 (1956), 79-114; 35 (1957), 302-7.

[5] Mather, *A Good Old Age* (Boston, 1726), p. 4.

[6] This according to recent work by Allan Kulikoff, "Tobacco and Slaves," unpubl. Ph.D. thesis, Brandeis, 1975. Similar findings have appeared in five other unpublished studies of mortality in the Chesapeake colonies.

[7] Much of that mortality occurred in childhood—in New England, about 20% of it during the first year of life and another 20% in the next 20 years. If we take another measure—life expectancy from age 20 to age 60—the results look a little different, but the major point remains. Only a minority reached old age. Of men aged 21 in the Chesapeake colonies during the 17th century, less than 30% (perhaps closer to 20%) survived to age 60. In Middlesex County, Mass., perhaps 50% did so. In the colonies generally, about 40% of the males survived from 21 to 60. Mortality among women was greater, particularly in the child-bearing years of young adulthood. Those estimates are consistent with the most recent work on the demography of the Chesapeake colonies, but different from the historiography of New England. See Appendix for statistical details.

Old age was highly respected in early America, perhaps in part because it was comparatively rare.[8] A large body of literature was devoted to the subject during the seventeenth and eighteenth centuries.[9] It was primarily a literature of prescription, which taught people how they were expected to behave toward their elders. Without exception, it prescribed the ancient ideal of deference and respect for old age. "These two qualities go together, the ancient and the honorable," wrote Cotton Mather. So closely were those ideas linked that they sometimes seemed to be one.[10]

[8] In Europe the effect was much the same. Goubert observed that in 17th-century France "Only about ten [in 100] ever made their sixties. The triumphant octogenarian, surrounded by an aura of legend that made him seem at least a hundred, was regarded with . . . superstitious awe. . . . His sons and daughters, nephews and nieces long dead, as well as a good half of his grandchildren, the sage lived on to become an oracle for his entire village. His death was a major event for the whole region." Pierre Goubert, *Louis XIV and Twenty Million Frenchmen* (New York, 1970), p. 21.

[9] See Job Orton [1717-83], *Discourses to the Aged* (Salem, Mass., 1801), and the works by Cotton Mather cited above. See also William Bridge, *Word to the Aged* (Boston, 1679); Increase Mather, *Two Discourses Shewing, I, That the Lord's Ears are Open to the Prayers of the Righteous, and II, The Dignity and Duty of Aged Servants of the Lord* (Boston, 1716); Cotton Mather, *Address to Old Men and Young Men and Little Children* (Boston, 1690). There is a vast sermon literature, particularly in the form of anniversary addresses, which often took up the same question.

[10] Mather, *A Good Old Age*, p. 4. The evidence of prescriptive literature is reinforced by another sort of literary evidence. For a social historian who wishes to discover normative patterns of thought, the most valuable indicators are not the thoughts that people advocated, but the thoughts that they betrayed. Early American literature contains much information of that kind. Anne Bradstreet, for example, began one of her poems with a meeting of the "four ages of man," in which childhood, youth, and middle age all naturally "make way" for "wise old age":

> And last of all, to act upon this stage:
> Leaning upon his staffe, comes old age.
> Under his arme a Sheafe of wheat he bore,
> A Harvest of the best, what needs he more.
> In's other hand a glasse, ev'n almost run,
> This writ about: *This out then I am done.*
> His hoary haires, and grave aspect made way:
> And al gave ear, to what he had to say.

Bradstreet, *The Tenth Muse* (London, 1650), p. 42.

The attitude which the young were expected to assume before their elders was unlike that in any other social relationship. Respect, honor, obligation, and deference were all involved, but there was something deeper than deference, something summarized in a word now largely lost from common usage—"veneration." Old age was to be venerated in early America. The *Oxford English Dictionary* defines veneration as "a feeling of deep respect and reverence," and its Latin root was the verb *veneror,* which meant "to regard with religious awe and reverence." Veneration was more than a form of respect. It was also a form of worship.[11]

Veneration was an emotion of great austerity, closer to awe than to affection. It had nothing to do with love. A man could be venerated without being loved—without even being liked very much. A good example is the Reverend Timothy Cutler (1684-1765), rector of Yale College, and later of Christ Church in Boston. Cutler was not a likeable character, but he was venerated by the people of New England. In his old age he was "haughty and overbearing in his manners; and to a stranger, in the pulpit, appeared as a man fraught with pride. He never could win the rising generation, because he found it so difficult to be condescending; nor had he intimates of his own age and flock. But people of every denomination looked upon him with a kind of veneration, and his extensive learning excited esteem and respect where there was nothing to move or hold the affections of the heart."[12]

Timothy Cutler's difficulties with "condescension" bring out another side of age relations. If youth was expected to venerate age, then age was required to respond with "condescension," a word which has reversed its meaning in the past two hundred years. To "condescend" in Cutler's gen-

---

[11] Veneration and respect were not categorical alternatives. Veneration was a specific form of respect. Respect was general; veneration was particular.

[12] John Eliot, *Biographical Dictionary* (Salem, Mass., 1809), p. 44.

eration was to treat one's social inferior with sympathy, decency, understanding, and respect. Its usage in this context tells us that age relations then functioned as a system of social inequality.[13]

But the veneration of age was more than merely a social idea. It was sacred in its very nature. As in many ancient and primitive societies, age relations were closely interwoven with religion. Respect for age was deeply embedded in the Judeo-Christian ethic of early America. Both the Old Testament and the New contain many passages which were themselves the most important literature of prescription in that society. "The hoary head is a crown of glory," reads the Book of Proverbs. That quotation became a cliché in colonial America.[14] The Fifth Commandment not only requires respect for one's parents as a sacred duty, but also offers the gift of long life as an appropriate reward—"Honor thy father and thy mother: that thy days may be long upon the land which the Lord thy God giveth thee." In other parts of Scripture the respect which is due a parent is broadened to include respect for all elders: "Rebuke not an elder, but intreat him as a father . . . the elder women as mothers. . . ."[15]

Veneration has always been an important idea in Chris-

---

[13] That usage also appears in the works of Jane Austen (1775-1817).

[14] The full quotation is a little different: "The hoary head is a crown of glory, if it be found in the way of righteousness" (Prov. 16:31, KJV), a qualification of some importance, as we shall see. One of the few biblical passages which fails to flatter age was expurgated from the King James Version. In Chapter 13 of Daniel there is a salacious story about Susannah and two elders, who were so taken with her beauty that while she bathed they lay in hiding and watched her, and then invited her to lie with them. When she refused they reported having seen her committing adultery, and she was sentenced to death. But young Daniel refused to believe the elders without cross-examining them. When he did so he found that they contradicted each other, and Susannah was saved. In Protestant Bibles that passage was suppressed; thus the King James Version of Daniel has only 12 chapters. Simone de Beauvior, *The Coming of Age* (New York, 1972), p. 141.

[15] Exodus 20:12; I Timothy 5:1-2. There are many similar passages. For Puritan glosses upon them see esp. Increase and Cotton Mather, cited above.

tianity, and still retains a special meaning for many denominations. In the Anglican Church "venerable" is a title given to church officers, especially to archdeacons. In the Roman Catholic Church veneration is reserved for holy men and women in the lowest of three degrees of sanctity—below beatification and sanctification. The Calvinist inhabitants of Anglo-America had nothing to do with Episcopal archdeacons or third degrees of sanctity, but as they moved from a Roman Catholic conception of sainthood to their own special idea of a "saint" as one of the Elect upon the earth, they enlarged upon the idea of veneration and gave it a new theological and social significance.[16] Puritan writers, more than others of their own time, made a cult of age. They argued that elderly people had "a peculiar acquaintance with the Lord Jesus," and that for younger people, therefore, "the fear of God and honouring the old man is commanded with the same breath."[17] The subject was an obsession with them; they returned to it again and again. Anne Bradstreet captured the intensity of their interest in a graceful verse:

> Who thinks not oft upon the Fathers' ages
> Their long descent, how nephews sons they saw
> The starry observations of those sages
> And how their precepts to their sons were law.[18]

[16] It must be remembered that Calvinism was the religion of most churchgoing Americans from 1640 to 1790. By actual count, as late as 1790, 62% of American churches held to the Five Points of Calvinism as defined by the Synod of Dort in 1619. In most important theological ways the Puritan Congregationalists of Massachusetts were no different from most other Protestant inhabitants of British America. Congregational, Presbyterian, Baptist, Dutch Reformed, German Reformed, and French Reformed Protestants broadly agreed upon the fundamentals of theology, and many Calvinist-Anglicans stood with them. The only sizable exceptions were Lutherans and Quakers.

[17] Quoted in John Demos, "Aging in Pre-Modern Society," p. 14.

[18] Bradstreet, "Contemplations," in *Several Poems compiled with Great Variety of Wit and Learning* (Boston, 1678). If the frequency of this theme in Puritan writing is any guide, the first four words of the stanza were more than a mere poetic conceit.

The importance of old age for the Puritans was ultimately derived from their cosmology. They believed that everything in the world existed for a purpose. Everything, without exception, was made to happen according to the divine plan of an all-seeing, all-knowing, all-powerful God. In a world where life was so precarious, they believed that great age was not an accident, but a special gift of God's pleasure. They saw the handful of godly men and women who survived to old age as the saving remnant of their race. "If any man is favored with long life," wrote Increase Mather, "it is God that has lengthened his days."[19] That attitude was sustained by an abundance of Scriptural authority. "Keep my commandments," the Bible promised, "for length of days and long life shall they add unto thee." At the same time, sinners were threatened with an early death: "The branch of the wicked shall be cut off before his day . . . bloody and deceitful men shall not live half their days."[20]

Old age, in short, was a sign. Puritanism had need of signs. The Calvinist doctrine of limited atonement—the idea that Jesus had not died for all men, but only for a chosen few—presented a truly formidable problem. How could the choice be known? The doctrine of Election posed the same dilemma. How could one recognize the Elect?[21] One indicator was old age. In early America, as in many

19 Mather, *Dignity and Duty of Aged Servants*, p. 52.

20 The Puritans qualified this connection, but only a little. "They who walk in the way of righteousness, shall be honoured with living to old age, when the wicked shall have their days shortened, which indeed many times happen to be so, yet not always." Mather, *Dignity and Duty of Aged Servants*, p. 50, quoting Job 15:32; Psalms 55:23. The King James Version is a little different.

21 Limited atonement and unconditional Election were two of the Five Points which became the cornerstone of Calvinist orthodoxy after the Synod of Dort. In the past 30 years historians have been persuaded by Perry Miller (beyond his own intention) that the New England Puritans were not Calvinist, or not really so. But in fact the "covenant" theologians whom Miller discussed were among the major architects of the Five Points.

other societies, survival to a great age was sufficiently un-common to seem unnatural or even supernatural. One way of making sense of such a world was to believe that age was itself endowed with supernatural properties. A person sur-vived to old age because God—or the Devil—had "length-ened his days." That attitude often appeared in primitive societies, where the elderly were often thought to possess important magic powers—not always for good. Witchcraft was commonly associated with old age, and particularly with old women.[22] And so also was the magic power for do-ing good which God gave to his saints upon the earth.

The exaltation of age in early America found its expres-sion in the iconography of Puritanism. The Puritans were, of course, hostile to religious icons in the literal sense. But they worshipped their word images as devoutly as any "pa-pist" prayed to his statues and stained-glass windows. Puri-tan writing was filled with stained-glass images which were the true icons of early America. God appeared to them, in Increase Mather's description, as a man with a white beard

[22] Of 15 witches accused at the Essex (England) Assizes in 1645, 2 were in their 40's, 3 in their 50's, and 10 in their 60's or older. "The likeliest age for a witch was between fifty and seventy," Alan Macfarlane has written. *Witch-craft in Tudor and Stuart England* (London, 1970), p. 161. Adult women accused of witchcraft tended to be younger in America. Of 165 people ac-cused of witchcraft in Essex County during the 1690's, the ages of 118 are known:

Age	Men	Women	Total
under 20	6	18	24
21-30	3	7	10
31-40	3	8	11
41-50	6	18	24
51-60	5	23	28
61-up	4	14	21
Total	30	88	118

In England a witch was most often a woman in her 60's; in America, she was in her 50's. The difference can be accounted for by a difference in age composition. See Macfarlane, ibid.; John Demos, "Underlying Themes in the Witchcraft of Seventeenth Century New England," *American Historical Review*, 75 (1970), 1315.

and a face that was older than time. We say, in our secular way, that God looks like an old man; the Puritans said that old men looked like God. "There is something of the Image of God in age," Increase Mather wrote.[23]

The seventeenth-century image of God as an old man survived to later periods of our history—even to our own time. But the Puritan image of Christ was very different from the Christ of our modern devotional painting. He was not a muscular young hippie with a handsome Haight-Ashbury beard, but the Christ who appears in the Book of Revelation, with hair "white like wool, as white as snow."[24] And their idea of an angel was a man in his seventies. When a white-haired septuagenarian suddenly appeared in the New England town of Hadley, some of the inhabitants mistook him for a heavenly messenger.[25] Those images were often employed by New England clergymen when they were instructing their congregations in their duty of respect for age.

The imagery of Puritanism itself showed something of the same spirit. Today Puritanism is personified by a solemn gentleman with a steeple hat, a suit of "sadd colours," and an expression to match. The female counterpart is a formidable lady in a mouse-gray gown and a clean white coif, with narrow eyes, puckered mouth, and parchment face. These stereotypes are not pleasing to New England historians of the twentieth century, who insist that all Puritans did not dress or look that way. Scholars have exhumed dusty inventories showing that suits of turkey red and even royal purple were surprisingly common in Puritan wardrobes. And they have produced business records revealing that Puritan women decked themselves with red penistones, blue duffels, yellow flannels, and green aprons.

23 Mather, *Dignity and Duty of Aged Servants,* p. 65.

24 Revelation 1:14, KJV; Mather, ibid.

25 John L. Sibley, *Biographical Sketches of Graduates of Harvard University* (Cambridge, Mass., 1873), I, p. 114.

All that is true. And yet *old* Puritans dressed precisely as the Puritan myth suggests. Clergymen in their sermons invariably instructed elders to behave with "becoming gravity" in dress and demeanor. "Levity in words, and much more in actions, is unsuitable and a shame to them, considering their age, and stains their glory," wrote Increase Mather. "For old men to be gay and youthful in their apparel, or if aged women dress themselves like young girls, it exposeth them to reproach and contempt."[26]

Those instructions were solemnly obeyed. Even such a man as John Winthrop Junior, who as a young man had been Puritan Boston's idea of a fop, in his old age carefully confined himself to suits of black or some other "sadd colour."[27] The stereotypical Puritan was given the manners and dress of old age. That image was as old as Puritanism itself. The polemical literature of the sixteenth century was full of it, and not only on the anti-Puritan side. It was also a self-image, which suggests much about the exaltation of age in early America.

The ideal of respect for old age was a continuing theme in American literature from the seventeenth century to the Revolution and beyond.[28] For nearly two hundred years it changed only by becoming more elaborately the same—by becoming stronger in its expressions. From the first American essay, by William Bridge, published in the middle of the seventeenth century, through the generations of Increase and Cotton Mather, to eighteenth-century moralists

26 Mather, *Dignity and Duty of Aged Servants,* p. 124.
27 Robert C. Black, *The Younger John Winthrop* (New York, 1966), p. 326.
28 In polemical exchanges, the authority of old age was sometimes used as a rhetorical weapon. For an amusing example, see *A Letter to the Clergy of the Colony of Connecticutt from an Aged Layman* (New Haven, 1760), which was trumped by Moses Dickinson, *An Answer to a Letter from an Aged Layman to the Clergy of the Colony of Connecticutt, in which the rights of the consociated churches are maintained . . . by an aged Minister* (New Haven, 1761). Both are in the New York Public Library.

such as Job Orton, old age became more exalted rather than less so.

◊◊◊

Early American literature provides copious evidence that veneration of old age was a social idea which was widely preached in that society. But was it also practiced? There are many tests. Most—though not all, as we shall see—suggest a similarity of attitudes and acts. One simple test can be made on the literature itself, where we find, besides the argument that the young should yield to their elders, an assumption that they would naturally tend to do so. The Puritans assumed that respect for age was an ordinary human impulse—even an instinct "written in their hearts by nature." Veneration of the aged was spoken of as natural and normal. Then as now, the strongest social habits were thought to be not cultural, but biological in their basis. Our memories are so short that we imagine our social arrangements have always existed, and that they are rooted in some deep, organic structure of our being. Today we tend to assume that youth will *not* venerate age. Modern psychology has taught us to expect trouble between age and youth. Freud believed that fathers would naturally exercise an arbitrary authority over their sons, and that sons would naturally resist. The Freudian model was, perhaps, an accurate description of generational relationships in central Europe at the end of the nineteenth century. But in the seventeenth century, the Puritans believed that exactly the opposite behavior was an immutable fact. "The light of nature teacheth men to honour age," one wrote, in a spirit that assumed the proposition to be self-evident. "The law written in their hearts by nature has directed them to give a peculiar respect and deference to aged men. In most civilized nations they have done so."[29] The Puritans assumed that youth *would* inevitably defer to age. Their assumptions, more than their prescriptions, tell us what to expect in their acts.

If we move beyond literature and study the thoughts that the Puritans betrayed in their social arrangements, we find that the ideal of veneration was not merely observed, but also institutionalized in many ways. Old age was ceremoniously honored on public occasions. The most important and solemn public gatherings in a New England town were the moments when the people met to worship together. In their meetinghouses they were carefully assigned seats of different degrees of dignity. The most honorable places did not go to the richest or strongest, but to the oldest. Families and neighborhoods were broken up and the congregation was seated according to sex and seniority. The places of highest honor went to men and women of the greatest age.

Only one seventeenth-century meetinghouse still stands in Massachusetts—Hingham's beautiful Old Ship Meeting, a few miles south of Boston. An historian has tried to establish the exact spot in the meetinghouse where each member of the congregation worshipped on a certain day, January 8, 1682. He has found that Hingham's meetinghouse seats were assigned primarily according to age and sex. Men sat on one side of the aisle, women on the other. The best seat was a single pew beside the pulpit, which was shared by the minister's wife and the aged widow of his predecessor. Next in honor was a bench below the pulpit, which belonged to the Elders. And their title was no euphemism. In 1682, the three Hingham Elders whose ages we know were seventy-three, eighty-six, and ninety-two. They held the bench of highest dignity, though their wealth was much below the average in the town.

The next best seats made a sort of inner circle around the pulpit. They were reserved for the wives and widows of El-

29 Increase Mather, *Dignity and Duty of Aged Servants*, p. 63.

ders and Deacons on the one side, and on the other the "old guard" that ran the town. Middle-aged men and their wives occupied the front rows in the gallery. Behind them, in an outer ring, were the young bachelors and maids. Young married couples with infants on their laps sat on the first floor and filled the middle of the meetinghouse, and the older children were seated on separate benches around the walls. The worst seats, tucked away in the back corners of the building, were reserved for blacks, Indians, and servants.

Hingham in 1682 was an elaborately stratified society, and its meetinghouse stood as an architectural model of its stratification system. Many different forms of inequality existed together in the Old Ship Meeting: inequalities of wealth, power, order, race, and sex were combined in a pluralistic stratification system of great complexity. It is impossible to say which criterion was most important, for care was taken to be sure that all were respected. The seating committee in Windsor, Connecticut, for example, was instructed that every man was "to be seated according to his age and rates, but no man was to lose his rank." But among all of those many distinctions none was more important than age.[30]

[30] John B. Coolidge, "Hingham Builds a Meetinghouse," *New England Quarterly,* 34 (1961), 435-61. Robert Gross has also studied the Concord, Mass., meetinghouse list of 1774. People were seated first by age, then within age groups by wealth, and finally within wealth groups by social status. For example:

	70 & up	60-69	50-59	40-49
1st bench				
richest 20%	5	5	0	0
middle 40	5	1	0	0
poorest 40	1	0	0	0
2nd bench				
richest 20	1	3	3	0
middle 40	0	6	0	0
poorest 40	4	0	0	0
3rd bench				
richest 20	0	0	3	7
middle 40	0	0	0	6
poorest 40	0	2	0	4

The practice of "seating" the meetinghouse was not confined to Puritan Massachusetts. It was followed everywhere in early America, from New England to the southern colonies and even on the far frontier. In Maury County, Tennessee, at the end of the eighteenth century the members of a Presbyterian church arranged themselves by sex and age. Their arrangements were necessarily a little different from those of the Puritans a hundred years before, for the church was really a glorified cabin and the seats were log puncheons. But old age was honored just as it was in New England. We are told that "the women with little children were seated nearest the fireplace—the old men were honored with seats near the wall where they could lean back—the young men and young ladies next in front of them, and the boys of restless, unruly age were placed in the center, where batteries of eyes could play on them from all quarters."[31]

Respect for age was institutionalized in other ways as well. Both in New England and in the southern colonies the principle of "eldershippe" was widely observed in the governance of Church and State. People generally agreed that "gray heads" were wiser than "green ones," as Increase Mather put it.[32] "It is presumed that old men know more

The list continued in that manner to the last and lowest bench, on which poor men in their 20's found their humble place. I am grateful to Robert Gross for permission to use this data. The Instructions to the Windsor seating committee appear in Henry R. Stiles, *The History and Genealogies of Ancient Windsor, Connecticut* (Hartford, 1891), p. 272-73.

[31] No mention is made of old women or middle-aged men, but perhaps the description would be complete if the "old men" were married to the "women with young children"—a hint that "old" may have meant "adult" on the frontier. William Stuart Fleming, *Historical Sketch of Maury County* (Columbia, Tennessee, 1876), p. 26.

[32] Mather, *Dignity and Duty of Aged Servants*, p. 58. As always among that highly fragmented group, there were exceptions. John Wise, who challenged

than younger ones," he asserted. "Aged persons are fittest to give counsel . . . fittest to be trusted with the greatest and most honourable offices."

One clergyman of the time described the early Congregational churches as "a speaking aristocracy in the face of a silent democracy." That "speaking aristocracy" was an elite of age, for the Puritan churches of the seventeenth century were run by an oligarchy of Pastors, Teachers, and Elders who were commissioned to join the minister of the community in all "acts of spiritual *rule* which are distinct from the ministry of the word and sacraments." The Elders were "guides and leaders to the church in all matters what-so-ever," whose duty it was "to see that none in the church live inordinately out of rank and place," or "without a calling," or "idly in their calling."[33] Theirs was the vital power to "open and shut the doors of God's house—the power of admission and excommunication, ordination and dismissal." They were instructed "to moderate the carriage in all matters of the church assembled, as to propound matters to the church, to order the season of speech and silence and to pro-

---

so many Puritan beliefs, challenged this one, too. He argued that "it is not how capable a person is, which is the main point. . . . If state policy did consist in Beards, then he-goats would do for ambassadors, as well or better than men. . . . I think it is not how long men have lived but how wise they are grown." But even as he argued against a necessary connection between age and ability, he conceded that the two were combined more often than not. "Theology as well as art, is a long study," he wrote. "Queen Elizabeth was wont to say of Bishops when she visited the Schools, 'Study hard children, study hard, for Bishops are old men.' So of necessity, all our Ministers must be very old men." Wise, *The Churches Quarrel Espoused* (1713), p. 88.

[33] Increase Mather, *Dignity and Duty*, p. 62. The best work on the subject is still I. N. Tarbox, "Ruling Elders in the Early New England Churches," *Congregational Quarterly*, XIV (1872), 401-16. In the churches of Massachusetts the "Pastor" and "Teacher" were together called "Teaching Elders." The Ruling Elders were laymen. Many churches also had Deacons and Deaconesses; the latter were commonly "ancient" widows aged 60 or over.

nounce sentence according to the mind of Christ with the consent of the church."[34]

In Separatist, Congregational, and Presbyterian churches, the Elders, "most forward and wise," customarily served for life. Men who were elected to office rarely resigned and hardly ever retired. They served until they died. So also did the clergy of Congregational New England. "Let the aged endeavor to be as useful as they can, even to the last," wrote one, who practiced as he preached. The Reverend John Brock (1620-88) of Reading, Massachusetts, continued in his ministry until his death. He had earlier "told one in his family, that he had besought this favour of heaven; to live but fourteen days after the publick Labours of his ministry should be finished." And he did just that.[35]

Michael Wigglesworth (1631-1705) kept working until he fell sick with the fever which ended his life. Cotton Mather, who preached the funeral sermon, created an indelible image of Wigglesworth as he was in his last year—"a little feeble shadow of a Man, beyond seventy, preaching usually twice or thrice in a week, visiting and comforting the afflicted; encouraging the private meetings; catechizing the children of the flock; and managing the government of the church; and attending the sick, not only as pastor but as physician too; and this not only in his own town, but also in all those of the vicinity. Thus he did, unto the last, and was but one Lords-Day taken off, before his last."[36]

34 On this subject compare Robert Browne, *Booke which Sheweth the Life and Manners of All True Christians* (Middelburg, 1582), with Williston Walker, *The Creeds and Platforms of Congregationalism* (New York, 1893), pp. 91-212. Walker suggests that the office of Ruling Elder was "speedily abandoned," but he appears to be mistaken. Evidence of its importance continued to appear into the 19th century. See also John Cotton, *Way of the Churches of Christ in New England* (n.p., 1645); *The Cambridge Platform*, Chap. VII; "Of Ruling Elders and Deacons: Heads of Agreement" (1648).

35 Sibley, *Harvard Graduates*, I, 128.

36 Mather, *A Faithful Man Described and Rewarded* (Boston, 1705).

Most New England ministers went on until they dropped. John Cotton kept working until the end, which came suddenly when he was sixty-eight years old. One winter day, as he was traveling from Boston to preach at Harvard College, he fell into the Charles River. Though he did not drown, he suffered severely from exposure. And yet even as he lay upon his deathbed he preached to a crowd of his parishioners, "many of whom added to their sincere mournfulness a desire to partake of the last words of a great saint."[37]

We should not assume that the idea of retirement was entirely unknown in early America; the word was occasionally used in something like its modern sense as early as the mid-seventeenth century.[38] In fact, the Puritan clergy instructed their listeners that sometimes there came a moment in life when retirement became a duty, and one to be borne as faithfully as work itself. Cotton Mather observed that "Old age is often very loth to be laid aside from stations and services. Old folks often can't endure to be judged less able than ever they were for Publick Appearances, or to be put out of Offices. But, Good Sir, be so wise, as to dissappear of your own Accord, as soon and as far as you lawfully may. Be glad of a dismission. . . . Be pleased with the Retirement which you are dismissed into."[39]

Occasionally, a man was forced into retirement. John

[37] Larzer Ziff, *The Career of John Cotton: Puritanism and the American Experience* (Princeton, 1962), p. 254; Joshua Scottow, *Old Men's Tears for their Own Declensions* (Boston, 1691); John Norton, *Abel Being Dead Yet Speaketh* (London, 1658); Mather, *Magnalia*, I, 285.

[38] Pepys, in his Aug. 30, 1667, diary entry, used it in the modern meaning. Arbuthnot, in 1712, made a character say "I have, indeed, a small Pittance left, with which I might retire." See *Oxford English Dictionary*, "retire," v., Ie. Another meaning, now lost, was more common—a retreat from society, often to the country. "My young gentlewomen like everything in the country except the retirement; they can't get the plays, the operas and the masquerades out of their heads; much less can they forget their friends." William Byrd to John Lord Boyle, Feb. 2, 1727, in Louis B. Wright (ed.), *The London Diary* (London, 1958), p. 38.

[39] Mather, *Good Old Age*, p. 28.

Mayo (1598-1676), minister of Boston's North Church and overseer of Harvard College, was dismissed in 1673 on account of age—apparently against his will.[40] But there was no fixed age at which retirement was formally required or generally expected. Retirement in that sense did not exist. Those who received the gift of power were commonly expected to keep it as long as they could. Old men worked until they were unable to continue or until they were "judged less able than ever they were."[41]

When old men were dismissed, it was commonly not for age, but for cause—as in the case of the Reverend Stephen Bachiler of Hampton, New Hampshire, who was excommunicated on a charge of sexual immorality at the age of seventy-eight. He returned to England, married for the third time, and died in 1660 at the age of one hundred. But unless something equally extraordinary happened, a seventeenth-century minister would remain in office until he died. Thirty-five clergymen's careers have been reconstructed: thirty-two of them died in office; only three retired.[42]

In a world without retirement as a normal event, superannuation sometimes became a serious social problem. What was a church to do when its minister was too old to do his duty? What, for instance, could it do about a man like Nathaniel Fisher? Fisher was ordained a minister in the town of Dighton, Massachusetts, in 1712 at the age of twenty-five, and he remained in office for sixty-five years, until his death in 1777. By the early 1770's that "aged and venerable pastor" was unable to preach, but unwilling to retire. When the town found a replacement for him, Fisher refused to

40 S. E. Morison, *The Founding of Harvard College* (Cambridge, Mass., 1935), p. 390.
41 C. K. Shipton, *Biographical Sketches of Those Who Attended Harvard College in the Classes of 1701-1712* (Boston, 1937), V, 312-14.
42 See Table 1.

Table 1.1
Frequency of Retirement Among New England Clergymen
1635-1700

Minister	Town	Retired Age	Retired Year	Died Age	Died Year
Allin, Thomas	Dedham			75	1671
Avery, Joseph	Marblehead			35	1636
Baker, Nicholas	Scituate			68	1678
Blakeman, Adam	Stratford	65	1663	67	1665
Brewster, William	Plymouth			77	1644
Browne, Edmund	Sudbury			76	1684
Bulkeley, Edward	Concord	80	1694	82	1696
Bulkeley, Peter	Concord			76	1659
Cobbett, Thomas	Ipswich			77	1685
Cotton, John	Boston			68	1652
Dalton, Timothy	Hampton			73	1661
Davenport, John	Boston			73	1670
Dunster, Henry	Charlestown			50	1659
Fiske, John	Chelmsford			69	1677
Green, Henry	Vineyard			30	1648
Harvard, John	Charlestown			31	1638
Higginson, Francis	Salem			44	1630
Hobart, Peter	Hingham			75	1679
Hooker, Thomas	Hartford			61	1647
Jones, John	Fairfield			57	1665
Lothrop, John	Barnstable			69	1653
Mather, Richard	Dorchester			73	1669
Maverick, John	Dorchester			58	1636
Mayo, John	Boston	75	1673	78	1676
Partridge, Ralph	Duxbury			79	1658
Phillips, George	Watertown			51	1644
Prudden, Peter	Milford			56	1656
Shepard, Thomas	Cambridge			44	1649
Sherman, John	Watertown			72	1685
Skelton, Samuel	Salem			41	1634
Stone, Samuel	Windsor			61	1663
Symmes, Zechariah	Charlestown			73	1672
Ward, John	Haverhill			87	1693
Wetherell, William	Scituate			84	1684
Whiting, Samuel	Lynn			82	1679

mean age at death 64.9
mean age at leaving office 64.7
mean age at retirement 73.3

Source: Calculated from data in Morison, *Founding of Harvard College,* Appendix B. All ministers in Morison's list are included for whom dates of

step down. Finally an ecclesiastical council persuaded him to accept a young man as "copastor." That arrangement continued until Fisher died, at the age of ninety.

Ministers were no different from other men with respect to retirement. Schoolmasters did not retire. Ezekiel Cheever (1615-1708) was master of the Boston Latin School until his death, and Elijah Corlet (1610-88) kept working at the Cambridge Grammar School from 1642 until he died.[43] Nor did men in ordinary occupations retire from their work. The court records of Massachusetts provide a startling example in the deposition of a certain "Henry Stitch, aged about 102 years" and still employed "in the mystery of coaling."[44] The political and economic leaders of New England behaved in much the same way. John Winthrop, according to his biographer, was "abroad and at his business every day, even when ill with fever in his last year."[45] Five out of the six Governors of Plymouth Colony continued to serve into old age: four died in office; the last was seventy-three when Plymouth was annexed by Massachusetts. The same was true of Assistants, who rarely "left their posts of their own accord, nor were they often voted out of office by their constituents. Usually their tenure was ended by death, which in some instances was very long delayed."[46]

In Rhode Island, Roger Williams (1603-83) was the patriarch of Providence until he died in his eightieth year. Though he was "lame" as early as the age of sixty-three, complaining sadly of "old pains, lamenesses, so that some-

---

birth, death, and departure from office are known—a procedure which was designed to bias the result in the direction of exaggerating the incidence of retirement. The result is an "upper-bound" estimate. Ministers who returned to England are omitted.

43 Cotton Mather, *Corderius Americanus* (Boston, 1708).

44 Demos, "Aging in Pre-Modern Society," p. 9.

45 Edmund S. Morgan, *Puritan Dilemma* (Boston, 1958), p. 204.

46 John Demos, *A Little Commonwealth: Family Life in Plymouth Colony* (New York, 1971), p. 174.

times I have not been able to rise nor goe nor stand,"[47] hobbling about the town with his great staff, his body bent and twisted with age and pain and misery, he still ran the colony until a few months before his death. Through the "long winter" of his old age he served as preacher, moderator of town meeting, and even tax collector. He wrote powerful polemics against the Quakers, and at the age of seventy he rowed from Providence to Newport to dispute with them. The journey took him a day and a night—thirty-eight miles of rowing! When he arrived, the Quakers in the audience heckled him, shouting, "old Man, old Man."[48] That radical sect, which made a religion of its contempt for inequality in every form, attacked the authority of age, as well as that of wealth and class.

For the southern colonies our evidence is scanty, but we know a great deal about the old age of one Virginia gentleman—William Byrd (1674-1744), Master of Westover Plantation. Byrd kept a secret shorthand diary during his late sixties. It reveals a man who was feeling his age in many ways. He was plagued by illness and worried about the decline of his mind. "God preserve my head," he wrote in 1740, "and grant I may not lose my memory and sense."[49] Yet his diary showed very little loss of activity. To the end of his life he actively directed the affairs of his plantation. He continued his career in politics, reaching his highest office in the last year of his life, when he was elected president of the Virginia council. It was an important office in the colony, second only to the governorship, and it came to Byrd precisely because of his age. He was a senior councillor and

[47] Ola Winslow, *Master Roger Williams: A Biography* (New York, 1957), p. 267.
[48] Perry Miller, *Roger Williams: His Contribution to the American Tradition* (New York, 1962), p. 244.
[49] Maude H. Woodfin (ed.), *Another Secret Diary of William Byrd of Westover, 1739-1741* (Richmond, Va., 1942), p. 50.

had been so for many years. But the incumbent president, William Blair, had clung stubbornly to life and office, sleeping in his council chair for many years until the end finally came at the age of eighty-nine, and Byrd, a mere stripling of seventy, inherited the office.

In his last years Byrd's private life was as full as his public affairs. He began each morning with lessons in Latin, Hebrew, and Greek, and took his exercise by dancing almost every day. In the evenings he proved himself a mighty trencherman, and at every hour of the day he was dangerous to any housemaid who came within reach:

> 9 May 1741   I played the fool with Sally, God forgive me.
>
> 15 June 1741   In the evening I played the fool with Marjorie, God forgive me.

Old age seems to have changed William Byrd's routine scarcely at all.

The public careers of men such as John Winthrop, William Bradford, Roger Williams, and William Byrd provide strong evidence that the prestige of age was often translated into political power. Old men in early America held the right of command in moments of crisis. At such times they had a way of materializing, as if from nowhere, to lead their younger neighbors. A classical example was William Goffe (c. 1607-79), a Puritan soldier who fought in the English civil war and was a "regicide" judge who condemned Charles I to death. In 1660, when Charles II returned to the throne, Goffe fled to New England and found a secret sanctuary there, first near New Haven, then in the town of Hadley, Massachusetts, where in 1675 he was living in hiding, unknown to most of the inhabitants. In that year an Indian war broke out, and all of the people of that frontier town repaired to their meetinghouse—all but Goffe, who remained in hiding. As he watched from a window, he saw an Indian war party stealing up on the town. At that moment he left his place of concealment and ran to the meetinghouse. As the ancient stranger raised the alarm a panic arose among the people; they had no idea what to do.

"I will lead," the old man said. "Follow me!"

The people of Hadley obeyed him instantly, even though he was a stranger to them. They had an old cannon, but knew not how to use it. Goffe taught them how to load it, and he trained it upon the Indians, who had taken refuge in an empty house. His first shot crashed against a chimney and sent the Indians running through a shower of brick and mortar. Goffe rallied Hadley's townsmen and ordered them in pursuit. When they returned they found that he had vanished as miraculously as he had appeared. Much later it was written that "His venerable form, silvery locks, mysterious appearance and sudden disappearance, with the disposition of the pious in those days to recognize in any strange event a special providence, led the inhabitants to regard their deliverer as an angel, who after fulfilling the purpose of his mission, had reascended to heaven. They very likely never knew who he was."[50]

That episode was perhaps the basis of Nathaniel Hawthorne's short story, "The Grey Champion," in *Twice Told Tales*. But Hawthorne used his literary license to transfer the event from King Philip's War to the Glorious Revolution; his "grey champion" was made to appear as if by miracle to lead the people of New England against Sir Edmund Andros.

The history of New England is filled with "grey cham-

[50] Sibley, *Harvard Graduates*, I, 114.

pions"—a theme which runs from William Goffe in 1675 to Samuel Whittemore and Josiah Haynes a century later, at the battles of Lexington and Concord. Whittemore and Haynes were household names in Massachusetts long after the Revolution. Samuel Whittemore was English-born—a captain of cavalry during the reign of George I. He migrated to Massachusetts, where he became a farmer. On April 19, 1775, at the age of seventy-eight or so, he took down his musket from the wall, belted on a brace of dragoon pistols, and went out to the Lexington road, where he made a one-man stand against the British army. He killed one soldier with his musket and two more with his pistols before being shot in the cheek and beaten and bayoneted by two infuriated British soldiers until they were sure that they had "killed the old rebel." But they were wrong; somehow he survived, and became a living legend in New England, where he finally died at the age of ninety-six.

Deacon Josiah Haynes was eighty on that same day. He turned out with the rest of the Minutemen of his town of Sudbury and marched eight miles to Concord bridge with blood in his eye and a long stride that left his younger neighbors puffing and straggling behind him. When his captain, a certain Nixon by name, hesitated to lead the men into battle, Josiah Haynes denounced him to his face.

"If you don't go and drive them British from that bridge," the old man spat, "I shall call you a coward."

And Haynes himself led his neighbors in the pursuit from Concord to Cambridge. Twenty-one elite companies of British infantry fled down the Boston road with an infuriated eighty-year-old Congregational deacon close at their heels—so close, in fact, that Josiah Haynes was shot and killed while reloading his musket, and another "grey champion" entered New England's folklore. The idea continued to have a resonance even to our own time. In New England during the nineteenth century John Quincy Adams, "Old Man Eloquent," became a "grey champion" of sorts. And Deacon Haynes's twentieth-century townsman is Archibald Cox, the "grey champion" of Watergate.[51]

The "grey champions" of New England were not merely a cultural myth. It is possible to observe statistical changes in the age of officeholders when moments of crisis came. In Concord and Brookline, Massachusetts, during the Revolution the age of officers—Selectmen and Revolutionary Committeemen alike—rose suddenly with the emergency, and fell when it ended. The change cannot be explained by the departure of the younger men to serve in the army, for it took place before they left town.[52] The same thing happened during the great sectional crisis of 1814, when a secessionist movement developed in New England. Once again the old men turned out and took command at the critical moment, then retired immediately after it was over.[53] The "grey champion" was a political reality in New England—an institution as well as an ideal.

---

[51] Mr. Cox lives in the town of Wayland, Mass., on land which was part of the original Sudbury settlement.

[52] The ages of Concord officeholders changed as follows:

	Mean Age	Median Age	% Over 60
Selectmen at 1st election, 1765-74	43.3	44.0	0
Revolutionary Committeemen, 1774-75	50.4	48.5	27.3
Selectmen at 1st election, 1775-84	44.0	47.0	0
Selectmen at 1st election, 1785-94	45.0	44.5	0

Data furnished by Robert Gross; similar results were obtained by Alisa Belinkoff in "Everyone who was Anyone in Brookline," unpubl. thesis, Brandeis, 1975.

[53] See my "Myth of the Essex Junto," *William & Mary Quarterly*, 3rd Series, 21 (1964), pp. 191-235, and *Revolution of American Conservatism* (New York, 1965; reprinted Chicago, 1975).

The most striking fact about those "grey champions" was that young people rallied freely behind them. But respect for age was not entirely voluntary. And where it was not freely forthcoming, it was forced. The most powerful form of coercion was economic. In that agricultural society, landed wealth was the basis for power, and parents retained both possession and control over their lands for a very long time—nearly to the end of their lives. Children tended to remain economic dependents long after they had reached physical maturity.[54] The reluctance of fathers to release their land was motivated in part by a concern for their own security in old age, but it went beyond material needs. Even wealthy fathers who could easily have provided for themselves and their children at the same time were slow to set those children free. Their disinclination suggests that land was used for something other than an economic purpose. And so it was; land was an instrument of generational politics—a way of preserving both the power and the authority of the elderly. Sons were bound to their fathers by ties of economic dependency; youth was the hostage of age.[55]

[54] It is possible that the authority of elders may have been even greater in America than it was in Europe, for here land was so abundant that most families were landed, and therefore nearly all fathers had a hold over their sons, who found it difficult to obtain a homestead in any other way. This irony was suggested to me by Peter Laslett. The practice has also been observed on the Canadian frontier. See S. Kohl and J. Bennet, "Kinship, Succession and the Migration of Young People in a Canadian Agricultural Community," *International Journal of Comparative Sociology,* VI (1965), 95-116. And the same pattern has been found in western Europe, where it survived even longer. In Achterhoek, the Netherlands, it was widespread until around 1875. "Almost every person in the community was economically dependent on his parents during the parents' lifetimes." Gerrit Kooy, *Het veranderend gezin in Nederland* (Leerdam, 1957); Kooy, *De Oude Samenwoning op het Nieuwe Platteland* (Assen, 1959). For a translation of this work, see "The Social System and the Problem of Aging," *Processes of Aging: Social and Psychological Perspectives* ed. by R. H. Williams *et al.* (2 vols., New York, 1963), II, 43-60.

[55] Parents apparently did not keep their children from marrying. There was actually a law in Massachusetts which forbade them to do so. According

New England fathers of the seventeenth century were especially slow to give their land to their sons. Typical in that respect was the Holt family of Andover, Massachusetts. The family patriarch was Nicholas Holt (1603-86), a prosperous yeoman with a handsome property and five sturdy sons to work it. And work they did, for almost as many years as their hardy father clung to life—and land. They married at the usual age in New England—twenty-six on the average—and each soon moved into a home of his own.[56] But their homes were built upon their father's property, and they did not even begin to receive land of their own until 1681, when Nicholas Holt was seventy-seven. The eldest son finally gained his independence at the age of forty, after having been married for twelve years! By 1685 all the sons had received their land, at an average age of thirty-two, which was very near the New England average. But even then it came with strings attached. Full financial independence did not really begin until Nicholas Holt died in 1686. There was, by the way, no sign of open hostility between fathers and sons in the Holt family, or in their town. The historian of Andover doubts that any such enmity existed. In seventeenth-century Massachusetts that pattern of generational relations seems to have been accepted by young and old as the way of the world.

Things remained very much the same in the eighteenth century as well. We might follow the Holt family through another generation. Nicholas Holt's second son, Henry, had eight sons. Seven of them married when they were twenty-five. But their land did not come to them until 1717, when

---

to Peter Laslett's unpublished research, in England orphans actually married later than did children whose parents were alive. Though the question has not been tested in America, the same pattern will probably appear here.

56 Philip J. Greven, *Four Generations: Population, Land, and Family in Colonial Andover, Massachusetts* (Ithaca, N.Y., 1970), pp. 143-44.

Henry Holt was seventy-three and four of his sons had been long married—from seven to seventeen years. Henry's seventh son, William, never married at all. It was he who received the original homestead (at the age of thirty) by a deed of gift that required him to "take ye sole care of his father Henry Holt and of his Naturall Mother Sarah Holt" for the rest of their days and to provide them with many things, all carefully spelled out in elaborate detail, even to the candles and hard cider. And if William had failed to supply "any one article aforementioned," he would have forfeited his property.[57]

It is significant that landed property often came to all the sons within a comparatively short period—when the eldest son was in his forties and the youngest was barely twenty and unmarried. It was a process which marked a kind of "retirement" by the father from the business of farming: not complete disengagement, but a passing on of the major responsibility for managing the family's lands. Final retirement came with the gift or sale of the homestead, often to the youngest son. Retirement in that special sense seems to have been normal among America's farming families in the seventeenth and eighteenth centuries. It was even universal, at a certain age. But that age was very advanced—around sixty-six or sixty-seven.[58] It was beyond the average age of

[57] Aged parents sometimes made tenants or sharecroppers of their children. In 1790 one man reported that it was "a common thing for parents in advanced age to let their farms on shares of produce, to young men making Provision for going to the West Country, by taking the Old Farms as annual tenants. The terms being mostly to accommodate both families in the house; thus the owner to retain the rooms and accommodation required for his reduced family, and land enough to keep the animals needed for his own use. The tenant to take as much produce of all kinds as he wanted for family use, all articles annually sold off to be for joint account; viz, one half of the proceeds paid over as rent." John W. Dyer, *Reminiscences* (Evansville, Ind., 1898), pp. 25-27.

[58] The average age of agrarian retirement in New England is estimated as follows: The mean age at which young men received land in the 17th century was 33. Their fathers, at the birth of the middle son, were 33 on

death for adult males. Most men never lived to reach it, and those who did usually died only a few years afterward.

In the late colonial period fathers tended to hold their land even longer than they had in the seventeenth century. A study of the movement of wealth in Concord, Massachusetts, during the eighteenth century shows that the upward mobility of young men and downward mobility of old men both declined from one generation to the next.[59] The primary cause was economic, but the importance of generational politics in these arrangements may be seen in sermons, which advised parents to hold back a sufficiency of "substance" for themselves. "Better it is thy children should seek to thee than that thou shouldest stand to their courtesy," wrote one of them.[60]

Such was the organization of that society that a parent

---

the average—or 66 when they gave their land to their sons. This estimate may be confirmed by a direct empirical measure. In Andover, Mass., the mean age of the father when he passed land to his sons is known to have been 67. (Greven, *Four Generations,* p. 135.) Final retirement—turning over the homestead—would occur after that age, which was beyond the mean age at death.

[59] The property mobility of men in Concord changed thus:

Age Group	% Moving Up		% Stable		% Moving Down	
	1746-70	1770-95	1746-70	1770-95	1746-70	1770-95
30 and Under	66	52	23	20	11	28
31-40	31	41	42	41	27	18
41 and Over	13	0	3	52	83	48

The median age of men by mobility status showed the same trend:

Median Age of Men

Period	No.	Moving Up	Stable	Moving Down
1733-57	81	27	29	41
1746-70	100	28	31	43
1770-95	74	28	41	44.5

Source: Robert Gross, *The Minutemen and Their World* (New York, 1976), pp. 208, 234; and unpubl. data kindly supplied by Mr. Gross.

[60] Job Orton, *Discourses to the Aged,* p. 39n.

was apt to be surrounded by "seeking" children nearly to the end of life. Just as there was no early retirement from work, so also there was no release from domestic tasks. The responsibilities of child-rearing normally continued to the end of life. Men married at twenty-five; women, at twenty-one. Normally the first baby was born within a year of the marriage; the last came when the wife was thirty-eight and her husband was forty-two. As a rule, the youngest child did not marry until the parents were sixty-four and sixty.[61] Men and women continued to live with their unmarried children nearly until the end of their lives. Very few old people lived alone; most remained in nuclear families with their own children still around them. Scarcely any of them lived in extended, three-generation households. Those who did usually had taken in a married daughter or son who had lost a spouse. When three generations lived together, it was more often the young who were in some way dependent upon the old than the old upon the young.[62]

[61] The life cycle of men in early America was roughly as follows:

Mean age at	1650	1700	1750	1800
First marriage	24	25	26	25
Last birth	42	42	43	42
Last child comes of age	63	63	64	63
Last child marries	65	64	66	67
Death	52	52	c52	c56

For women it was a little different:

Mean age at	1650	1700	1750	1800
First marriage	20	21	23	22
Last birth	38	38	39	39
Last child comes of age	59	59	60	60
Last child marries	60	61	63	64
Death	c50	c50	c50	c56

See Appendix.

[62] These generalizations rest upon an extraordinary local census of Surry, N.H., taken in 1806 by the local clergyman, who carefully recorded the residence and exact age of everyone in town. There were 25 men and women 65 or over. None of them lived alone; only 1 lived with another family; 20

Even after sons became economically independent, their fathers did not hesitate to control and correct them, though both might be full-grown. Samuel Sewall Senior often criticized his son Samuel Junior about his behavior. "I warn my eldest son against going to taverns," Samuel Senior wrote in 1716, when he was sixty-four and his son was thirty-nine!

---

continued to live in their own nuclear family, 12 with unmarried children, 8 without. Only 4 lived in extended families which spanned 3 generations, and in every case the elderly parents had taken in a daughter who had infant children but no husband. The residence patterns were as follows:

Households Including Elderly Residents (65 and up)	Other residents and their relationship to elders
Abiel and Elizabeth Allen (aged 73, 71)	daughter (aged 40)
Benjamin and Joanna Carpenter (76, 77)	daughter (50)
Jedidiah and Mary Carpenter (73, 67)	none
Eliphalet and Ann Dart (65, 62)	daughter (37)
Jeptha and Mary Dawes (68, 70)	son (45)
Joshua and Joanna Fuller (79, 72)	none
Thomas and Grace Harvey (66, 63)	daughter (38) & 4 grandchildren (6-11)
Lemuel and Abigail Holmes (64, 67)	daughter (26)
John and Lydia Hill (67, 56)	daughter (20)
Samuel and Elizabeth McCurdy (85, 82)	daughter (55) & grandson (16)
Dinah Armstrong (67)	in household of Thos. Redding (55) no relation (?)
Abner and Susannah Skinner (67, 68)	daughter (26)
Abiel and Ruth Smith (87, 85)	none
Zebulon and Tabitha Streeter (67, 69)	son (31) & daughter (26)
Obediah and Sarah Wilcox (82, 72)	none

Source: "A Census of the Inhabitants in the Town of Surry, in the County of Cheshire, State of New Hampshire, taken in the Summer of 1806 by Rev. Perley Howe," in F. B. Kingsbury, History of Surry, New Hampshire (Surry, 1925), pp. 64-77.

In England during the 17th and 18th centuries similar patterns prevailed. Nearly 90% of elderly married people lived in nuclear households. In central and eastern Europe, on the other hand, residence patterns were different. Households tended to be larger and more complex. Elderly people often lived with married children, and both "stem" families and "extended" families were common. For a summary of the evidence, see Peter Laslett, "Historical Sociology in Relation to Aging," unpubl., pp. 27-37. The extent to which the central European pattern was introduced by German immigrants to the middle colonies remains to be established.

The father also interfered often in his son's domestic arrangements, and referred to him paternalistically as "my Samuel." Yet the son in his turn showed no outward resentment toward his "honored father."[63]

Parents such as Samuel Sewall the elder showed much concern for the welfare of their children, but little regard for their wishes. One early American adolescent pathetically described the helplessness of youth and its despair of being noticed or even consulted in family decisions. "O think of me sometimes!" William Little exclaimed in his diary, as his father arranged the affairs of the family.[64] The hierarchy of age had a tone similar to that of the hierarchy of orders— "the common people and children" were linked together in a single phrase by Jonathan Edwards. On the other side, betters and elders were combined in their power and authority.[65]

The powers and privileges of old age were firmly anchored in the society. Wherever we turn we find it—in the arrangement of the meetinghouse, in patterns of officeholding and landholding, in family organization—in fact, the exaltation of age was a central part of a *system* of age relationships, a set of interlocking parts. That exaltation functioned as an instrument of conservatism in that tradition-bound society. "The honor we owe to our parents and ancestors obligeth us to attend to that which our fathers have told us," Samuel Dexter wrote. "Let us endeavor to recover that spirit of family government and authority which our fathers had;

---

[63] Milton Halsey Thomas (ed.) *Diary of Samuel Sewall* (2 vols., New York, 1973), *passim*, esp. pp. 815, 707, 705-6n.

[64] W. B. Little, Diary, Apr. 6, 1805, MS, New York Public Library.

[65] See e.g. Jonathan Edwards, *Freedom of the Will*, in Clarence H. Faust and Thomas H. Johnson (eds.), *Edwards* (New York, 1935), p. 299.

they ruled their houses well, and had their households in good subjection; children and servants knew their places and kept their distances."[66] Veneration thus created continuity, stability, permanence, constancy, and order in the society. We do not commonly think of continuity as something which needs to be created. Too often we assume that there is a law of inertia in history—that historical conditions, like physical objects, tend to stay at rest until they are set in motion. But that is surely a mistake, for the world is made of motion. Change is normal in human affairs. Stability is a human invention; continuity, when it exists, is an artifact which men have created. And among the many instruments of its creation in early America was the system of age relationships.

The system worked, partly because the number of the aged was so small. In that world of high fertility and high mortality, where the population was very young and the odds against surviving to a ripe age were great, respect for age was enhanced by its comparative rarity. Ancestors are always more easily worshipped at a distance. The authority of elders was increased by the fact that most of them were sleeping safely in their graves. High mortality and low life expectancy were surely not sufficient in themselves to produce that functioning system of age relations, but they helped to maintain it.

But even as the ideal of veneration was being acted out in so many ways, there were signs that things were not always as they were meant to be. Many writers commented upon lapses in proper behavior, lamenting that such things should happen. Increase Mather observed that "to treat Aged Persons with disrespectful and disdainful language only because

---

[66] Samuel Dexter, *Some Serious Thought on the Foundation, Rise and Growth of the Settlements in New England* (Boston, 1738), pp. 255, 269-70.

of their age, is a very criminal offence in the sight of God: yet how common it is to call this or the other person *Old Such An One,* in a way of contempt on the account of their age."[67]

An historical phenomenon is never understood until its limits are established. The veneration of age in early America had its social boundaries. It is generally true that people were ranked according to their years, and that "older" meant "better" and "oldest" meant "best." But people were also ranked in many other ways—by sex and race, wealth and learning, "order" and "estate," beauty and brains. Though age operated as a system of social inequality, we must always remember that it also coexisted with many other inequalities, each of which served to qualify the rest. Age stratification was sometimes narrowly limited by those other distinctions.

Respect for age ran strongest among the elite of powerful and prosperous males who dominated early American society. It probably existed within most families where the husband and father was healthy and active. But around the edges of the society there was a marginal population for whom it scarcely existed at all. It did not exist for the poor. To be old and poor and outcast in early America was certainly not to be venerated, but rather to be despised. In some strange and paradoxical way, old age seems actually to have intensified the contempt visited upon a poor man. A rich old man was the more highly respected because he was old, but the aged poor were often scorned.

To be very low in any sort of status was to be removed from the protection of society, far more than today. The elderly poor of early America were treated very badly. Perhaps it is fortunate that there were so few of them, for their sufferings were great. Unattached old people often met with

67 Increase Mather, *Dignity and Duty,* p. 98.

much brutality. A New Jersey law of 1720 instructed justices of the peace to search arriving ships for "old persons" as well as "maimed, lunatic, or any vagabond and vagrant persons," and to send them away in order to prevent the growth of pauperism in the colony.[68] Every now and then an individual emerges from the anonymous mass: An old man on a coasting sloop, sick and penniless, ignored by his fellow passengers and finally picked up by the crew and put ashore on a barren and uninhabited island, where he was left to die by himself. An old man living alone like an animal in the woods, dressed in tattered garments of green leather, his gray beard dirty and matted, taking shelter in a pile of brush and eating whatever he could steal from farms or forage from the forest. A drunken, crippled old man living in the alleys of a seaport town, sleeping by day in a deserted cellar, scavenging at night along the empty wharfs. Those were the *untermenschen* of early American society. In that hierarchical world the people who suffered most were not those with low status, but those with none at all. There were not many of them. In 1790 it was observed (and widely believed) that "in America there are few without families, and the ease of procuring subsistence removed all apprehensions of suffering in old age."[69] But if the aged poor were only a small minority, their misery was great.

Others were exceptions in a different way. They were not so much an under class as an outer class—quarrelsome, ungodly people who always seemed to be doing battle with their neighbors, going to the law against them, and generally reacting with hostility to the norms of the community. They were surprisingly numerous—a minority, but a large one. In New England towns they were the people who

[68] James Leiby, *Charity and Corrections in New Jersey* (New Brunswick, N.J., 1967), p. 7.
[69] *Annals of Congress*, 1st Cong., 2nd sess., col. 1233, Feb. 12, 1790.

rarely attended church: Hingham's Old Ship Meeting could seat no more than five hundred people in 1682, but there were seven hundred in the town. In many New England towns there was an outer ring of non-Calvinist and anti-Calvinist inhabitants who mocked the ideals of the majority and were despised in turn. For them the normal standards of the society were inverted. Such people often appeared in the court records of seventeenth-century Massachusetts. One deposition tells us of a certain Nathaniel Parker, aged twenty-three, saying to another New Englander, aged sixty-five, "God damn me, if thou wert not an old man, I would bat thy teeth down thy throat." The way in which Parker began his remark suggests that he was not on the best of terms with the culture of the Puritan majority, and the way he ended it shows that he rejected its attitudes toward age.[70] There were many such men in early America—a human flotsam whose attitudes were particularly brutal toward the aged. In them we find an exception to almost every civilized rule.

Some old women (not most) were also exceptions to the general exaltation of age. To be a poor widow in early America was not to be venerated. Many a widow was protected against poverty by her husband's will, which commonly assigned her a third of the estate and required children to furnish food, clothing, and shelter on pain of forfeiting their inheritance. But the wealthy widow was largely a fictional figure. Few were affluent; many were miserably poor. The desperation of widowhood appears in one episode which caused much talk in Boston in 1667. When

[70] Legal records are a treacherous source for social history. They may be used to reverse any generalization about the majority. The evidence is valuable and important if it is properly used, but any attempt to reconstruct social history primarily from court records is comparable to a modern sociologist's trying to reconstruct normal patterns of life today from a police blotter. Many people who appear in the legal records were not criminals, but witnesses. Nevertheless, a deviant class is more thoroughly covered than its numbers would warrant.

the headmaster of Boston Latin School died, his widow took possession of the schoolhouse and refused to leave until the town awarded her an annuity of £8 per annum. But that sort of provision was rare, and a widow without it was sometimes reduced to dependency and degradation. Old widows rarely remarried in America.[71] Their children sometimes turned away from them: Increase Mather complained that there were children who were apt "to despise an *Aged Mother.*"[72] For most old women—married, or propertied, or respectable—the normal attitude of veneration for old age seems to have applied. In Hingham, the minister's widow had the best seat in the meetinghouse. But poor, widowed, and base-born women were treated with a contempt which was deepened all the more by their womanhood. Some were actually driven away by their neighbors, who feared an increase in the poor rates. The legal records of the colonies contain many instances of poor widows who were "warned out" and forced to wander from one town to another.[73]

[71] Daniel Scott Smith has estimated that the percentage of widows ever remarrying changed as follows in Hingham, Mass.:

Marriage Cohort	Age at Widowhood		
	20-39	40-59	60 & up
before 1760	57.4	13.7	0.0
1761-1800	35.7	5.2	0.0
1801-1840	35.5	2.3	0.0

For males the chances of remarriage were much better:

	20-39	40-59	60 & up
1761-1800	93.3	74.6	18.8
before 1760	90.5	46.9	8.8
1800-1840	85.4	46.0	7.1

Source: Smith, "Population, Family and Society in Hingham, Mass," unpubl. Ph.D. thesis, Berkeley, p. 281.

[72] Mather, *Dignity and Duty*, p. 100.

[73] For evidence of warnings out, which were legal notices sometimes accompanied by physical removals, see Douglas Jones, "Geographic Mobility and Society in Eighteenth-century Essex, Mass.," unpubl. Ph.D. thesis, Brandeis, 1975.

Finally, in the southern colonies, there was a fourth exceptional group: old slaves, who were kept working as long as possible. "Negroes in their sixties were not very productive, but they usually did enough work at least to pay for their support."[74] But what of those who could not work? The treatment of superannuated slaves varied greatly from one plantation to another. Given the fragmentation of slaveholding society into so many sovereign units, we may assume that the range of practice was as broad as the range of possibility. Some masters undoubtedly served their aged slaves with every possible consideration; others resorted to the most cruel and callous brutality. The critical problem concerns the distribution of that practice.

Here we find a conflict of testimony. Many slaveholders insisted that their aged slaves lived out the twilight of life in serene retirement, with all needs attended to, and many wants as well. More convincing is the testimony of the slaves themselves, who asserted that planters tried to sell off their aged workers, or even to free them before they became a burden upon the plantation. When that expedient failed (laws against manumission were designed to prevent it), an old slave was often turned loose to fend for himself, without food, without clothing, without shelter.

One slave testified: "When my mother became old, she was sent to live in a little lonely log-hut in the woods. Aged and worn-out slaves, whether men or women, are commonly so treated. No care is taken of them, except, perhaps, that a little ground is cleared about the hut, on which the old slave, if able, may raise a little corn. As far as the owner is concerned, they live or die, as it happens; it is just the same thing as turning out an old horse. Their children, or other

74. Kenneth M. Stampp, *The Peculiar Institution: Slavery in the Antebellum South* (New York, 1956); Charles Sackett Sydnor, *Slavery in Mississippi* (Gloucester, Mass., 1965), p. 66.

near relations, if living in the neighborhood, take it by turns to go out at night with a supply saved from their own scanty allowance of food, as well as to cut wood and fetch water for them; this is done entirely through the good feelings of the slaves, and not through the masters' taking care that it is done. On these night visits, the aged inmate of the hut is often found crying on account of sufferings from disease or extreme weakness, or from want of food or water in the course of the day: many a time, when I have drawn near to my mother's hut, I have heard her grieving and crying on these accounts; she was old and blind too, and so unable to help herself. She was not treated worse than others: it is the general practice. Some good masters do not treat their old slaves so: they employ them in doing light jobs about the house and garden."[75]

Another slave described a different episode: "The young mistress came out to see how things were done on her plantation, and she soon gave a specimen of her character. Among those in waiting for their allowance was a very old slave, who had faithfully served the Flint family through three generations. When he hobbled up to get his bit of meat, the mistress said he was too old to have any allowance: that when niggers were too old to work, they ought to be fed on grass. Poor old man! He suffered much before he found rest in the grave."[76]

Still others described a tendency among slaveholders to sell off their slaves before they became too old to work. One wonders what species of men were purchasers, and how they gained by their investment.

A third slave remembered: "My old master also sold a dear brother and a sister, in the same manner as he did my

[75] Moses Granby, "Life," in W. L. Katz (ed.), *Five Slave Narratives* (New York, 1968), p. 32.

[76] Harriet Jacobs, *Incidents in the Life of a Slave Girl* (Boston, 1861), p. 142.

father and mother. The reason he assigned for disposing of my parents, as well as several other aged slaves, was, that 'they were getting old, and would soon become valueless in the market, and therefore he intended to sell off all the old stock, and buy in a young lot.' A most disgraceful conclusion for a man to come to, who made such great professions of religion!"[77] That testimony referred not merely to occasional incidents, but to the "usual manner" of dealing with "old, worn-out slaves."[78]

A fourth slave wrote: "Question: What do they do with old slaves, who are past labor? Answer: Contrive all ways to keep them at work till the last hour of life. Make them shell corn and pack tobacco. They hunt and drive them as long as there is any life in them. Sometimes they turn them out to do the best they can, or die. One man, on moving to Missouri, sold an old slave for one dollar, to a man not worth a cent. The old slave was turned out to do the best he could; he fought with age and starvation a while, but was soon found, one morning, *starved* to death, out of doors, and half eaten up by animals. I have known several cases where slaves were left to starve to death in old age. Generally, they sell them south, and let them die there; send them, I mean, before they get very old."[79]

Even for the majority of the white population the reality departed from the ideal. Scholars who should know better sometimes romanticize the social relationships of earlier times. But in fact those relations were often painful and difficult for both young and old alike. The weight of re-

[77] William and Ellen Craft, *Running a Thousand Miles for Freedom; or, the Escape of William and Ellen Craft from Slavery* (Miami, 1969), p. 10.
[78] Granby, "Life," p. 10.
[79] Lewis G. and Milton Clark, *Narratives of the Sufferings of Lewis and Milton Clark* (Boston, 1846), p. 112.

sponsibility rested heavily upon the aged—more heavily than we may easily imagine. We must remember that just as mortality was higher than it is today, so morbidity was also great beyond our own experience. It is sometimes asserted that the few who survived to a ripe old age were more hardy and healthy than the elderly are today. But that was not the case. To be old in early America was to be wracked by illness. It was to live in physical misery, with pain as a constant companion. A protracted life, wrote one clergyman, "is not so properly called living, as dying a lingering death."[80]

We may choose an example at random from old men whose lives are fully documented. Benjamin Franklin suffered terribly in his last years. He was afflicted with infirmities for which medicine knew no remedy—most of all "the stone" and gout—and endured them only by taking opium in massive quantities. "Opium gives me ease when I am attacked by pain," he wrote in 1789, "and by the use of it I still make life at least tolerable."[81] When Washington was elected President of the United States, Franklin sent him a letter of congratulations. "For my own personal ease I should have died two years ago," he wrote, "but though those years have been spent in excruciating pain, I am pleased that I have lived them, since they brought me to see our present situation." The agony of old age afflicted Franklin with a *tedium vitae* which was widespread in early America. As he lay in misery upon his deathbed, his daughter tried to console him with the hope that he would live many years longer. "I hope not," he replied.[82]

Washington, Adams, Jefferson—almost any other promi-

80 Eliab Stone, *A Discourse Delivered at Reading* (Boston, 1811), p. 8.
81 Franklin to Benjamin Vaughn, Nov. 2, 1789, in A. H. Smyth (ed.), *Writings* (10 vols., New York, 1905-7), X, pp. 49-50.
82 Carl Van Doren, *Benjamin Franklin* (New York, 1938), p. 779. Heavy drinking in old age was also common: "Wine is thought to be old-men's milk." Charlestown, S.C. *Gazette*, Apr. 2, 1741.

nent American of that era might equally serve as an example. Scarcely anyone experienced a serene old age. And the worst suffering was perhaps not physical, but emotional. Because old age was so very rare, the aged also suffered from a sense of isolation, loneliness, and emptiness more than they do today. When John Lathrop, a Yankee clergyman, gave his anniversary address in 1811 he expressed a feeling of being totally alone in the world. In fact, he still led a full and active life in the town, but it scarcely seemed to be his town any more. "Let us look around among our neighbors. Where are they who lived here 60 or 70 years ago? They are generally gone. . . . Who now occupy the lands, and dwell in the houses which we see?"[83] For Lathrop, his own descendants were a new race; his old town belonged to strangers.

Nevertheless, the aged were endlessly instructed to be up and doing. "Though your infirmities be never so many and great, yet you have peculiar honour that is twisted with your infirmity, for it is called the Crown of old Age," said William Bridge.[84] And since the hoary head was a crown of glory, Cotton Mather added a clerical command: "Let none of our Old People be so unhappy as to abdicate their Crown." They were to live with great dignity and restraint, "sober, grave, temperate, sound in faith, in charity, in patience," said Mather. "A light and a Gay sort of an Air, in old age, 'tis as improper, as for the winter solstice to pretend unto all the airs of midsummer."[85] The righteousness of their conduct must be such as to "compel a reverence from our juniors."[86] They were to be always a living example of the good old way for the public. And for themselves, their spiritual accounts were always to be kept in balance. Their

[83] Joseph Lathrop, *Old Age Improved* (Springfield, Mass., 1811), p. 4.
[84] William Bridge, *Word to the Aged,* p. 5.
[85] Mather, *A Good Old Age,* pp. 8, 24.
[86] Ibid., p. 27.

model was to be President Chauncey of Harvard, who, according to Increase Mather, "seldom saw a day in which he was not with God at least six times." They were to "maintain religion in their houses" and be active in public affairs. "An old man should, like old Bradford, be always doing of some good. . . . You are to do a little more service and be serviceable until you are by your great master called away."[87]

While the aged were forbidden to lay their burden down, the young were not allowed to take it up. They were kept on leading strings long after their maturity. And though they were often treated as dependents to an extraordinarily advanced age, yet they were forbidden to show resentment or hostility directly by some of the deepest prohibitions of their culture. Such hostility did exist, but it was muted in America; it had none of the intensity that appeared so often in Continental Europe. There is no known American expression comparable to the common *canard* for French fathers who held onto their land—"*père qui vit trop,*" the father who lives too long.[88] There was none of the cold and bitter fury of a German peasant song, which might be translated:

> Papa, when will you give me the farm?
> Papa, when will you give me the house?
> When will you finally move to your little room
> And tend your potato patch?[89]

[87] Mather, *Dignity and Duty*, p. 139.
[88] John R. Gillis, *Youth and History; Tradition and Change in European Age Relationships, 1770-Present* (New York, 1974), p. 41.
[89] Lutz Berkner, "The Stem Family and the Development Cycle of the Peasant Household: An Eighteenth-Century Austrian Example," *American Historical Review*, 77 (1972), 398-418. In the local dialect the verse is:

> Voda, wann gibst ma denn's Hoamatl,
> Voda, wann gibst ma denn's Haus,
> Wann gehst denn amol in dein Stuberl ein,
> Und grobst da bra Erapfoln aus?

Still, there were resentments which found their way to the surface, not in any form which appeared as direct hostility, but in other ways. One of them was drama. In English Restoration comedy, which was often performed in America, "crabbed old age" was a common target of bitter satire, just as it had been for Aristophanes and Plautus. Once again, the vices of old age were attacked as the vices of power. Old men were portrayed as rich and covetous misers who cruelly exploited the young. At the end of the plays they are still rich and covetous, but they have been brought low, and often cuckolded by their young victims. Old men appeared as lecherous, obscene creatures who tormented their beautiful and innocent young wives (though not so innocent as not to have married them in the first place). They were drunken fools, doddering, senile imbeciles, absurd old hypocrites, silly misanthropes. Senility itself became a sort of slapstick. In all these ways the aged were attacked indirectly, even as they were being venerated formally. Ridicule, we must remember, is often a form of rage.[90]

Even the Puritan clergy complained of the vices of age while they celebrated its authority. They recognized that old age had its "moral infirmities." And in that world, where shame was stronger than guilt as the moral cement of society, the moral failings of old age were thought to be the worse because they were the more visible. William Bridge made the point with a simile of extraordinary power: "When the leaves are off the trees, we see the birds' nests in

---

[90] In Restoration drama old age and Puritanism were commonly linked together: consider such characters as Sir John Brute in Vanbrugh's *Provok'd Wife,* Alderman Gripe in Wycherley's *Love in a Wood,* Heartwell in Congreve's *Old Bachelor,* Desbro in Aphra Benn's *The Roundheads,* and Tickletext in *The Feigned Curtezans.* For other examples, see Elisabeth Mignon, *Crabbed Age and Youth: The Old Men and Women in Restoration Comedy of Manners* (Durham, N.C., 1947).

the trees and bushes. Now in our old age our leaves are off, then therefore we may see these nests of sin, and lusts in our hearts and lives, which we saw not before, and so be sensible and repent of them."[91]

The moralists compiled long catalogues of vices and errors to which old people were thought to be especially susceptible. Even so, the lists were shorter for the old than for the young, and their vices were not the most serious in any hierarchy of sin. Cotton Mather wrote that "Old age is often too covetous, too sparing, too hoarding and ready to lay up. . . . Old folks often seem to grasp the hardest for the world, when they are just going out of it: an evil release."[92] The folk myth of the old miser was a powerful theme in early American thought. The miserliness so often attributed to old age may have had a solid foundation in fact. One elderly man wrote to his brother, "I had nobody this last sickness to tend me because it would have cost 12 shillings a week. Some scare me by telling me that I shall live 20 years longer, but I hope I shall not, for I am weary already. . . . I cannot work but contrive not to spend too fast, but pinch what I can. I did not think I should live so long."[93] His fear of destitution was quite real.

Bridge also made a list of the moral infirmities to which old age was sometimes liable. Once again, covetousness led the list. The elderly were also "apt to be too touchy, peevish, angry and forward." They suffered from the sin of pride, and "think they know more than others." They were "Hard to please," "full of complaints," "impenitent," "uncharitable to the sins of youth," and "full of suspicions." And again we find that the vices of age in the seventeenth century were not the vices of weakness, but the vices of

91 Bridge, *Word to the Aged,* p. 6.
92 Mather, *A Good Old Age,* p. 29.
93 Quoted in Demos, "Aging in Pre-Modern Society," p. 12.

power. In early American sermons, an old sinner sinned with authority.

There was still another difficulty in growing old—a difficulty closely connected with the exaltation of old age. Beyond the physical infirmities and the social stresses which were inherent in old age, there were also psychic infirmities, which were often quite severe. The evidence of their existence is not very clear. It appears as an undercurrent in the literature—as an insubstantial shadow which falls across the page.[94] Nevertheless, it seems that old people in early America often had a special kind of difficulty in coming to terms with others and perhaps with themselves. Even as most (though not all) elderly people were apt to hold more power than they would possess in a later period, they were also apt to receive less affection, less love, less sympathy from those younger than themselves. The elderly were kept at an emotional distance by the young. If open hostility between the generations was not allowed, affection was not encouraged either. Veneration, after all, is a cold emotion. The elderly often complained that they had lived to become strangers in their own society, aliens in their own time. And so they were, in a psychic sense—strangers in the hearts of their own posterity, aliens from the affection of their own kin.

At the same time, the restless striving of Puritan elders suggests still another kind of psychic difficulty. Old people in early America were also apt to be at odds with themselves. Psychic serenity in old age was very rare. There was a continuing anxiety which people carried to their deathbeds. Were they fulfilling their social obligations? Were they keeping faith with their God? Growing old was full of

[94] On this elusive subject I owe much to John Demos, who generously shared his own thinking and writing with me. See also A. Lipman, "Prestige of the Aged in Portugal: Realistic Appraisal and Ritualistic Deference," *Aging and Human Development*, I (1970), 127-36.

psychic pain in Puritan America. Here was the great and final irony—that the extraordinary social power of the aged in early America was accompanied by a crushing psychic weakness. Old age was exalted by law and custom, but it was wounded in the heart. Those two sides of its condition were combined in a pattern of great complexity.

For nearly two hundred years that pattern persisted in America. The system of age relations continued to operate in the same way. The clergy continued to deliver their sermons on the exaltation of age. Youth was still instructed to venerate the old, and age was urged to "condescend" to youth. The people of New England still "dignified" the seats of their meetinghouses, and gave the highest dignity to the aged. Old men still occupied high offices until they died in them. Fathers still waited until they reached their sixties before releasing land to their grown sons. And the dynamics of family relationships still favored the power of the old.

But late in the eighteenth century there were growing signs of strain in the system of age relations. In the 1760's, just as the colonies found themselves increasingly in opposition to what they called the "mother country," there was growing trouble between the generations in some American families. In both cases the problems were political—they were problems of liberty and power.

Consider the history of one American family, and two men within it—Landon Carter of Sabine Hall (1710-78), a great Virginia planter, and his eldest son, Robert Wormeley Carter (1734-97). In 1766, the year that Parliament passed its "Declaratory Act" over the colonies, Robert Carter was thirty-two years old and married, with money of his own but not enough for independence. He continued to live in his father's house, and under his father's authority. But he was growing restless. The father at the same time was increasingly disturbed by the conduct of his "graceless son," who seemed to have a "constant genius for contradiction" and deliberately did "everything to thwart me." The father was conscious of giving more than he owed; the son, of receiving less than his due.

In July of 1766, on one of those humid, hot Virginia days which try the most serene temper, the trouble between the two men suddenly burst into the open. It started trivially, with an argument over a teapot. The father sent a slave to fetch a pot of tea, and the son muttered something which might have been an accusation of extravagance. The father exploded.

"What, Sir!" he said, "Can't I spend my own money?"

"By God," replied the son, "You will have none to spend soon."

Words began to fly faster than thoughts. "He said abundance more, and I replied tauntingly," the father wrote remorsefully in his diary. "Perhaps we are equally unhappy in temper. I am old, but . . . sons are determined against the least indulgence to the Grey hour of a parent."

If that was a "Grey hour," there were black ones in the years ahead. After the teapot-tempest, the enmity between father and son began to feed upon itself. There were many bitter arguments, and nearly all of them could be traced to a single cause—the son's continued dependence upon his father. The father, for his part, wrote once in his diary, "I would have indulged the brute, could his behavior have been any other but absolute control in my house, which I don't care to give up to a son who will not nor ever does behave with any kind of respect."

Every trivial difference became a symbolic test of

strength. When the father ordered ale for dinner, the son requested beer instead, and was refused. At the next meal the father ordered beer, and the son refused to drink it. It went on that way for ten years. Then, in 1776, when the son invited some friends for an evening of gambling in the house, the father peremptorily ordered the cards and tables removed, and was utterly astonished by his son's response. "I was told by a forty-year-old man he was not a child to be controulled," the father recorded in his diary. And the son called his father a "bashaw," an Oriental despot, in language which Americans were learning to apply to George III in that year.

Feelings grew so high that the two men came close to physical blows. The father began to fear for his life, and went about his own house armed with a pistol. "Surely it is happy our laws prevent parricide," he wrote in his diary, "or the devil that moves to this treatment, would move to put his father out of the way. Good God! That such a monster is descended from my loins!"[95]

The struggle took a heavy toll of both men. The father began to spend more time in the solitude of his own sitting room, drinking heavily. "Nothing but spirits seems to be able to restore such a lost tone in old age," he wrote. The son, on the other hand, went roistering about the country, and the neighbors gave him the nickname of "Wild Bob." Peace came to Sabine Hall only with the death of the father in 1778.

The parallel between the family wars of the Carters and the American War for Independence was too close to have been coincidental. Both conflicts developed out of questions of authority and independence. At the same time that

---

[95] All this is from Jack P. Greene (ed.), *Diary of Colonel Landon Carter of Sabine Hall, 1752-1778* (2 vols., Charlottesville, Va., 1965), pp. 250, 310, 315, 713, 763, 1004, 1102.

America was fighting for autonomy, Robert Wormeley Carter was waging his own private war of independence from his father. Relations between the generations had been deeply affected by the same principles which led to colonial resistance. A new set of social ideas had found a sudden release in the American air, and the traditional system of age relations could not long coexist with them. A revolution was in the making, which is the next chapter of our history.

II. THE REVOLUTION IN AGE RELATIONS
1770-1820

I can never forgive New York, Connecticut or Maine for turning out venerable men of sixty or seventy . . . when their judgment is often the best.

John Adams (1735-1826)

It is reasonable we should drop off, and make room for another growth. When we have lived our generation out, we should not wish to encroach upon another.

Thomas Jefferson (1743-1826)

LATE in the eighteenth century the western world experienced a social revolution which was more powerful in its causes and more profound in its effects than any comparable happening in modern history. The American War of Independence and the French Revolution were both parts of that great upheaval; the Russian and Chinese revolutions would be its echoes in the outer world. But the great revolution itself was something larger than those mighty events, and something deeper than the political disturbances which it caused. It was a fundamental change in world culture, which began in the western nations and spread swiftly to every human society on the face of the earth. In Anglo-America, where its full effects were first felt between 1770 and 1820, radical changes simultaneously appeared in demography and economics, politics and law, stratification and association, ideology and psychology, eth-

ics and aesthetics. Every sort of human relation was transformed by it: relations between nations, classes, races, sexes
—and also generations.

The great revolution was, among other things, a revolution in age relations. It was the end of an *ancien régime*
which was also a *régime des anciens,* and the beginning of a
new order of things built upon a different principle. The
revolution created a world without "veneration" on the
one hand or "condescension" on the other; a world without
eldership or primogeniture. On the surface it introduced
a spirit of age equality, which reached its most dramatic expression in the famous public *fêtes* of the French Revolution, where a symbolic harmony of youth and age was celebrated in elaborate rituals. In those public festivals, the old
men distributed gifts of figs and raisins to the youths; in
turn, the young women presented baskets of bread and fruit
to their elders.[1] But beneath that surface a new sort of inequality was being born, a new hierarchy of generations in
which youth acquired the moral advantage that age had
lost.

In America the first small signs of change began to appear
as early as the middle of the eighteenth century. Among the
first to be challenged was the custom of "seating the meeting" according to age. In a few New England towns that
practice had begun to grow weak early in the century.
Northampton, Massachusetts, for example, was still operating according to the old way in 1707, when it instructed its
seating committee "first to have regard to a person's age,

[1] Mona Ozouf, "Symboles et Fonction des Ages dans Les Fêtes de l'Époque
Révolutionnaire," *Annales Historiques de la Révolution Française,* 42 (1970),
569-93.

second to estate, and third to have some regard to men's usefulness." Thirty years later the town decided to reverse the relative importance of age and wealth. In 1737 its seating committee was instructed to "have respect principally to men's estate. 2. to have regard to men's age. 3. voted that there be some regard and respect to men's usefulness but in a less degree."[2]

Northampton was not a typical town. Most others continued to use age as the primary criterion for ranking until the end of the eighteenth century. But then, one by one, they stopped seating their meetinghouses in the traditional way. The transition began slowly in the mid-eighteenth century, reached its peak in the 1790's, and was largely completed by 1830. When the towns stopped "dignifying the seats," they did not abandon the practice of seating altogether. Instead of assigning the seats by age, estate, and place, the committees often sold them at auction, and the best bench in the meetinghouse went to the highest bidder. In that way, the towns shifted from a pluralistic system of stratification to a unitary system based primarily on wealth alone. Rank and status in the meetinghouse thereafter rested upon material possessions, without regard to age.[3]

[2] John R. Trumbull, *History of Northampton* (2 vols., Northampton, 1898-1902), I, 517; II, 74.

[3] The practice of seating the meeting in Massachusetts was abolished by the following dates:

Watertown	1775	Townshend	1780	Ludlow	1797
Wenham	1765	Stow	1790	Newton	1800
Needham	1775	Weston	1791	Acton	1808
Amherst	1775	Middlefield	1791	Dover	1812
Topsfield	1780	Concord	1792	Deerfield	1820
Manchester	1780	Framingham	1794	Northfield	1830
Princeton	1780	Boxborough	1796	Pittsfield	1836

Source: Robert J. Dinkin, "Provincial Massachusetts: A Deferential or a Democratic Society," unpubl. Ph.D. thesis, Columbia, 1968, pp. 195-99; J. E. A. Smith, *The History of Pittsfield, Mass.* (2 vols., Boston, 1869-76), II,

That was mainly a ceremonial change in the prerequisites of old age. Another innovation made at the end of the eighteenth century reached directly to its power. Between 1790 and 1820, American legislatures for the first time began to require public officials to retire from office at a predetermined age—usually sixty or seventy. That policy of compulsory retirement was first introduced for judges. The earliest instance appears to have been a provision in New York's constitution of 1777, which was a response to a specific problem created by the senility of a sitting judge. No other state acted at the same time, but within a few years many others began to do so. In 1792 New Hampshire required judges to leave the bench at seventy. Connecticut enacted a similar law in 1818, and New York in 1821 lowered its limit to sixty. By 1820 at least six other states had passed retirement laws.[4]

Those statutes infuriated former President John Adams, who, at the age of eighty-nine, expressed his indignation in the letter quoted briefly at the beginning of this chapter. "I can never forgive New York, Connecticut, or Maine," he wrote, "for turning out venerable men. . . . To turn out such men to eat husks with the prodigal or grass with Nebuchadnezzar ought to be tormenting to the humanity of the nation."[5] For Adams, it was not merely a question of humanity, but of the common good. He quoted a curious phrase from Sir Edward Coke which rings so strangely in a

---

p. 312; Susan Kurland, "A Political History of Concord," unpubl. senior thesis, Brandeis, 1972, p. 148.

Each town was apt to differ in detail. Some communities adopted seating assignments based explicitly on wealth, without having an auction. Others sold special pews to the wealthiest people in town, while at the same time distributing most seats in the traditional way.

[4] F. N. Thorpe, *Federal and State Constitutions* (7 vols., Washington, D.C., 1909).

[5] Lester J. Cappon, *The Adams-Jefferson Letters* (2 vols., Chapel Hill, N.C., 1959), II, p. 582.

modern ear that it tells us something of the enormous social distance between their world and our own. Adams believed that "None were fit for Legislators and magistrates but 'sad men.' " And who were those sad men? he asked. "They were aged men who had been tossed and buffeted by the vicissitudes of Life, forced upon profound reflection by grief and disappointments, and taught to command their passions."[6]

Adams's correspondent strenuously disagreed. Thomas Jefferson was also an octogenarian—only eight years younger than Adams—but he shared the new spirit of that revolutionary era in a way that Adams could not. While living in Paris during the 1780's Jefferson had made two great discoveries for himself. The first was the tyranny of one class over another, which he learned by observing French society, where everyone seemed to be either "a hammer or an anvil," either a "sheep or a wolf." The second was an idea taught him by an English radical named Richard Gem— that another great tyranny was one of generations. Jefferson took up Dr. Gem's idea with an evangelical enthusiasm, and set himself to converting others. The result was one of the most extraordinary and powerful cycles in his epistolary writing, in which he argued that "the land belongs in usufruct to the living," that one generation had no right to bind another, and that the constitution of a republic and all of its laws should be rewritten at least once every nineteen years.

Jefferson's American friends were not receptive to his new enthusiasm. James Madison, who had just survived the agony of framing one constitution (Jefferson had been in France at the time) observed mildly that the idea of having to do it over again every nineteen years was "liable in practice to some powerful objections." Jefferson's doctrine never

6 Ibid.

became popular in its pure form, but it was established in substance by those American states which made regular provisions for revising their fundamental laws as often as they pleased. And the regularity with which Americans rewrote their political rules in the nineteenth century reflected a deep change in attitudes toward change itself.[7]

A similar change simultaneously occurred in attitudes toward age. Changes in popular attitudes are perhaps the most elusive of historical events, but, if we use a little ingenuity, we find that they are susceptible to empirical study, and even to statistical measurement. One quantitative test of attitudes toward age is made possible by a happy quirk of human nature: when people report their ages to census takers they are apt to bend the truth a bit. The result is a pattern of systematic distortion in age statistics which is called "age heaping." To a demographer, age heaping is an inconvenience, but to an historian it is an opportunity, for it allows him to measure the intensity of age bias as it has changed through time.

Two kinds of age heaping commonly exist in census data. One is a tendency of people to round off their ages and to report them as twenty, thirty, or forty, rather than the odd years in between. In seventeenth-century America that kind of age heaping was very common, either because people did not know how old they were or because they did not care.[8] But as literacy increased, and America became a nation of

---

[7] In the late 18th century, words which described change reversed their values. Then, "novelty," "innovation," and "modern" were all pejoratives. But by the early 19th century they had become praise words. See Raymond Williams, *Keywords* (New York, 1976), p. 174.

[8] It is probable that they cared very much. When John Hull, the Puritan goldsmith and merchant, went to England, one of the first things he did was try to discover how old his wife was. "Being in England, I went to town where my wife Judith was born, and took her age out of the register, born September 3, 1626." Hull, "Diary," *American Antiquarian Society Transactions and Collections,* III (1857), 152.

clock watchers and calendar keepers, age heaping of that sort slowly declined. Today it scarcely exists, at least by comparison with the distant past.

But at the same time, another kind of age heaping has actually increased. Today it is common for people to pretend to be younger than they really are. They prefer to be listed in the census as thirty-nine rather than forty or forty-one, and sometimes they remain thirty-nine for several years—perhaps until they are suddenly forty-nine. Contrary to popular belief, men are more vain about their age than women. The "thirty-nine" syndrome is a masculine weakness, not a feminine one. It is also strongest in what we call middle age—rising through the thirties and forties, peaking at about fifty, and declining thereafter, but never entirely disappearing. Even octogenarians in America today prefer to be seventy-nine, according to the most recent evidence. In the twentieth century that foible has become a staple joke for stand-up comedians such as Jack Benny. The humor rests upon the assumption that most people have always wanted to be younger than they are, and probably always will.

But if we examine the history of age heaping in America, we discover that attitudes have changed remarkably through time.[9] The evidence is flawed in many ways: continuous

[9] Our quantitative test rests upon a ratio between actual and reported ages. Actual ages are computed as a 10-year moving average of reported ages, thus:

$$R_x = \frac{10A_x}{\displaystyle\sum_{i=(A_x-5)}^{n=(A_x+5)}(A_n - A_x)}$$

Where no age heaping exists, actual and reported ages are the same, and the ratio $(R_x) = 1.000$. When ages are over-reported, ratios rise above 1.000; when under-reported, they fall below it. If no age heaping exists in the reporting of ages, then age ratios for 39, 40, and 41 will be the same. Where

data reach backward only to 1880. For information before that date we must rely upon small samples and local census lists.[10] Nevertheless, the evidence at hand clearly shows that the pattern of age bias has changed greatly over the past three centuries. In early America, people did not try to make themselves out to be younger than they were; they tended to represent themselves as older instead. That tendency was weakest in early life, but existed at all age levels, and grew much stronger in the eighteenth century. (See Table 2.1.) In the nineteenth and twentieth centuries, on the other hand, people tended to represent themselves as younger than they actually were. That bias toward youth grew steadily stronger with each succeeding census, from the late eighteenth century to the late twentieth.[11] (See Ta-

the reporting is biased against old age, more people tend to report themselves as 39 and fewer as 41. Thus age ratios fall below 1.000 for 39 and rise above it for 41. Where bias toward old age exists, the opposite pattern appears:

Age	No Bias	Bias Toward Old Age	Bias Toward Youth
39	1.00	0.90	1.10
40	1.00	1.00	1.00
41	1.00	1.10	0.90

10 The test works badly for the 17th century, because age heaping to ages ending in zero was very great, and numbers of people reporting ages ending in 9 or 1 were very small. As a result the figures are unstable. We have three 17th-century studies, each done by slightly different methods. One shows a general bias toward age rather than youth; another shows that pattern only at advanced ages; a third is inconclusive. On balance, the 17th-century material suggests a bias toward age which was weaker than that of the 18th century. Two other censuses are available for Westchester County, N.Y.: Bedford and New Rochelle (c. 1698). See Robert Wells, *The Population of the British Colonies in North America before 1776* (Princeton, 1975), p. 117. But the numbers are too small to be useful. Wells, who has made a more careful study of early American census materials than anyone else, writes that, other than the Maryland, New Haven, and Westchester census tracts, he knows of no data indicating exact ages before 1790.

11 Exact ages were first recorded in the federal census of 1850, but totals for each age were not calculated until 1880. To make such a calculation it is necessary to return to manuscript census schedules and add each age individually, an enormously tedious task. Helena Wall was assigned the job of

TABLE 2.1
The Exaltation of Age in Early America
Age Heaping Ratios, c. 1636-1787

Age	Prince George's County, Md. 1776	New Haven, Conn. 1787	Middlesex County, Mass. 1661-75	Essex County, Mass. 1636-72
29	.981	.798	.617	.793
30	2.266	1.575	1.944	2.716
31	.561	.949	.597	.498
39	.732	1.014	.166	.503
40	3.264	1.557	2.449	3.939
41	1.067	.879	.392	.363
49	.594	.585	.222	.669
50	2.029	1.934	4.286	4.161
51	.875	.923	.541	.254
59	.467	.522	.416	.327
60	3.818	2.456	6.875	4.139
61	1.400	.902	.385	.365
69				.345
70				3.354
71				.384
n	5292	5085	251	4106

Sources: Prince George's County, Md.: John Modell, unpubl. compilation of ages reported in two parishes, 1776, from Gaius M. Brumbaugh, *Maryland Records*, I, 1-89. (Blacks are omitted, on the assumption that their ages were reported for them.) Essex and Middlesex counties are calculated from Carol Shuchman, "Examining Life Expectancies in Seventeenth Century Massachusetts," unpubl. paper, Brandeis, 1976, and from data kindly furnished by John Demos.

ble 2.2.) In brief, the evidence of age reporting shows that attitudes toward age have been continually changing throughout American history. But the pattern of change itself was changed sometime between 1790 and 1850.

---

drawing a small sample from the census of 1850. She found a pattern of age heaping which is consistent with the trend from 1880 to 1950. Her age heaping ratios (ages 29-81) were as follows: ages ending in 9, .893; ages ending in 0, 1.437; ages ending in 1, .815. She found a strong pattern of age heaping to even years ending in zero (30, 40, 50, etc.) and a moderate bias toward youth. If the sample is accurate, then the transition occurred before 1850.

TABLE 2.2
The Growth of Youth Bias in Modern America
Age Heaping Ratios, 1880-1950

Age	1880	1890	1900	1910	1920	1930	1940	1950
29	.873	.897	.957	.945	.969	.993	1.016	1.040
30	1.296	1.253	1.143	1.164	1.119	1.073	1.027	1.000
31	.779	.803	.877	.850	.873	.896	.919	.942
39	.927	.944	.994	.979	.996	1.014	1.031	1.048
40	1.345	1.303	1.159	1.219	1.176	1.133	1.089	1.045
41	.791	.807	.874	.839	.855	.871	.887	.903
49	.897	.919	.975	.964	.985	1.007	1.029	1.051
50	1.372	1.332	1.214	1.252	1.211	1.170	1.128	1.087
51	.817	.828	.936	.851	.862	.873	.884	.895
59	.820	.851	.943	.910	.940	.969	.998	1.027
60	1.320	1.284	1.169	1.209	1.172	1.134	1.095	1.057
61	.787	.799	.879	.821	.833	.844	.855	.866
69	.878	.897	.941	.936	.955	.974	.994	1.013
70	1.197	1.172	1.096	1.123	1.098	1.073	1,048	1.023
71	.782	.800	.891	.836	.853	.871	.889	.906
79	.858	.879	.909	.922	.943	.964	.985	1.006
80	1.142	1.119	1.008	1.075	1.052	1.030	1.007	.985
81	.808	.822	.913	.851	.865	.879	.892	.906

These are the numbers by which reported ages must be divided to obtain true ages. The magnitudes of these divisors measure the amount of age heaping at each given age. A value of 1.000 indicates that reported ages equal actual ages. Values above 1.000 indicate that more people report themselves to be that age than are actually so. Values below 1.000 indicate the opposite. See Ansley J. Coale and Melvin Zelnick, *New Estimates of Fertility and Population in the United States* (Princeton, 1963), pp. 127-28.

At the same time, a parallel pattern appeared in other evidence—that of costume. During the seventeenth century, and even more so in the eighteenth, male fashions flattered age; that was one of its primary purposes. The intent was to make young men look older than they actually were. Hair styles were particularly important; natural hair was hidden beneath a wig, or powdered and made white as if by old age. The cut of men's clothing had a similar purpose. During the eighteenth century clothes were cunningly tailored in such a way that the shoulders were made narrow and rounded, the hips and waists were actually broadened, and the backs of the coats were designed to make the spine appear to be bent by the weight of many years. Only one part of the body was revealed—the lower leg, which is, perhaps, an old man's last anatomical advantage. During those two centuries these tendencies became stronger rather than weaker; the pattern of bias toward old age in men's clothing actually grew more intense.

But between 1790 and 1815, men's dress was revolutionized. Artifice remained, but its effect was reversed. The French Revolution introduced fashions that flattered youth. Wigs were replaced by hairpieces and toupees, which were designed to make old men look young again. The white powder that had been used to give men the appearance of age, yielded to hair dyes, tints, and preservatives. The cut of a coat was designed to flatter a youthful figure. It was pulled in at the waist and puffed out at the shoulders, and the back was made straight and broad. Knee breeches were replaced by trousers, which was primarily a statement about class relations, but the design of the trousers also made a point about age. The trousers were tightly trimmed, and if they were a bit more trim than the men who wore them, there were corsets for men as well as for women. From about 1790 to our time, fashion has attempted in its endless variety of ways to make old men look young again.

During the transition there was a thirty years' war of the sartorial generations, and a deadly struggle it was, deeply disturbing to those who lived through it. Many old men were left behind by the change—men such as Samuel Curwen (1715-1802), a Salem merchant who had been born in the reign of George I and died in the administration of Thomas Jefferson. By the early nineteenth century he had become a famous sight. "He appeared in our streets, much like a Patriarch," wrote a local clergyman. "The English tye-wig, the long scarlet cloak, the heavy rings, and gold-headed cane attracted notice after the war, tho' it was best dress before it, for persons of condition."[12] Samuel Curwen, tottering feebly through the streets of Salem, was an object of respect before the Revolution; afterward, he was a curiosity instead. But the change was most cruel in its effects upon the generation that came after Curwen's—the generation whose unhappy fate it was to be young in an era when age was respected and old in a time when youth took the palm.

The transition occasionally had its amusing moments. In Concord, Massachusetts, an elderly gentleman named Abiel Heywood was, according to his biographer, "the last man in the town, excepting the Reverend Dr. Ripley, who wore the old-fashioned knee-breeches, or small-clothes. When about marrying, he for the first time procured a pair of pantaloons, and informing Mr. Nathan Brooks of the fact, inquired of him how they were to be put on. Mr. Brooks told him he believed that people generally drew them on over their heads, but whether the doctor tried that mode does not appear; if he did, he never made public the result of the experiment, and it is only known that he succeeded in some way or other in getting the strange garment on, became reconciled to the fashion and thereafter followed it." It is interesting to observe that Heywood adopted the new fashion on the eve of his marriage at an advanced age.[13]

The history of women's dress is far more complex than that of men's. The primary purpose of feminine fashion was to express a spirit of sexual subordination, and even to

12 William Bentley, Diary, II, 423.

13 Francis R. Gourgas, "Memoir of Abiel Heywood," *Memoirs of Members of the Social Circle in Concord. Second Series, From 1795 to 1840* (Cambridge, Mass., 1888). I owe this anecdote to the kindness of Robert Gross.

promote it. But behind that purpose, attitudes toward age also appeared. We have discovered from some of the earliest feminine costumes which have been found that old women and young women dressed very differently thousands of years ago. Clothing that has survived (by a miracle of preservation) in prehistoric burial mounds shows that young women dressed in a most extraordinary way for that cold climate. The body of a handsome Danish girl of twenty was buried in a brief tunic which barely covered her breasts, and low upon her hips she wore a remarkable short skirt— made not of cloth, but of loose-hanging cords—which revealed more than it concealed. Very different is an old woman's costume which has also survived from the same period. She wore a long skirt, made of closely woven cloth, which rose to meet a bodice and fell nearly to the ground. Thus ancient fashion flattered both youth and age by shrouding an old body in flowing drapery while revealing the grace of a young one.

In the modern era we find a different pattern: Feminine costumes were more or less the same for women of all ages. There were many small differences—caps for married women and other symbols of rank, status, and condition, which were codified in what were called "sumptuary laws." But in the seventeenth and mid-eighteenth centuries, every woman's body was hidden beneath her dress—all but the shoulders and breasts, which are parts of the body that a mature woman may show to advantage. Torsos distended by twenty years of child-bearing were carefully camouflaged, and hips broadened by six or eight deliveries were buried in flowing skirts. Legs were made totally invisible—a service to old age. Women wore wigs and powdered their hair just as men did, and with the same effect. Women's clothing in the early modern era was designed to flatter age rather than youth.

That pattern prevailed until the late eighteenth century.

Then the dressmakers of post-Revolutionary Paris began to produce the first feminine fashions in modern history that were designed primarily for youth. The diaphanous gowns of the "Directory" style enormously flattered a youthful body and cruelly mocked an old one. When a Baltimore beauty married the brother of Napoleon, one observer remarked that her wedding gown was so insubstantial that it could be squeezed into a snuffbox! That style was widely adopted by young women in America during the early nineteenth century despite the stern disapproval of their elders.

But it soon ended. Feminine fashion also had its Thermidor—perhaps because the primary purpose of women's dress was still to show the subordination of women rather than the superiority of youth. The old style returned, and retained its hegemony until the 1920's, when women's clothing suddenly began to be oriented unequivocally toward youth instead of age, with more exposure and less support, higher hemlines and lower necklines. From the 1920's to the 1970's, in summer fashions especially, hemlines moved intermittently higher and necklines progressively lower. In the summers of 1973 and 1974, designers added (or subtracted) bare midriffs; in the summers of 1975 and 1976, bare backs. A social historian may await the future with some anticipation.

Still another kind of evidence of the changing attitude toward age is linguistic. As elderly people began to lose their social status, the world developed a more elaborate vocabulary with which to abuse them. The result was the invention of a new language to express contempt for old people. If we consult the *Oxford English Dictionary*, we discover that most of the pejorative terms for old men appeared for the first time in the late eighteenth and early nineteenth centuries. Some were old words which had earlier carried an honorific meaning—*gaffer*, for example. *Gaffer* had been a title of respect, even a term of endearment, in seventeenth- and eighteenth-century England. It probably arose as a contraction of godfather. But by 1820 *gaffer* (usually *old gaffer*) had been converted from a praise word into a pejorative expressing general contempt for old men. Another such word is *fogy*, which before 1780 meant a wounded military veteran. By 1830 *fogy* had become a "disrespectful appellation for a man advanced in life." The term was put to heavy use in American politics during the 1850's, at the time of the "Young America" movement: the rhetoric of the movement reviled *fogyism* (the characteristic thought of fogies), *fogydom* (the genus of fogies), and *fogyish* behavior in all its forms.

Shakespeare sometimes used the word *greybeard* to describe an honorable old man, and "greybeard counsell" as a synonym for wisdom. But every example from the nineteenth century in the *Oxford English Dictionary* carries a negative connotation. In 1815 *old guard* was a descriptive phrase which was worn like a decoration by Napoleon's soldiers; its first English translations carried the same meaning. By 1880 *old guard* had become an American expression used to describe reactionary, corrupt, and aged politicians.

Superannuated seems also to have shifted its meaning. In the seventeenth and eighteenth centuries, according to the *Oxford English Dictionary*, it referred to people of various ages who were disqualified from some particular service or activity by reason of their age—old maids in their forties, half-pay officers in their thirties, aging courtiers in their twenties, and boys in their teens who had passed the age for school admission were all called *superannuated*. But in the nineteenth and twentieth centuries, *superannuated* increasingly referred to men and women in their sixties, and implied a kind of generalized incompetence.

At the same time that old words changed their meanings, new ones were invented, thus enlarging the vocabulary of abuse. They began to appear in the late eighteenth century and multiplied rapidly in the nineteenth. One example is *codger,* a slang word of urban origin, which probably was derived from the verb *to cadge,* or beg. The first clear example given in the *Oxford English Dictionary* dates from 1775. By 1796, *codger* was being used as a specialized pejorative for a "mean stingy miserly old fellow."[14]

In the next century many other terms of specialized abuse were invented. *Old cornstalk* (1824) was an Americanism for "an ineffectual old man."[15] *Old goat* meant a lecherous old man, *fuddy-duddy,* a pompous old man, *granny,* a weak old man; *mummy,* an ugly old man; *geezer,* an eccentric old man; *goose,* a silly old man; *galoot,* an uncouth old man; *bottle-nose,* an alcoholic old man; *back number,* an anachronistic old man.[16] Still another set of words was invented to express an indiscriminate contempt for age—*baldhead* (1800), *baldy* (1820), *oldster* (1829), *oldliner* (1855), *old womanish* (1775), and *old womanism* (1828). Those words entered the language at the same time that others, opposite in connotation, were disappearing from use—*progenitor, eldern, beldam,*[17] *grandame, grandsire, forefather, gramfer, granther, grannam.*

The worst pejoratives were rude and vulgar salutations which any arrogant young man might use to greet any old

---

14 The word *cojer* may have meant the same thing as early as 1756.

15 See Mitford M. Mathews (ed.), *A Dictionary of Americanisms* (Chicago, 1951), p. 1153.

16 Note the shift in the vices associated with age. Where once they were the vices of strength, they soon became the vices of weakness.

17 In the 18th century *beldam* was an honorable title for grandmother. In the 19th century it became a pejorative, like *hag* or *virago.*

one—words such as *old-timer* (1824) and *pop* (from at least 1889)—which signaled in advance that an elderly man was about to be treated as a member of a generational proletariat. In the eighteenth century, on the other hand, there was a language, now lost, which was the generational equivalent of apple-polishing. Then, *grandfather* was a verb; *to grandfather* meant "to flatter with an excess of veneration." In 1748 Richardson used it that way in his *Clarissa:* "Nor would I advise that you should go to grandfather your cousin."[18]

The semantical pattern we find in the changing language of age relations is similar to all our other evidence. But it is important to observe that words describing old women have a different history. Virtually every term of abuse used for old women appears to be as old as the English language itself. *Hag* was a common term in the fourteenth century; it was used to describe a woman suspected of practicing witchcraft, and also any repulsive and ugly old woman. *Crone* is equally antique. *Old maid* meant nothing good as early as 1530, when she was described as "the most calamitous creature in nature." *Old trot* appears in Shakespeare's *Taming of the Shrew.*[19] The fact that such language existed long before a similar set of words appeared for men strongly suggests that old women were despised not so much for being old as for being women. On the other hand, the language of abuse for old men dates only to about 1800. Before that time there was instead a special vocabulary of abuse for young men—words such as *yongling* and *skipper*—which has become extinct. Dr. Johnson was heard to complain of impudent *puppies* and Mr. Pickwick of *young upstarts*. All of those terms have disappeared from common usage. It is difficult to think of any twentieth-century words that imply

[18] Samuel Richardson, *Clarissa Harlowe* (London, 1768), I, 331.
[19] I. ii. 79.

contempt explicitly for youth. Some are specially reserved for young people—*young punk,* for instance. But young punks are contemptible because they are punks, not because they are young. Modern words that were originally invented as pejoratives for youth have tended to be transformed by usage into praise words. The word *kid* meant something rude in the early twentieth century, but by the next generation its connotation had been reversed. On the other hand, praise words invented for old people are quickly turned the other way—euphemisms such as *senior citizen* are often laden with a heavy freight of sarcasm. Thus the evidence of language shows, once again, the same pattern and timing of change as the evidence of age bias in census tracts and men's fashions.

Still another sign of change in attitudes toward age appears in a visual form. Group portraits of American families necessarily expressed an ideal of age relationships. The artist, in solving his problem of composition, made each portrait a statement about generations. These statements changed through time, and in an interesting way.[20]

[20] Historians today sometimes offer three categorical objections to the use of literature and painting as evidence in social history: that it is elitist, that it reflects artists' conventions rather than societal customs, and that it is "impressionistic." All of those complaints (as caveats, at least) are incorrect. The first is empirically mistaken, for in Anglo-America formal culture was not restricted to a small elite. Literacy, book ownership, library membership, the social origins of artists, and the origins of their clientele show roughly the same pattern. From 1750 to 1850, the top 60 to 70% of the population (ranked by wealth) participated in cultural affairs. Only a minority was excluded. Intensity of participation was uneven, but not as much as one might expect. Undoubtedly, other societies were very different, but in America literary evidence is not necessarily "elitist." Second, the objections to an inference from "art" to "life" rest upon an error in logic— a fallacy of false dichotomy. Aesthetic conventions, after all, are the conventions of the culture in which they arise. A family painting is secondary

No family portraits are known to have survived from seventeenth-century America. The earliest we have is Feke's *Royall Family,* painted in 1741. Only a few have come down to us from the eighteenth century, but before 1775, all except one portrait had the same composition. The father stood above his family—a stern, unbending, proprietary figure. His wife was seated below him, with other women of the household. And the children were placed below the wife. That vertical composition represented a hierarchical relationship between sexes and generations.

After about 1780, another arrangement began to appear: all the members of the family were placed upon the same horizontal plane. No longer was the father a patriarchal figure, brooding above his wife and children; he and his wife were now on the same level—and so also were the children. That horizontal style remained conventional until the twentieth century; in fact, every family painting we have found from 1820 to 1890 was composed in precisely that way. (See Table 2.3.) Then, in our own time, a pluralistic pattern of composition arose, in some family paintings, the children were actually placed above their parents—and a new idea of generational inequality was displayed. Once again, we see the same lines of change—this time reflected in the evidence of American art. The timing of that change was precisely the same as that in our census data, fashion history, and social vocabulary.[21]

---

evidence of that family's activities, but primary evidence of the artist's idea of the family. His idea is often highly conventional—but for our purposes conventionality is a strength, not a weakness, for it is the social convention that we wish to discover. Third, such evidence is not impressionistic if we clearly establish the boundaries of our inquiry in advance, and include all available evidence that falls within it, on both sides of the question.

[21] A similar test might also be made of age relations in American drama and fiction—difficult because there was so little of it before 1790, but enough to be useful. The plays of Munford and Royal Tyler are full of references to age relations.

TABLE 2.3
Composition of Family Portraits, 1729-1871

Date	Painter	Subject	Age Composition Vertical	Horizontal
1729	Smibert	Bishop Berkeley & entourage	X	
1741	Feke	Isaac Royall family	X	
1747	Greenwood	Greenwood-Lee family	X	
1750	Copley	John Temple family	X	
1755	Blackburn	Winslow family	X	
1771	C. W. Peale	Lloyd family	X	
1772	C. W. Peale	Cadwalader family	X	
1772	C. W. Peale	Johnson family	X	
1774	Williams	Denning family		X
1775	Dawkins	Burroughs family	X	
1777	Copley	Copley family	X	
1777	Trumbull	Trumbull family		X
1789	Savage	Washington family		X
1791	C. W. Peale	Unknown		X
1793	Wright	Wright family	X	
1795	Jas. Peale	Peale family		X
1800	Anonymous	Sargent family	X	
1800	West	Hope family	X	
1804	Earl	Unknown		X
1804	Johnson	McCormick family		X
1806	Trumbull	Vernet family		X
1815	Pinney	Cottle family		X
1820	Harding	Smith family	X	
1830	Davis	Unknown		X
1832	Smith	Talcott family		X
1835	Davis	Unknown		X
1836	Knight	Unknown		X
1840	Field	Moore family		X
1850	Hollingsworth	Hollingsworth family		X
1871	Johnson	Hatch family		X

I am grateful to Mr. Lewis Kachur for his assistance in assembling this evidence. This includes all family portraits he could find in which the father, mother, and children appeared together. He did not use paintings which showed only fragments of a family.

Still other evidence appears in the history of inheritance customs. In early America, attitudes toward age fixed the flow of power not merely between generations, but also within them. In a world where "older" meant "better," the eldest child received advantages denied to others. The first-born son was better born than any of his brothers. New England, as well as the southern colonies, actually practiced a modified system of primogeniture by which the eldest son commonly inherited the largest share of the property. He rarely received the entire estate, but was favored over his brothers in material possessions, marriage chances, and many other things.

There was no necessary economic reason for favoring the first-born son. The collective interest of the family could have been met by another arrangement, in which the youngest child received the largest share instead. That system was, in fact, actually practiced in some parts of England.[22] In one way it was more workable than primogeniture. When the father died the eldest son had already set up a household for himself, while the youngest was often the child who looked after the parents in their last years and still lived on the homestead. But Americans used a modified form of primogeniture more often than any other method of inheritance. The southern colonists practiced a fullblown form of primogeniture, while in New England the conventional arrangement was for each child to receive an equal share of the property except the eldest son, who was given

[22] It was called "Borough English," or, in law, ultimogeniture. See George C. Homans, *English Villagers of the Thirteenth Century* (Cambridge, Mass., 1942), p. 123; Frederick Pollock and Frederic William Maitland, *The History of English Law Before the Time of Edward I* (2 vols., Cambridge, Eng., 1923), II, p. 280.

a double share. That combination of primogeniture and partible inheritance (called "double-partible inheritance") continued to be used from the seventeenth century until the end of the eighteenth. Then it suddenly disappeared—both in law and in custom. Between 1775 and 1800 most states repealed the laws which had given an advantage to the first-born son. At the same time there was also a change in actual wealth-holding. Daniel Scott Smith, in studying the town of Hingham, Massachusetts, recently made an ingenious test of that change. He found that eldest sons had a significant material advantage over their brothers in early America, and maintained it during the late eighteenth century. If anything, primogeniture became stronger rather than weaker from 1650 to 1800. But early in the nineteenth century, eldest sons suddenly lost their advantage. They have never regained it. After 1810, the wealth of elder and younger sons was virtually the same. The advantage of the elder sons had rested entirely upon age prejudice—upon the premise that older was better. When that premise was destroyed, as it was in so many ways at once, primogeniture and double-partible inheritance vanished overnight.[23]

Patterns of descent changed in names as well as in prop-

[23] Smith tested the relationship by comparing the wealth of fathers and fathers-in-law of first and younger sons. He measured the advantages which birth order brought to chances for a fortunate and prosperous marriage. The results were as follows:

Date of tax list		Same wealth quintile as father		Higher wealth quintile than father		Lower wealth quintile than father		
fathers	sons	1st	last	1st	last	1st	last	n
1647	1680	25	29	58	29	17	43	26
1749	1779	30	33	44	26	25	41	94
1779	1810	26	30	55	27	18	43	117
1810	1830	36	27	30	36	34	37	139
1830	1860	34	35	34	30	32	34	138

Source: Daniel Scott Smith, "Parental Power and Marriage Patterns: An Analysis of Historical Trends in Hingham, Massachusetts," Journal of Marriage and the Family, 35 (1973), 424.

erty. An indication of that trend appears in the frequency with which children were given the same names as their grandparents. The proportion of grandparents honored in that way actually increased from the seventeenth to the late eighteenth century, then fell sharply between 1790 and 1830, and fluctuated at low levels during the nineteenth century. The timing and direction of that change conforms closely to that in other evidence.[24]

⟨⟩

All of our evidence suggests that a revolution occurred in attitudes toward age between 1770 and 1820. It manifested itself in many ways at once—in the abolition of "seating the meeting" (c. 1770-1820), in the first mandatory old age retirement laws (1777-1818), in the pattern of age preference revealed by census data (1787-1850), in the age bias of costume (1790-1820), in the changing language of age relations (c. 1780-1820), in the inheritance of property (1775-1810), and in the descent of names (1780-1820). Many other kinds of evidence might be added,[25] but enough has been introduced to make the point.

[24] Daniel Scott Smith has studied naming practices in Hingham, Mass., with the following results:

Marriage cohorts	Sons	Daughters
pre-1700	14.0	13.5
1701-1720	18.7	17.8
1721-1740	11.8	18.5
1741-1760	6.2	19.7
1761-1780	11.3	16.2
1781-1800	15.0	13.8
1801-1820	10.8	13.0
1821-1840	7.6	6.8
1841-1860	8.1	12.0
1861-1880	8.5	8.3

Source: D. S. Smith, unpubl. data.

[25] Another fascinating test can be made by studying the changing taxonomy of age. When old age was more highly respected than youth, common conceptions of life-stages tended to be more elaborate at the end than

This great transition will be misunderstood if we think of it as a moment when one static system suddenly replaced another. There are no static systems in history. Change is eternal in the world—the only unchanging historical fact. But if the existence of change is constant in history, its rhythm is variable. The pace and direction of change are apt to be profoundly different from one historical period to the next—and those differences become the basis of "periodization" schemes by which historians give pattern and meaning to the past.

Historical revolutions might best be understood not as moments when one stasis succeeds another, but rather as changes in the pattern of change itself—as moments of "deep change." "Deep change" may be defined as change in the *rate* of change—an alteration which is at once discontinuous in its nature and transforming in its effect. We live in three spatial dimensions, and a fourth of time. There is also a fifth dimension, in which change itself changes. Deep change is change in the fifth dimension. It customarily happens abruptly, but its full effects are often felt very slowly on the surface of history.

Age relationships have changed in precisely this way. During the first two hundred years (roughly 1607-1820) the pattern of change was involutionary—age relationships changed primarily by becoming more elaborately the same.[26] The exaltation of age became more intricate, and

---

at the beginning. On the other hand, in the modern world, where youth receives more attention than old age, those stages are more elaborate at the beginning than the end of life. Two or three of Shakespeare's "seven ages of man" are devoted to the years before adulthood. The rest are reserved for maturity and old age. In our time the most widely cited taxonomy of age is Erik Erikson's "eight stages of man"—"oral-sensory," "muscular-anal," "loco-motor-genital," "latency," "puberty and adolescence," "young adulthood," "adulthood," and "maturity." In that taxonomy, five stages out of eight are reserved for the years before adulthood; only one for advanced age.

[26] Involution, an ancient idea in science and theology, has been popularized in social science by Clifford Geertz. See his *Agricultural Involution: The Processes of Ecological Change in Indonesia* (Berkeley, Calif., 1963).

certainly more intense. Our indicators of change show that the authority and power of age became stronger rather than weaker during that period.[27] The exaltation of age became more highly rationalized and institutionalized as the years went by. But there was also an undercurrent of increasing inner hostility and even hatred of age.

Then, during the decades between 1780 and 1820, there was a process of revolutionary change—deep change, transforming change. The authority of age began to be undermined, and at the same time the direction of age bias began to be reversed. Cultural institutions which had rested upon a hierarchical conception of age relations began to disintegrate, and an ideal of age equality appeared. That ideal did not last long, however, for it masked a different sort of inequality. The revolution came to an end by 1820, and a new pattern of change emerged—a process of continuous, stable, evolutionary change in which gerontophobia became progressively more intense. The development of a new system of age relations was not completed in the revolutionary period, but it was everywhere begun. And from that beginning it steadily unfolded over the next hundred years. Thus, the history of age relationships in America first ran through a period of involutionary change in which the exaltation of age became more elaborately developed; then through a period of revolutionary change, which occurred during the era of the French Revolution; and then through a period of evolutionary change in which status of old age steadily declined.

The timing of the revolutionary change tells us many things about its cause. First, it tells us what its cause was *not*. In America, at least, it was not industrialization, urbanization, and the growth of mass education—not "modernization" in the ordinary meaning of the term. We know

[27] The pattern of bias in age heaping moved in that direction; so also did the practice of primogeniture and naming customs.

that because there is one clear and simple law of causality which always operates in history: if event B happened after event A, it cannot have been the cause of A. That is one of life's few certainties. The great transition in age relations began in America before urbanization, industrialization, and universal education could have had any effect.

The structure of the American economy changed very little from 1760 to 1790. The older generation retained its control of the land, and land retained its economic importance, even as attitudes toward age began to be transformed. Roughly 90 per cent of the population dwelled on farms and earned their living from the soil. The means of production (in a Marxian sense) remained much the same, and so also did the material order of the society. Intensive industrialization and urbanization began later. We must, therefore, reject "modernization" in that sense as the cause of change in attitudes toward age, and find another explanation.

If not modernization, then what? Another possible explanation is demographic. Some scholars have suggested that change in the status of the aged was due at least in part to changes in the age composition of the population. Let us apply our time test to this hypothesis, and see if it works. There was, in fact, a very great change in the age composition of American society—a demographic transition which was *almost* contemporary with the revolution in age attitudes. From the seventeenth century to the early nineteenth century, age composition in America remained constant. The median age was the same whenever it was measured before 1790. It was sixteen when the first federal census was made in that year, sixteen again in 1800, and sixteen once more in 1810.

But in 1820, when the census takers made their rounds again, they recorded a change. It was not very great—so small, in fact, that nobody seems to have noticed it. But the American population had grown slightly older. Its median age had advanced from sixteen to about sixteen and a half.[28] The change was trivial in itself, and yet it marked a great divide in American demographic history. After 1810 the population began to grow older, and continued to do so for a very long time. The median age advanced to nineteen by 1850, twenty by 1870, twenty-five by 1920, and thirty by 1950.

Obviously, the decade 1810-20 marked a deep change in American demography. For more than a century and a half before 1810 the age composition of the population had remained extraordinarily stable. But after 1810 there appeared a different pattern, one of stable and continuous change, by which the median age advanced at a constant annual rate (roughly 0.4 per cent per year) until about 1950.

Then the change patterns broke again. In the two decades from 1950 to 1970, the median age fell for the first time since 1810—not by very much, but enough to break the continuity. The significance of that break is doubtful. It is possible that the age distribution of the population has reached a new stability—for nearly thirty years now the median age has been fluctuating in the neighborhood of thirty. But, on the other hand, it is possible that a rising tendency was briefly interrupted, and will resume in the late 1970's. The census of 1980 will certainly show the median age has begun to rise again. Many professional demographers predict that the population will continue to grow older in the future as it has in the past. But the American people have so

---

[28] That figure is for the white population only. But an estimate for the black population can be made from later federal census counts and from earlier state data. By extrapolation we may make an educated guess (no more) that the median age of the entire population changed in almost the same proportion, from 16.2 to 16.7.

seldom behaved according to demographic expectations that any prophecy must be entertained with suspicion. The actual trend will not be clear for another thirty or forty years.[29]

Median age is merely the most crude and simple statistical measure of age composition. If we ask what proportion of Americans were elderly, we find an answer which is summarized in Appendix Table III. The sources are much scattered, but show a consistent trend. Before 1810, the proportion of people who could be called elderly changed very little. Less than 2 per cent of Americans were sixty-five or older. After 1810, that number began to rise. The relative proportion of people over sixty-five in America grew continuously, from less than 2 per cent in 1810 to more than 10 per cent in 1970. The largest part of the change has come within the past fifty years. Those demographic changes first occurred in New England, and then spread slowly to the South and West. In Surry, New Hampshire, as early as 1810, 4.6 per cent of the population was sixty-five or over— a proportion not matched by the nation as a whole until the 1920's.[30]

What caused that growth in the proportion of the elderly? In demographic terms, a change in age composition is the result of changes in fertility, mortality, and migration. Intuitively, we might expect that the American population began to grow older primarily because of a decline in death rates. But in fact the population grew older primarily be-

[29] According to one estimate, if zero population growth is achieved at present mortality levels, the median age will stabilize at approximately 37, and the proportion of the population aged 65 and over will be about 17%. *New York Times*, June 1, 1976.

[30] Racial differences also existed. The median age of the white population began to rise before that of blacks did: it was not until after Emancipation that the median age of blacks advanced significantly. In the 20th century, particularly since 1950, racial differences in age composition have grown greater rather than smaller.

cause of a declining birth rate.[31] A falling birth rate caused a reduction in the number of young children in American society; it was that tendency more than any other which made the major difference in the distribution of ages.

If we turn to the history of fertility in America, we find that birth rates were very high before 1810. They fluctuated a little because of wars and changing economic conditions, but were generally remarkable for their stability. Then, in the decade 1800-1810, fertility began to fall, and continued to do so for the next one hundred and fifty years. The trend reversed with the "baby boom" of the 1940's and 1950's, but resumed in the 1960's and 1970's. Changes in fertility and age composition have run together in American history. Fertility has changed first, with changes in age composition coming close behind, like a statistical shadow. Mortality and migration also had their effects, but not very great ones. Eighty per cent of the change in age composition was caused by a falling birth rate, less than 20 per cent by a fall in death rates.[32]

[31] There is an enormous literature on this question. The classical work is Ansley J. Coale, "The Effects of Changes in Mortality and Fertility on Age Composition," *Milbank Memorial Fund Quarterly*, 34 (1956), 302-7.

[32] The relative importance of fertility and mortality as determinants of age distribution may be compared. If fertility in a stable population is held constant and life expectancy increases from 30 to 70, then the proportion of people over 60 rises only by 10 to 20%. But if mortality is constant and the gross reproduction rate falls from 3.0 to 1.0, then the proportion of the elderly rises by more than 400%:

Life Expectancy at Birth Is:	% of Population 60 & Over When Gross Reproduction Rate Is:		
	3.0	*1.5*	*1.0*
30	4.1	11.5	18.7
70	4.5	13.1	21.9

See Joseph Spengler, "Some Economic and Related Determinants Affecting the Older Worker's Occupational Role," in Ida Simpson and John McKinney (eds.), *Social Aspects of Aging* (Durham, N.C., 1966), p. 7. The beginning of the decline in mortality may actually have lowered median age rather than raising it, by reducing death rates in the early years of life.

Though mortality made little difference in the age distribution of the population, it did have a major impact in another way. A very large drop in death rates over the preceding two hundred years meant that an increasing proportion of the American population lived to experience old age. Two hundred years ago, life expectancy at birth was less than half of what it is today. But beginning in the late eighteenth century, life expectancy began to rise. By 1830 there was already a substantial improvement, and a significant increase in the number of Americans who survived to old age. More than a third of Americans born in that year lived to the age of sixty (see Appendix Table V).

The cause of the improvement in life expectancy in the late eighteenth and early nineteenth centuries is unclear. Medicine probably contributed little, except in its conquest of smallpox, which had been a major scourge of the American population. Improvements in diet and sanitation probably had some effect. But the larger part of the rise in life expectancy in the western world was more likely the result of something over which mortal man has virtually no control—a change in the virulence of disease itself. It was probably that change which accounted for a good deal of the improvement in life expectancy.

In any case, the pace of that improvement accelerated in the late nineteenth and twentieth centuries, when a variety of human efforts (in sanitation more than medicine) began to make a difference. But once again, changes in the severity of disease itself may have been more important than we imagine. Whatever the reason, the trend is quite clear. In 1830, about one-third of all native-born Americans survived to the age of sixty; in 1900 more than half did; in 1940, two-thirds; in 1960, three-quarters; and in 1975, four-fifths. That demographic trend caused a profound change in the rhythm of individual lives. We can see something of its impact in the history of the life cycle in America in Appendix Table V. From 1650 to 1800 (approximately), the life cycle changed very little. Almost everyone married in early America, and once the responsibilities of a family were taken up, they were not laid down until the end of life. The first baby was born within a year of the marriage, and the last when the parents were in their mid-forties. Children were a continuing presence; usually the last child did not leave home until after one or both parents had died. That pattern prevailed until 1800. It changed only in the direction of an even greater extension of the time of dependency, as childhood mortality declined faster than adult mortality, and age at last birth increased a little.

But then the major break occurred—another deep change in the pattern of change itself. From 1800 to the mid-twentieth century, as both fertility and mortality declined, the life cycle was transformed, and dramatically so. Early in the nineteenth century parents began to live beyond the period of their children's dependency. In 1850, they did so only by a year or two on the average. But by 1950 the last child was grown and gone from home when most parents were still in their forties—and still in the full vigor of adult life. A new period of life had come into being: that between adulthood and old age.[33]

Those demographic changes in fertility and mortality were profoundly important. But they cannot explain the revolution in age relationships any better than industrialization or urbanization. It is likely that they helped to main-

[33] The timing of those trends was very different in other modern societies, but generally speaking, revolutions did not occur simultaneously in demography, economics, and attitudes toward age. Peter Laslett observes that in Britain "the really extensive changes in the proportions of the aged in the population took place a century or more after the onset of industrialization and the onset of the dissolution of traditional society." Laslett, Historical Sociology in Relation to Aging," p. 12.

tain its momentum, once it had begun. The general improvement in mortality may have had the effect of creating a closer relationship between old age and death. That connection had always existed in some degree: a Puritan clergyman observed in the seventeenth century that "all men may die, but old men must." Still, the connection was weakened by the frequency of death at an early age. As mortality rates dropped in childhood and the middle years of life, old age became more closely linked with death. At the same time, the growth of a secular spirit made death seem more empty and destructive than before. In that way, the mortality revolution may have deepened the change in attitudes toward old age. But it could not have set the change in motion.

There is one explanation which might account for both of these great processes. I offer it only in a summary form, for its demonstration requires a volume much larger than this one. But the main lines might be summarized in the span of a few pages.

The major change we wish to explain first took place in Anglo-America during the eighteenth century, and spread swiftly to Britain and France. During the nineteenth century it slowly advanced into central and northern Europe and Latin America, and was carried to Oceania by English colonists. In the early twentieth century it reached eastern and southern Europe, and in the mid-twentieth century, the great Asian civilizations. Only some of the cultures of Africa remain largely unchanged by it. But it was in the northern colonies of Anglo-America that the great change first appeared.[34]

---

[34] We are beginning to see some agreement upon this descriptive pattern of diffusion. See e.g. Edward Shorter, *The Making of the Modern Family* (New York, 1975), Chapter 7 *passim*.

In the mid-eighteenth century, well before the revolution in age relations, Anglo-American society began to change in several ways at once. First, there was a radical expansion of the idea of equality—not equality of possessions, but equality in Tocqueville's special sense, that is, equality of condition, equality of legal status, equality of social obligation, equality of cultural manners, equality of political rights. Prior to that time, the authority of age had rested upon a hierarchical conception of the world. But the intoxicating idea of equality—"lovely equality," Jefferson called it—destroyed the hierarchy of age, just as it destroyed the hierarchy of social orders and called into question hierarchies of sex and race as well.

Second, there was an extension of the ancient idea of liberty. In the early eighteenth century "liberties" were considered to be specific exceptions to a condition of prior restraint. But in the eighteenth century, American society became a world in which "Liberty" (now a singular noun, and capitalized) was itself a prior condition for most men (slaves and paupers excepted). The growth of that idea destroyed the authority of age by dissolving its communal base, for the power of elders in early America had rested upon a collective consciousness—upon the submergence of individuality into the family, the town, the church. The growth of a spirit of social atomism snapped the ties of obligation between generations as well as between classes.

The growth of those ideas in Anglo-America was caused primarily by the interaction of English Protestant ideas with the American environment. The vast abundance of fertile land and a favorable climate were necessary, but were not sufficient conditions of that growth. The culture which the English colonists carried to America contained strong libertarian and egalitarian tendencies—in the political institutions of East Anglia, in the legal idea of fee-simple possession, in the economics of closed-field farming, in the theology of Protestantism. But in seventeenth-century English culture all of these tendencies had their opposites, which were also introduced into America. The physical dangers of the New World, the psychic effect of isolation, the intense military insecurity, the anxiety inherent in a colonizing venture—all those factors, at the beginning, created a world of small, closed settlements which tended to be authoritarian, highly collectivistic, and hierarchical. By the mid-eighteenth century those closed societies had begun to impinge upon one another. As long as they had been separate, each of them could be authoritarian and collectivistic in its own way. Then, as they began to interact, a libertarian frame came to be increasingly important to the maintenance of internal restraints and repressions. In the 1760's, imperial authority challenged those little communities to assert the libertarian side of their cultural inheritance—liberty against imperial control, equality against an imperial elite. And once those great principles were set loose in the world, they developed an irresistible power.

That great process alone might or might not have produced the vast social revolution which America experienced. But it was also accompanied by another great change. The northern colonies in the seventeenth and eighteenth centuries had been a world of extraordinary equality of wealth—the people of early America were more nearly equal in their distribution of wealth than those of any other society in which wealth distributions have ever been measured. But during the 1760's, at exactly the same time that the American colonists were developing a rhetoric of equality and liberty, the inequality of wealth distribution began to grow. Its cause was neither industrialization nor urbanization, but rather the growth of markets and systems of exchange. The growth of inequality in the distribution of wealth began to come into conflict with inequalities of other kinds—began to undercut the pluralistic system of stratification which had prevailed in early America. Further, those inequalities placed an increasing stress upon families at both the top and the bottom of the society. If wealthy fathers gave land to their sons at an early age, then the collective structure of the family grew a little weaker. If they did not, tensions of the sort that shattered the domestic peace of the Carters disrupted the family in another way. In either case, the bonds were loosened. Poor families, on the other hand, experienced a different kind of internal stress, for their resources were insufficient to supply the needs of the next generation.

At the same time, the accumulation of wealth among the elite encouraged a spirit of social atomism among the leaders of society, and as a result they developed a tendency to turn from public service to their own private affairs. In all of those ways, the growth of wealth inequality increased the internal tensions and the development of heterogeneity in American society. The unity of early American communities had been sustained by their internal homogeneity. But in Puritanism, in the web of local English institutions, and in the operation of the American economy there was a powerful and potentially dangerous dualism between individuality and community. Both elements coexisted in Protestant America. And as long as most individuals were more or less the same, then there were no necessary contradictions. Autonomous individuals could join easily in a strong community as long as all of them were roughly alike. But as internal differences developed, conflicts erupted between individual autonomy and community.

Social structures are highly resilient—not easily disrupted. They are apt to contain within themselves many compensatory mechanisms by which internal stresses of various kinds are corrected and equilibrium restored. But between 1760 and 1790 American society was pulled in two different ways at once. It was impossible for the social system to adjust to one challenge without at the same time making the other even more severe. As a consequence, the system was torn to pieces.

The events of the American War of Independence were not enough in themselves to cause the great transition. Most of our indicators show that the major movement occurred a little later—primarily in the 1790's. But it was the War of Independence which engendered a revolution in western Europe, and in turn, that European revolution was itself introduced to America. The triumph of the new system came faster in the New World—more so than in any other society—because here the old régime was weak. It did not have the strength to resist.

The cause of the revolution in age relations was complex —a cluster of countervailing tendencies which together destroyed the structure of early American society and created a new social system in its place. The "deep change" in attitudes toward old age which we have detected was merely one aspect of a sweeping transformation.

III. THE CULT OF YOUTH IN MODERN AMERICA
1780-1970

> *Nature abhors the old, and old age seems the only disease; all others run into this one. We call it by many names—fever, intemperance, insanity, stupidity and crime; they are all forms of old age; they are rest, conservatism, appropriation, inertia; not newness, not the way onward. We grizzle every day. I see no need of it. Whilst we converse with what is above us, we do not grow old, but grow young.*
>
> *Ralph Waldo Emerson (1803-82)*

> *I have lived some thirty years on this planet, and I have yet to hear the first syllable of valuable or even earnest advice from my seniors. They have told me nothing and probably cannot teach me anything.*
>
> *Henry David Thoreau (1817-62)*

FROM Thomas Jefferson's era to our own time, the lines of change have been straight and stable. For two hundred years American society has changed with dizzy speed, but the pattern of that change has been remarkably regular. An historical movement, mysterious in its origin but unmistakable in its effect, began at the end of the eighteenth century and continued to the late twentieth. It was like one of those powerful Pacific waves the Japanese call a *tsunami,* which begins beneath the bottom of the sea and rises swiftly to the surface, destroying everything within its reach. In much the same way, a great historical wave was set in motion two hundred years ago by a mysterious disturbance hidden deep beneath the surface of events. For two centuries it has expanded outward in a great circle which is now nearly as wide as the world itself. Only in our own time has it begun to approach its natural limits.

That great historical wave changed age relations in several ways at once. First, it multiplied the numbers of the aged. In American society the elderly part of the population, those who were sixty-five and over, grew steadily from less than 2 per cent in 1800 to more than 10 per cent in 1970. This, as we have seen, was mostly the result of falling birth rates. At the same time, falling death rates also had an effect; they increased the chances of reaching old age. In 1750, only one American out of five survived to the age of seventy. By 1970, four out of five did so. For many millennia old age had been an experience limited only to a few. Suddenly, in the space of a mere two centuries, it has become the normal expectation of many.

But at the same time that old age came to be more common, it also came to be regarded with increasing contempt. Where the Puritans had made a cult of age, their posterity made a cult of youth instead. The clergy of New England, who were the intellectual elite of that society, had made veneration a sacred duty. But the great New England literati of the nineteenth century began to offer their readers opposite instructions.

The Transcendentalists, for example, expressed at least three different sets of opinions on the subject of old age. Only one of them had been heard before. Writers such as Theodore Parker still preserved something of the traditional attitude of respect for age. One of Parker's most successful sermons was devoted to the subject. He argued that old age was good, but only when it was associated with other good things. "It is only a noble, manly life, full of piety, which makes old age beautiful," he wrote. Without virtue, old age was ugly and foul. "The old age of the sensualist, the miser, of him who worships only place and fame and power—what a judgment it is against the sin."[1] His classical cautionary example was Aaron Burr—"the worst great man Young America ever gendered in her bosom." In Theodore Parker's sermon, the leaven of time was necessary for true moral greatness, but insufficient in itself.

Parker's attitudes on the subject of age were not very different from some which had been expressed by Puritan moralists such as John Wise, whose way of connecting age and virtue had become a cliché in the early modern era.[2] But among the Transcendentalists, Theodore Parker occupied what might be called the right wing, at least in his attitudes toward age. John Wise, on the other hand, had occupied the left wing of Puritan thought. In both the seventeenth and the nineteenth centuries, attitudes toward old age constituted a range or spectrum of belief which cannot be reduced to a single idea. But by the mid-1800's, that spectrum had shifted in such a way that the left edge in Wise's generation had become the right edge in Parker's.

At the other extreme of Transcendentalism was Henry David Thoreau. At the arrogant age of thirty, Thoreau expressed the most perfect and finished contempt for all his seniors: "Age is no better, hardly so well, qualified for an instructor as youth, for it has not profitted so much as it has lost. One may almost doubt if the wisest man has learned anything of absolute value by living. Practically, the old have no very important advice to give the young, their experience has been so partial, and their lives have been such miserable failures, for private reasons, as they must believe; and it may be that they have some faith left

[1] Theodore Parker, "Of Old Age," sermon preached Jan. 29, 1854, *Collected Works* (14 vols., London, 1875), III, pp. 92-109.
[2] See above p. 41n.

which belies that experience, and they are only less young than they were."[3]

Here was a total reversal of traditional attitudes—a complete and decisive rejection of the ideal of "veneration" and the institutions of "eldership." For Thoreau, "the old," as he called them, were experienced only in the ways of failure, finished only in their forms of corruption. He expressed an attitude of alienation from many things—from all his seniors, to be sure, but also from much more. To say that youth can learn nothing from age is to reject not merely age, but also learning. To doubt that the wisest old man has learned anything by living is to doubt not merely old men, but wisdom. It was a corrosive creed that Thoreau invented in the woods of Walden—a kind of moral anarchism. But it was one that appealed to many Americans in the nineteenth century.[4]

Among the Transcendentalists, Thoreau was an ethical extremist. The man at the center was Ralph Waldo Emerson. In a history of old age, his works can be quoted on every side of the question. Even so, there is a consistency of sorts in his opinions. On the subject of old age, Emerson offered both testimony and judgment. He bore witness to the "creed of the street" in nineteenth-century America—a creed which was, in his description, unfavorable to age: "In short, the creed of the street is, old age is not disgraceful, but immensely disadvantageous." With that opinion Emerson did not really disagree. His works were filled with passages such as the one with which this chapter begins. In

3 *Walden* (New York, 1937), Chapter I, p. 8.
4 On a visit to the library of the Frick mansion in New York, I noticed that an expensive edition of the collected works of Henry David Thoreau was in a place of honor. My first reaction was one of surprise—that a man who made simplicity into a system of morality should be celebrated in such opulent surroundings. But then again, there was a natural affinity between the ethical anarchism of Henry Thoreau and the economic acts of Henry Frick.

Emersonian writings, Nature abhorred old age, and Emerson agreed with Nature. "Frankly face the facts and see the result," he wrote. "Tobacco, coffee, alcohol, hashish, prussic acid, strychnine are weak dilutions: the surest poison is time."

But Emerson was most of all a moralist. Even as he abhorred old age, he argued strenuously against abhorrence of the aged. To maintain both of those opinions, he found it necessary to insist that a person could grow younger in spirit even as he grew older in every other way. It was a silly sort of argument. The idea of "growing younger" is an absurdity in the same way that so much of Emerson is absurd when the clouds of rhetoric are stripped away. But that is what makes Emerson so fascinating as an historical phenomenon—a first-class mind caught by the contradictions of a transitional era. Yet even in its absurdity the idea was an intelligent contradiction—exquisitely sensitive to the demands of two profoundly different traditions which met (without mixing) at the center of Emerson's thought.

In the larger context of nineteenth-century American literature, the Transcendentalists were all men at the center. Some major American writers were much more conservative on the subject of age. Nathaniel Hawthorne was one; he filled his stories with old characters who ranged in status from the great "grey champions" we have already met to the pathetic "white old maid" who was so miserably absorbed in her past that she died clutching "a lock of hair, once sable, now discolored with a greenish mold." There were also Hawthorne's old friends in the Customs House: "The white locks of age were sometimes found to be the thatch of an intellectual tenement in good repair," he wrote. "But, as respects the majority of my corps of veterans, there will be no wrong done, if I characterize them generally as a set of wearisome old souls, who had gathered nothing worth preservation from their varied experience of life. They seemed to have flung away all the golden grain of practical wisdom, which they had enjoyed so many opportunities of harvesting, and most carefully stored their memories with the husks."[5]

But Hawthorne thought more favorably of old age than most of his contemporaries did. His aged characters are rarely attractive, but always interesting. Hawthorne was one of a handful of modern novelists—Dickens was another, and Balzac a third—who allowed his aged characters to possess a truly individual existence. Most modern authors make old people into cardboard characters—stereotypical figures put together from the prejudices of the age. Hawthorne, on the other hand, was in the fullest sense sympathetic to old age. So was Longfellow, who cultivated the appearance of old age with his grizzled beard, and prepared a poem on the subject of aging for the fiftieth anniversary of his graduation from Bowdoin College. In *Morituri Salutamus* (the gladiator's motto—"We who are about to die salute you") he did his best to celebrate old age. But the exaltation of elders which had come so easily to the Puritans was uphill work for a poet in nineteenth-century New England:

> Whatever poet, orator, or sage
> May say of it, old age is still old age.
> It is the waning, not the crescent moon;
> The dusk of evening, not the blaze of noon;
> It is not strength, but weakness; not desire,
> But its surcease; not the fierce heat of fire,
> The burning and consuming element,
> But that of ashes and of embers spent,
> In which some living sparks we still discern,
> Enough to warm, but not enough to burn.

[5] Hawthorne, *The Scarlet Letter* (Boston, 1900), Introduction.

What then? Shall we sit idly down and say
The night hath come; it is no longer day?
The night hath not yet come; we are not quite
Cut off from labor by the failing light;
Something remains for us to do or dare;
Even the oldest tree some fruit may bear;
Not the Oedipus Coloneus, or Greek Ode,
Or tales of pilgrims that one morning rode
Out of the gateway of the Tabard Inn,
But other something, would we but begin;
For age is opportunity no less
Than youth itself, though in another dress,
And as the evening twilight fades away
The sky is filled with stars, invisible by day.[6]

Hawthorne and Longfellow were as favorable to old age
as any major literary figures of their era. At the other extreme, far beyond even Thoreau in his contempt for age,
was the older Walt Whitman. For Whitman, age was a species of spiritual affliction. The poems he wrote on the subject when he himself had reached old age are suffused with
alternate and ugly moods of anger and self-pity. Walt Whitman was unable to accept the thought that old age was actually happening to him. Every anniversary introduced a
spasm of pain to his poetry:

As I sit writing here, sick and grown old,
Not my least burden is that dullness of the years,
          querilities, ennui
May filter in my daily songs.

Again, in "Queries to my Seventieth Year" (aet. 69):

Thou dim, uncertain spectre—bringest thou life or death?
Strength, weakness, blindness, more paralysis and heavier
Or placid skies and sun? Wilt stir the waters yet?

6 Longfellow, *Poetical Works* (Boston, 1886), pp. 310-14.

> Or haply cut me short for good? Or leave me here as now,
> Dull, parrot-like and old, with cracked voice harping,
>   screeching.

And in "A Carol Closing Sixty-Nine" (aet. 70):

> O me myself—the old jocund heart yet beating in my breast,
> The body wrecked, old poor and paralyzed—the strange
> inertia falling pall-like round me,
> The burning fires down in my sluggish blood yet not extinct,
> The undiminished faith—the groups of loving friends.

In short, attitudes toward age in nineteenth-century America spanned a broad spectrum of belief. There were a few clergymen in the first third of the century who continued to deliver "centennial addresses" in the spirit of Job Orton and Joseph Lathrop.[7] Those antique figures were men who had been boys before the Revolution and who still scorned the new ways of a world which they disliked and distrusted. But most major literary figures who published in America between 1820 and 1890 broke decisively with the attitudes of their ancestors on the subject of old age. The break was more radical in some writers than in others, but in almost all of them it took place.

Even the works which attempted to celebrate old age were forced to recognize the change. Lydia Maria Child, for example, published one of her many potboilers on the subject of old age, an anthology called *Looking toward Sunset*

---

[7] See e.g. Ebenezer Burgess, *A Centennial Discourse delivered in the New Meeting House of the First Church in Dedham* (Boston, 1840), which was not very different from Samuel Dexter, *Some Serious Thoughts on the Foundation, Rise and Growth of the Settlement in New England* (Boston, 1738).
Another good example of the persistence of traditional attitudes is Timothy Farrar Clay, *Honorable Old Age: A Discourse Occasioned by the Centennial Anniversary of Hon. Timothy Farrar* (Andover, 1847). Once again, Proverbs 16:31 was put to work. But the argument was that of John Wise rather than the Mathers; old age was not honorable in itself, but only with right conduct.

(Boston, 1865), which consisted mostly of the works of recent authors that were offered as a literature of consolation. So also had been the sermons of Puritan clergy, but the arguments had changed. In 1865 Mrs. Child offered as the principal consolation of old age the fact that it would soon be over. "The more the world diminished and grew dark," one author in her anthology wrote, "the less I felt the loss of it; for the dawn of the next world grew even clearer and clearer." (pp. 42-43).

Another author suggested that old age was happy because it was a time of disengagement from the affairs of the world. "It is then that we have nothing to manage," he concluded. Still others, in an Emersonian way, argued that it was possible to grow young. And the Reverend Edmund Sears, in an essay on "everlasting youth," proposed "the wonderful paradox" that "the oldest people are the youngest. To grow in age is to come into everlasting youth. To become old in years is to put on the freshness of perpetual spring. We drop from us the debris of the past, and breathe the ether of immortality" (p. 62).

Mrs. Child's volume on old age was representative of a genre of "gathered gems for the aged" which appeared in the mid-nineteenth century—anthologies filled with salutes to old maids, and grandfathers' reveries, and romantic odes to the autumn of life.[8] As the number of the aged began to

---

[8] See also S. G. Lathrop, *Fifty Years and Beyond; Or, Gathered Gems for the Aged* (Chicago, 1881); S. Holmes, *Light at Evening Time* (New York, 1871); Margaret Eliot White, *After Noontide* (Boston, 1888); William E. Schenk, *Nearing Home* (Philadelphia, 1868); Cora S. Nourse, *Sunset Hours of Life* (New York, 1875); John Stanford, *The Aged Christian's Cabinet* (New York, 1829); Amelia Edith Barr, *Three Score & Ten; A Book for the Aged* (New York, 1915); Adolf L. Vischer, *Old Age, Its Compensations and Rewards* (London, 1947); J. Lathrop, *The Infirmities and Comforts of Old Age* (Springfield, Mass., 1802).

Another genre consisted of works such as Frank M. Mills's *Notings of a Nonagenarian* (Boston, 1926)—Ciceronian essays by aging celebrities. The

increase, commercial publishers in New York and Boston were quick to discover that new market. The new magazines, such as *Littell's Living Age* and *The Atlantic Monthly*, exploited it greedily. But those attempts to celebrate old age were themselves evidence of the way in which attitudes had changed. Where seventeenth-century works had assigned an active role to the aged in society, the nineteenth-century essays worked upon an opposite assumption —that old age would be a time of rest and disengagement, serenity and peace. Veneration of the old had been an idea at the center of American society in the seventeenth century; in the nineteenth century, old age existed increasingly on the margin of society.[9]

If we leap ahead one hundred years to American literature in the mid-twentieth century, we find once again a broad spectrum of belief on the subject of old age. But that spec-

---

last growl of many a literary lion was often an essay on old age. See Lydia H. Sigourney, *Past Meridian* (New York, 1854); Elizabeth Cady Stanton, *The Pleasure of Age* (n.p., n.d., *c.* 1885); M. C. (Mathew Carey?), *Excerpts from the Commonplace Book of a Septuagenarian; Reflections on Shakespeare's Seven Ages of Man* (Philadelphia, 1835); George Frisbie Hoar, *Old Age and Immortality; An Address Delivered before the Worcester Fire Society* (Worcester, Mass., 1904); William Dean Howells, *Eighty Years and After* (New York, 1921); Charlotte Conover, *On Being Eighty; and Grow Old and Like It* (Yellow Springs, Ohio, 1938); Nicholas Murray Butler, *De Senectute* (New York, 1937).

Some of these arguments were very ingenious. Hoar, for example, wrote a thoughtful essay on the Websterian theme that "old Age . . . brings every man to his individuality." But most of them pathetically concluded with something like Butler's advice—"Try to keep youthful, Old Man."

9 A parallel movement appears in American painting. 17th-century portraits of old men stressed authority and active engagement in the life of the community. In the 19th century, the dominant theme appears in a Currier and Ives print called "Old Age," in which that stage of life is a time of retirement and rest. In the realistic paintings of the 1920's and 1930's, a mood of gerontophobia was generally evident.

trum has again shifted to the left. And the last traces of veneration have disappeared. Even the most sacred texts of the Judeo-Christian religion are rejected out of hand. Robert Service did not even hesitate to take on the Ten Commandments: "I respectfully submit that whoever made up the Ten Commandments might have done a better job. Take the fourth. One is exhorted to honor one's parents, with a bribe of longevity. Honor to whom honor is due, I say. I have known very few men worthy of it, and I could never see why parents should be honored just because they are responsible for our existence. I know it is considered bad taste to criticize them, and I do not want to be lacking in respect; but I have always felt that it should be the other way about—that it is the parents who should honor the children; for if the race is really advancing, the new stock should be better than the old."[10]

In the seventeenth century, Anne Bradstreet had asked, "Who thinks not oft upon the Fathers' Ages" and of "the starry observations of those sages?" In the twentieth, Ira Gershwin asked another sort of question:

> Methus'lah lived nine hundred years
> Methus'lah lived nine hundred years
> But who calls that livin'
> When no gal will give in
> To no man what's nine hundred years?

In major works of twentieth-century American literature, old age has rarely been a central theme. When it has appeared at all, it has usually been cast in one of four major

---

[10] Robert Service, *Ploughmen of the Moon* (New York, 1945).

There were, of course, notable exceptions, such as George Santayana's *Minuet on Reaching the Age of Fifty*, Sarah Orne Jewett's *Country of the Pointed Firs*; Edwin O'Connor's *Edge of Sadness*; John Updike's *Poorhouse Fair*; Arthur Miller's *Death of a Salesman*; Louis Bromfield's *The Farm*; Maxwell Anderson's *Night Over Taos*. For an extensive list see Constance E. Kellam, *A Literary Bibliography on Aging* (New York, 1968).

motifs. First, and most favorable to age, is the theme of Ernest Hemingway's *Old Man and the Sea*, one of the few modern American novels in which an old man is the protagonist. The hero is an unlucky fisherman named Santiago, whom Hemingway calls simply "the old man." We are told that "everything about him was old except his eyes and they were the same color as the sea and were cheerful and undefeated." The action can be summarized in a sentence. After eighty-four days without a single catch, the old man killed a great fish, one too big to bring into his little boat; as he sailed home he fought to keep the sharks away from his prize, but slowly lost all except the bones to them, and yet arrived in triumph with the great skeleton as proof of his success.

The rhetorical trappings of that little book belong very much to its own time. It is filled with bloodshed and brutality and all of the other staple ingredients of twentieth-century literary realism. The author even manages to introduce a little sex into his story—no easy matter when his subject is an old man alone in an open boat. But if the rhetoric is realist, the message is pure romance—even Emersonian romance. The old man with the young eyes fights the sharks and loses, but fights his age and wins. His muscles ache with age and weariness; his mind is a cloud of vagueness and confusion. But the young spirit conquers the old body, and the novel ends on a classical note of Emersonian triumph. In its theme, *The Old Man and the Sea* is almost identical with the argument of Emerson's essay, "Circles."

But Hemingway, unlike Emerson, was not the man at the center of twentieth-century letters. In his attitudes toward age relations he occupied the right wing. More common were the other three themes, which even Thoreau might have found excessively gerontophobic. The first and most common of them was the pathos of age. Old age in modern American literature is not the stuff of tragedy. A truly tragic hero must have strength and dignity and purpose. But old age in twentieth-century fiction has been denied all of those qualities. When old age appears at all in a literary work, it is apt to be not tragic, but pathetic. The central theme is the weakness and dependence of age.

A classical example is the dying old man in John Steinbeck's *The Grapes of Wrath*. We meet him only two pages before the end of the book, and are never even told his name. We see him dimly, lying on his back in the gloom of an old barn, slowly starving to death. "He was about fifty," Steinbeck wrote. "His whiskery face gaunt, and his open eyes were vague and staring." The solitude of the barn is suddenly shattered by the arrival of an Okie family distracted by its own misfortunes. They are seeking shelter for a daughter, Rose-of-Sharon, who had just given birth to a dead child. The family sees the starving old man. A boy who is tending him explains: "I didn't know. He said he et, or he wasn' hungry. Las' night I went an' bust a winda an' stoled some bread. Made 'im chew 'er down. But he puked it all up, an' then he was weaker. Got to have soup or milk. You folks got money to git milk?"

Everyone leaves the barn but the old man and the girl.

> For a minute Rose-of-Sharon sat still in the whispering barn. Then she hoisted her tired body up and drew the comfort about her. She moved slowly to the corner and stood looking down at the wasted face, into the wide, frightened eyes. Then slowly she lay down beside him. He shook his head slowly from side to side. Rose-of-Sharon loosened one side of the blanket and bared her breast. "You got to," she said. She squirmed closer and pulled his head close. "There!" she said. "There." Her hand moved behind his head and supported it. Her fingers moved gently in his hair. She looked up and across the barn, and her lips came together and smiled mysteriously.

There is nothing in the old man—no personality, no humanity. He is merely a bag of bones, helpless and totally dependent. The girl picks up his old head in her young hands and *makes* him take her milk. "You got to," she commands. It is a horrible scene—one of the most powerful and hideous in modern American fiction.[11]

There are many similar scenes in twentieth-century American writing. In Robert Frost's "Death of the Hired Man," a "poor old man" named Silas returns to a farm where he used to work. The farmer's wife finds him "huddled against the barn-door fast asleep, a miserable sight and frightening too," and takes him into her kitchen. While the farmer in his living room loudly expresses his contempt for the old man, Silas sits quietly by the kitchen stove and dies.

The pathos of old age is not the worst of its permutations in modern literature. A more corrosive theme is the emptiness of old age. That is the central idea of T. S. Eliot's "Gerontion," a dark description of the empty misery of "an old man in a dry month," who lacks even the solace of a strong and happy memory. Even the grandfather's reveries of romantic fiction are denied to him. He is merely an "old man, a dull head among windy spaces," an "old man in a draughty house," a "dry brain in a dry season." In Eliot's poem, old age appears as merely an aching void.

Beyond Eliot there is still another ugliness, more finished and complete. For the Irish writer Samuel Beckett, in *Krapp's Last Tape*, the emptiness and misery of old age become a revelation of the absurdity of life itself. In Beckett the circle is closed. The misery of old age extends to embrace us all.[12]

---

[11] John Steinbeck, *The Grapes of Wrath* (New York, 1939), pp. 617-19. Reprinted by permission.

[12] Robert Frost, *Complete Poems* (New York, 1964), pp. 49-55; T. S. Eliot, *Collected Poems 1909-62* (New York, 1963), pp. 29-31; Samuel Beckett, *Krapp's Last Tape* (New York, 1960). American literature is very different

In short, the major works of modern literature have generally conformed to a consistent pattern of complex change in attitudes toward old age. At any single moment, a broad spectrum of opinion was expressed, but from the early nineteenth century to the mid-twentieth century each successive spectrum shifted toward the left, toward an increasing antipathy for old age.[13]

The literary elite led the transition; other writers followed at a distance. Many essays and poems were written on the subject of old age in nineteenth-century America. It was a favorite theme in literary periodicals, religious journals, and popular magazines.[14]

At least four scholars have studied that literature in a systematic way. All of them have found more or less the same

---

from European writing in its discussions of age. We find nothing in America like Dylan Thomas's spirited advice:

> Do not go gentle into that good night
> Old age should burn and rave at close of day
> Rage, rage against the dying of the light.

The "celebration of man" which Thomas identified in his "poetic manifesto" as the greatest joy and function of poetry was also the celebration of an old man. Thomas, "Do Not Go Gentle into that Good Night," *Collected Poems, 1934-1952* (New York, 1971), p. 116.

[13] A further complexity was introduced by variations within the career of each writer, most of whom tended, like Emerson, to offer more than one opinion on the subject, and also, like Whitman, to become more gerontophobic as time passed. If we were to plot expressions with time as the ordinate and age bias as the abscissa, then the attitude of most individual authors would appear not as a point, but as a parallelogram.

[14] See e.g. N. C. Frothingham, "Old Age," *Christian Examiner*, LVII (1854), 61-77; "Respect Due to Old Age," *Albany Bouquet*, I (1835), 46; "Growing Old Gracefully," *Graham's American Monthly Magazine*, 51 (1857), 42; Mary Deming, "Old Age," *The Ladies' Repository*, 18 (1858), 603; "Growing Old," ibid. 281; C. M. Kirkland, "Growing Old Gracefully," *Sartain's Union Magazine of Literature and Art*, 8 (1851), 258; A. K. H. Boyd, "Concerning Growing Old," *The Living Age*, 66 (1860), 136; "An Essay on Old Age," *The Atheneum*, 9 (1828), 398; James Payn, "The Backwater of Life," *Living Age*, 205 (1895), 572; B. Hendrick, "The Superannuated Man," *McClure's Magazine*, 32 (1908), 115-27; B. A. Crankenthorpe, "The Plaint of the Old," *Living Age*, 200 (1894), 606, and many more.

pattern—a continuing decline in the literary status of old age. Traditional attitudes disappeared more slowly from popular writing than from high literature, but the direction of the trend was more or less the same. The pace of change accelerated steadily as time passed—moving slowly in the early nineteenth century, faster in the late nineteenth, and fastest in the early twentieth. According to one scholar, the literature also tends to show "a shift in the sociological prime of life from mature middle years (1890) to young adulthood (1955)."[15] Also, in nineteenth-century literature aged characters maintained "a fair number" of close associations with young adults, while in twentieth-century literature there has been an increasing sense of isolation.[16]

[15] Martin U. Martel, "Age-Sex Roles in American Magazine Fiction, 1890-1955," Bernice Neugarten (ed.), *Middle Age and Aging*, p. 56.

[16] The four projects covered different periods, by different methods, with slightly different results. Jean Bertrand, in a senior essay on attitudes toward death (unpubl., Univ. of Michigan, 1975), studied attitudes toward old age from 1820-90. She attempted to measure shifting opinions in a quantitative way, and found a trend which extended through the entire period, accelerating toward the end of it.

Yosef Riemer, in an essay on attitudes toward old age from 1828 to 1860 (unpubl., Brandeis, 1975), found a broad spectrum of belief, most of it shifting toward gerontophobia. A few writers still exalted old age as the Puritans had done in the 17th century; many others defended it as "the golden sunset," the "autumn of life," "life's happiest time," a period of "rest." Still others actually attacked it as "decadence."

W. Andrew Achenbaum, "The Obsolescence of Old Age in America," *Journal of Social History*, 8 (1974), 48-62, confined his inquiry to 1865-1914, arguing that age was increasingly perceived to be a "burden, not a blessing." Old age was seen as "obsolescent" by a "cult of youth which swept late nineteenth-century America in dramatic counterpoint to its deprecation of old age." Achenbaum argued that the transition from "veneration" to "deprecation" of old age happened primarily during 1865-1914. But that is certainly erroneous.

A fourth study is Martin U. Martel, "Age-Sex Roles in American Magazine Fiction, 1890-1955," Bernice Neugarten (ed.), *Middle Age and Aging*, pp. 47-57. Martel finds the process of change moving strongly through the 20th century. He also adds interesting observations on a "shift in the sociological prime of life from mature middle age (1890) to young adulthood (1955)." And he finds that aged characters tended to have close associations with younger people in the literature of the 1890's but not so much in the

The growth of gerontophobia also appeared in popular culture during the nineteenth and twentieth centuries—in its timing, one step behind the mass media and two steps behind the high literature.[17]

In America, the proverb is not merely a medium of expression, but a mode of thought. It is a form of packaged wisdom, for people on the go. American proverbs reduce whole philosophies to a single sentence. They are a species of abbreviated wisdom which are especially suitable to a culture that allows neither leisure for reflection nor taste for learning nor time for sustained study.

The philosophy of Emerson especially lent itself to popular proverbs. "You are only as old as you think," Americans like to say—as if even aging is a form of voluntary action. Thoreau's philosophy was also easily translated into epigrams—"no fool old fool," "old dog, new tricks," and the Ozark folk song:

> Never mind the old folks
> Old folks, old folks.
> Never mind the old folks
> For they don't care.

The elaborate arguments of the literati were reduced to pithy proverbs which epitomized the fashionable wisdom of the age. "Age before beauty," Americans were apt to say when two generations met in passing.[18] In that popular say-

---

1950's. Again, Martel enters special claims for 1890-1955 as *the* time of the change, and urbanization as its cause. But those assertions are mistaken.

[17] Few motion pictures have old men as their protagonists. On the rare occasions when they are the central figures, they are usually made to be lonely, weak, pathetic, and obsessed with the past—Rod Steiger in *The Pawnbroker*, consumed by his memory of his sufferings; Ace Bonner, the alcoholic ex-rodeo champ dominated by the memory of his success in Peckinpah's *Junior Bonner;* and, most powerful of all, the Swedish doctor in Bergman's *Wild Strawberries*. One of the few movies to present an old man as a protagonist in a favorable way is *Harry and Tonto*.

[18] To which Dorothy Parker once replied, "And pearls before swine."

ing, age and beauty are formed in a dichotomy, with the implication that age is ugly and beauty is young.

Mass attitudes quickly appeared in mass politics. Highly self-conscious youth movements began to grow throughout the western world in the nineteeth century. In 1828 James Fazy issued a polemic, *On Gerontocracy*, in which he attacked government by elders.[19] In Italy the cry was taken up by Mazzini and the "Young Italy Movement." In America there was a parallel in Stephen Douglas's "Young America movement," a highly charged group of ambitious young politicians within the Democratic party who attacked "Fogyism" in all its forms.

A political contest between the generations seemed inevitable to nineteenth-century Americans. So also did its outcome. Oliver Wendell Holmes, Sr., wrote that "Each generation strangles and devours its predecessor. The young Fijian carries a cord in his girdle for his father's neck. The young American bears a string of propositions or syllogisms in his brain to finish the same relative."[20]

But the new attitude was more an exaltation of youth than an attack upon the aged. One indication of mass attitudes is the national mythology. Americans have personified their culture in mythic figures, as all peoples do. In early American history, those figures were often elderly. Puritanism was personified by an elderly gentleman. The soldiers of the Revolutionary War were old men in the memory of Oliver Wendell Holmes, Jr., but in fact the Minutemen of Concord were, on the average, the same age as the draftees of World War II. The leaders of the early Republic are remembered as "Founding Fathers"; it is always surprising to discover how young some of them were.

Since the nineteenth century, America's hero figures have

19 Gillis, *Youth and History*, p. 37.
20 Oliver Wendell Holmes, Sr., *Mechanism in Thought and Morals* (Boston, 1871), p. 98.

tended to be young men. As the "backcountry" was transformed into the "frontier," Americans began to identify with "cowboys," and the heroes of the West were often endowed with the eternal youth of men such as George Armstrong Custer, the "boy general." In the Civil War, the Union was defended not by old men with flintlocks, but by "our boys in blue." The American empire was personified by Teddy Roosevelt charging up San Juan Hill with his regiment of young roughriders close behind him. In the 1920's Americans made a national hero of Charles Lindbergh, who was celebrated not least for his youth.

America itself, as late as the mid-twentieth century, still thought of itself as a young nation even though it was more than three centuries old—in fact, the oldest independent republic in the modern world. "The youth of America is their oldest tradition," wrote Oscar Wilde. "It has been going on now for three hundred years." But Wilde was not correct. The "youth of America" is, in fact, a modern idea. When the American settlements were really young, its inhabitants tried to think of themselves as older than they were. Plymouth celebrated itself as the "Old Colony" long before the Revolution. Virginia proudly took the name "Old Dominion" before it was even a state. In fact, as early as the seventeenth century a writer referred to Virginia as "his Majesty's most ancient colony and dominion."[21]

One curious rhetorical irony appeared in a new application of the adjective "old": in the nineteenth century it became a sort of political slang word. When American politics was democratized, virtually every major politician acquired a nickname. There had been none in the seventeenth or eighteenth centuries—nobody dared to speak of the Governor of Massachusetts as Johnny Winthrop, or the Proprietor of Pennsylvania as Billy Penn. The earliest political nickname of any prominence was "Old Hickory,"

21 *Calendar of Virginia State Papers,* I, 63.

which was first applied to Andrew Jackson around 1815. Thereafter, almost every American politician had to have one. John Quincy Adams was known, not very folksily, as "Old Man Eloquent" by 1846. Lincoln, of course, was "Old Abe" (1860). Halleck was "Old Brains" (1863), and Buchanan was "Old Buck" (1861), or, incredibly, "Old Public Functionary." Thomas Hart Benton was "Old Bullion" (1841) and Winfield Scott "Old Chippewa" or "Old Chapultepec" (1850, 1852). Stephen Van Rensselaer was the "Old Patroon," Grant "Old Three Stars," Harrison "Old Tip," Horace Greeley "Old White Hat," and Zachary Taylor "Old Rough and Ready" or simply "Old Zach." Stevens was "Old Thad," and Stonewall Jackson was in his own time known both as "Stonewall" and as "Old Jack." And Joseph Heister, a Pennsylvania politician, was improbably called "Old Sauerkraut."

It is interesting to observe that men who were not called "old" were often called "little." McClellan was "Little Mac," Martin Van Buren "Little Van," and Steven Douglas the "Little Giant." We can find in this parallel a key to the meaning of "old," which commonly operated as a democratic diminutive in American politics. The function of a political nickname after Andrew Jackson's time was to establish its leaders upon a footing of social equality with the electorate. "Old," like "little," was a way of cutting a statesman down to size.

A cult of youth developed in America during the nineteenth century and grew rapidly in the twentieth.[22] It became most extreme in the 1960's, when mature men and women followed fashions in books, music, and clothing which were set by their adolescent children. This historian observed a Boston matron on the far side of fifty, who might have worn a graceful palla in ancient Rome, dressed in a

<hr />

22 R. L. Rapson, *The Cult of Youth in Middle Class America* (Lexington, Mass., 1971).

miniskirt and leather boots. He saw a man in his sixties, who might have draped himself in the dignity of a toga, wearing "hiphugger" jeans and a tie-dyed T-shirt. He witnessed a conservative businessman, who in an earlier generation might have hesitated each morning, wondering whether to wear black or charcoal gray, going to the office in white plastic shoes, chartreuse trousers and cerise shirt, purple aviator glasses, and a Prince Valiant haircut. Most astonishing were college professors who put aside their Harris tweeds and adopted every passing adolescent fad with an enthusiasm out of all proportion to their years. One season it was the Nehru jacket; another, dashikis; the next, railroad overalls. In the early 1970's it was love beads and leather jackets. Every twist and turn of teen-age fashion revolutionized their costumes. But always, old was out and young was in. There was a pathos in those scenes—because the worshippers of youth succeeded only in displaying their age. The desperation in their acts was described by Judith Viorst in a volume of poetry called *It's Hard To Be Hip Over Thirty*.[23] Another indication of the popular attitude is the development of a false consciousness about age in America. Just as most Americans imagine themselves to be "middle class" even when they own nothing but their debts, so also most Americans of advanced age imagine themselves to be "middle-aged." A twentieth-century survey taken in Elmira, New York, found that only a little more than a third of people over sixty thought of themselves as old. Nearly two-thirds called themselves "middle-aged."[24]

That false consciousness of Americans about their own age is sometimes extreme. E. B. White, in 1969, confessed to a particularly bizarre form of this delusion. "Old age is a special problem for me," he said, "because I've never been able to shed the mental image I have of myself—a lad of

23 Judith Viorst, *It's Hard To Be Hip Over Thirty* (New York, 1968).
24 Zena Blau, *Old Age in a Changing Society* (New York, 1973), p. 100.

about nineteen." He was then seventy![25] One wonders how many old men and women still think of themselves as adolescents. Probably more common (because less extreme) is the attitude held by Bernard Baruch,[26] who somewhere wrote that "Old age is always fifteen years older than I am."

Gerontophobia is a highly destructive attitude, destructive most of all to those who adopt it—for in the end it is always directed inward upon the mind it occupies. Gerontophobia begins as a loathing of something in others; it ends as a loathing of something in oneself. In the end, the discovery that one is old is inescapable. But most Americans are not prepared to make it. Instead, their age suddenly becomes apparent to them in a brutal way which allows no vestige of dignity or pride to survive the discovery. The result is an orgy of self-pity and contempt. In an interview, one old woman spoke piteously of her age. Her appearance filled her with pain; the image in her mirror had become her enemy. Even the sounds she made filled her with self-loathing.

> What is the sound I make when I am old? Shuffling for sustenance, napping for strength, dressing for no one, waiting for one certain visitor, I am a diminished me. No capital *I*. No self to fling free, a bird sailing skyward. There is only a small *i*, shriveled within the layers of the years. . . . Somewhere in the early sleepless morning, when daylight still brings flicker of promise, I lie young on my scarcely wrinkled bed and am warmed by the feel of husband-hands caressing me knowingly or of child-fingers on my face or of friend-touch on my hands. But these moments pass. Daytime brings no warmth, and at last I rise because I have always risen and go to prepare myself for a day which stays too

---

[25] *New York Times*, July 11, 1969; quoted in Blau, *Old Age in a Changing Society*, p. 103.
[26] I have been unable to verify the attribution.

shortly and a night which comes too soon. I am an island, barren, surrounded by the waters of my plight.[27]

In the end, the cult of youth consumes all of its believers.

∿∿∿

At the same time that attitudes toward old age changed, the social and economic conditions of aging were also transformed. Most important was a revolution in the relationship between age and employment—a great change which consisted primarily in the growth of retirement. Forced retirement at a fixed age was very rare in early America, and first appeared for public offices in the late eighteenth century. But not until the late nineteenth century did mandatory retirement become common in most occupations.

That revolution was a highly complex process—more intricate than merely the growth of retirement itself. The first and most important change was the opposite of what we might expect. From at least 1800 to our own time, the age of people in most jobs actually increased. If we take a cross section of the American economy at different eras, we discover that the average worker was older in 1875 than in 1775, and older again in 1975 than in 1875. Maritime occupations are a good example. We imagine that men who went down to the sea in wooden ships must have been a grizzled set of old salts and their captains as ancient as Ahab himself. But it was not so. We have a typical ship's roster, one for the *Globe,* a whaler which sailed from Martha's Vineyard in 1822. The crew was young, incredibly so. The captain was the oldest man aboard—twenty-nine years old! (He had spent sixteen of those years at sea.) The mates were twenty-six, twenty-five, and twenty. The average age of the ship's officers was only twenty-five. But even so, it could rule

[27] "An Old Woman Speaks," Bert K. Smith, *Aging in America* (Boston, 1973), pp. 3-4.

with the authority of age, for the average age of the crew was only nineteen, not counting the ship's boys, who were fifteen and fourteen. The oldest man who sailed before the mast was twenty-four.[28]

As mortality declined and length of life advanced in America, so also did the average age of its work force. From the early nineteenth century to the twentieth, the members of every major profession have grown steadily older. The pace of change was slow, but its proportions were substantial. The age of political leaders is a good example. In the early Republic the median age of Cabinet officers was forty-seven. In the mid-twentieth century it was sixty.[29] At the same time the median age of United States Senators advanced from forty-five in 1799 to fifty-seven in 1925. There was a similar trend in most other occupations. The highest ranking generals in the Revolution and the War of 1812 were thirty-nine on the average at their time of service. In the Civil War they were forty-nine, and in World War II

[28] William Lay and Cyrus M. Hussey, *A Narrative of the Mutiny on Board the Whaleship Globe*, ed. by Edouard A. Stackpole (New York, 1963), pp. viii, xiv. A paper by Ira Dye, "A Quantitative Study of the Early American Seaman," to be published in The American Philosophical Society's *Proceedings*, will provide more information about the age of seamen.

[29] Between 1879 and 1945 the median ages of Cabinet members changed as follows:

Position	1789-1824	1825-1849	1850-1874	1875-1899	1900-1924	1925-1945	Entire Period
Sec. of State	53.00	54.67	61.75	61.70	59.75	68.50	59.13
Sec. of Treasury	44.00	50.17	56.00	61.75	58.50	52.50	54.00
Sec. of War	45.33	53.50	53.33	54.00	49.75	50.50	50.23
Attorney General	41.75	51.00	54.15	57.25	53.38	59.50	53.29
Postmaster General	46.50	49.83	49.50	52.50	53.50	58.00	50.70
Sec. of Navy	47.83	48.25	48.25	61.17	54.00	66.50	53.00
Sec. of Interior	—	—	48.38	61.50	60.50	64.00	58.00
Sec. of Agriculture	—	—	—	62.67	58.00	50.00	54.00
Sec. of Commerce & Labor	—	—	—	—	56.50	57.75	57.00
Entire Group	46.88	51.45	51.80	59.70	55.18	60.15	53.66

Harvey Lehman, "The Age of Eminent Leaders, Then and Now," *American Journal of Sociology*, 52 (1947), 345.

fifty-nine.[30] Leaders in twentieth-century America are not merely older on the average, they also tend to vary less in their ages. From 1900 to 1940, no Speaker of the United States House of Representatives was elected under the age of sixty except Nicholas Longworth, who in 1925 was chosen at the age of fifty-six.

In this century the word "young" has begun to take on a new meaning in the higher reaches of the Republic. In 1975, for example, the newspapers reported a movement on Capitol Hill in which a group of "Young Turks" attacked the congressional gerontocracy and succeeded in turning out an elderly committee chairman—Representative Wright Patman, who was eighty-one years old. His successor, Representative Henry Reuss, was called one of the most promising "young" members of Congress—he was sixty-two![31]

[30] Harvey Lehman, *Age and Achievement* (Princeton, 1953), p. 280.
[31] *New York Times,* Jan. 23, 1975. The ages of United States Representatives change from 1799 to 1975 as follows:

Year	Number of Individuals	Median Age	Mean Age
1799	108	43.50	43.29
1825	217	41.81	43.08
1849	241	42.81	43.93
1875	301	47.48	47.75
1899	373	47.97	48.67
1925	436	53.46	53.25
1950	347	48.90	50.11
1975	403	48.50	49.06

In the Senate, a similar pattern appeared:

Year	Number of Individuals	Median Age	Mean Age
1799	39	45.25	45.19
1825	63	46.50	47.10
1849	70	49.50	50.79
1875	82	51.50	52.50
1899	75	58.17	56.83
1925	108	57.50	56.95
1950	83	54.50	61.95
1975	94	52.50	54.59

Sources: For 1799-1925, Harvey Lehman, "The Age of Eminent Leaders: Then and Now," *American Journal of Sociology,* 52 (1947), 343; for 1950-1975, compiled by Helena Wall from *Congressional Directories.*

But another change took place in the opposite direction. As the age of workers has tended to rise in modern America, the age at which they have done their most valued work has tended to fall. A test is provided by a study of change in the ages at which men have made their major contributions to knowledge in the western world. In the eighteenth century they tended to make their major contributions when they were in their forties. In the nineteenth and twentieth centuries they have done so in their thirties. The difference has appeared in every major field of human endeavor. This was discovered by Harvey Lehman in his study of age and achievement.[32] He did not expect to find it and was unable to offer an explanation. It is indeed a very strange and curious fact. People have begun to make their major contributions at younger ages, even as they are growing older on the average. The most creative period of life has grown shorter even as life itself has grown longer. This is so despite the

[32] The median age of men making major contributions in certain fields changed as follows:

Field	Period I		Period II	
	Born Before	Median Age	Born	Median Age
Physics	1785	43.5	1785-1867	34.6
Geology	1800	46.2	1801-1857	41.1
Math	1748	42.7	1748-1848	34.0
Practical Invention	1750	39.6	1830-1850	33.4
Pathology	1773	47.0	1773-1871	39.0
Medicine	1759	48.5	1760-1850	40.2
Public Hygiene	1749	43.9	1750-1850	38.4
Literature	1807	43.9	1807-1851	40.3
Economics & Politics, major	1791	45.0	1791-1850	41.4
Economics & Politics, minor	1790	46.2	1790-1851	42.0
Electrical Engineering	1845	40.3	1845-1875	33.9
Philosophy	1763	42.2	1764-1850	40.1
Botany	1800	43.5	1800-1854	40.3
Education	1743	43.7	1744-1849	42.4
Music	1814	43.4	1815-1850	38.7

The periodization varies from one field to another because Lehman divided each field into two equal groups, one early and one late. Lehman, *Age and Achievement,* Chapter 18.

fact that the modern world generally requires a more extended period of preparation for almost every career, and that the sum of human knowledge has grown greater, so its mastery should be more protracted. These trends should lead us to expect that major contributions should have been made at an older age rather than younger one in the modern world. But the opposite is clearly the case.

This pattern may perhaps be explained by the fact that human knowledge has changed its epistemic texture. In almost every field the structure of thought has shifted toward increasingly formal systems of reasoned proof. Knowledge based upon experience and tradition has been replaced by logic and empiricism. It has often been demonstrated that most human beings reach their highest levels of ability in the manipulation of abstract reasoning, mathematics, and symbolic logic in young adulthood. Other forms of intelligence—for instance, vocabulary, memory, and judgment— are apt to reach their peak later in life. Also, the pace of growth in knowledge has been accelerating rapidly in the modern world. "Old" knowledge becomes outmoded more quickly. It is increasingly difficult for anyone to stay on the frontier of a field for any length of time.

The problem has been compounded by the growth of educational inequality between age groups. Here was an irony of progress: as education improved in America, the relative condition of elderly Americans grew steadily worse. Employers began to establish educational qualifications for their employees—first a grade school certificate, next a high school diploma, then a college degree. Inequality between the generations would not have developed if education had not improved in the twentieth century. But the better things became for most people, the worse they were for elderly people.[33] Middle-aged workers who lost their jobs

[33] According to the Census of 1960, levels of attained education have changed as follows in twentieth-century America:

often found it difficult to get another. An intense age prejudice appeared in employment opportunities. Simone de
Beauvoir did a study of job notices in American newspapers
and discovered that 97 per cent of them fixed the upper
limit at the age of forty.[34]

In the late nineteenth century social commentators began to speak of the uselessness of old men. The classical instance is Sir William Osler's farewell address to The Johns
Hopkins University in 1905. His argument was so extraordinary that it deserves to be quoted at length:

> I have two fixed ideas well known to my friends.
> . . . The first is the comparative uselessness of men
> above forty years of age. This may seem shocking, and
> yet, read aright, the world's history bears out the state-
> ment. Take the sum of human achievement in action,
> in science, in art, in literature—subtract the work of
> men above forty, and, while we should miss great
> treasures, even priceless treasures, we should practi-
> cally be where we are today. It is difficult to name a
> great and far-reaching conquest of the mind which has
> not been given to the world by a man on whose back
> the sun was still shining. The effective, moving, vital-
> izing work of the world is done between the ages of
> twenty-five and forty years—these fifteen golden years
> of plenty, the anabolic or constructive period, in which
> there is always a balance in the mental bank and the
> credit is still good. . . .

Age	Birth Years	Median School Years Completed
25-29	1931-1935	12.3
30-34	1926-1930	12.2
35-39	1921-1925	12.1
40-44	1916-1920	11.8
45-49	1911-1915	10.6
50-54	1906-1910	9.7
55-59	1901-1905	8.8
60-65	1896-1900	8.6
65+	-1895	8.3

[34] Simone de Beauvoir, *The Coming of Age* (New York, 1972), pp. 338-39.

My second fixed idea is the uselessness of men above sixty years of age, and the incalculable benefit would be in commercial, political and professional life, if, as a matter of course, men stopped work at this age.[35]

Osler's generalization about the history of the world is, of course, erroneous. One cannot resist answering his question, "What would have been left if we subtracted from history the work of men over forty?" We would have physics without Newton's *Principia*, economics without Adam Smith's *Wealth of Nations*, social theory without Marx's *Das Kapital*, and philosophy without Kant's *Critiques*. America without the work of men over forty would be a Puritan settlement without John Winthrop, a Revolutionary movement without Samuel Adams, a War of Independence without George Washington, a new nation without Thomas Jefferson, a Civil War without Abraham Lincoln, a New Deal without Franklin Roosevelt, and a Watergate without Richard Nixon. But, then again, how could there be an America at all without men over forty? Christopher Columbus sailed when he was forty-one! Osler's argument is inaccurate even as a version of his own history. His most important contributions were made during his career at Johns Hopkins, which he began at the age of forty.

But if Osler's statement was not an accurate description of the past, it was a good indicator of how attitudes toward old age were changing in his own time.[36] Public opinion

35 *Scientific American*, 92 (1905), 243.

36 A similar argument was made by George Beard, an influential American psychologist of the nineteenth century. Beard argued that no less than 70% of the world's work had been done by men before they were forty-five, and that the most fertile period of life fell between the ages of thirty and forty-five. See Beard, *Legal Responsibility in Old Age, Based on Researches into the Relationship of Age to Work* (New York, 1874). A counterargument was made by another psychologist, G. Stanley Hall of Clark University. Hall was the scholar who was largely responsible for inventing our modern idea of adolescence. In his last major work (which he wrote when in his 80's) he developed a parallel idea, called "senescence." Hall argued that the "last half of life" was itself a positive and even creative period. Stanley Hall's

was, of course, more than a little shocked by his argument (particularly when several newspaper accounts represented him as proposing a policy of senecide). But a similar outlook, in a form less extreme, was becoming very widespread in the world. And its popularity rested in part at least upon an empirical reality, which appears in Professor Lehman's statistics.

By the social standards of the age, old men were working longer, but young men were working better. The inevitable solution to this contradiction was the growth of mandatory retirement. We have already observed its small beginnings in the period between 1777 and 1820. During the nineteenth and twentieth centuries it gradually spread to other fields. Little is known about the history of retirement from 1820 to 1870. It was probably growing steadily but slowly through that period. As late as 1870 only one-fourth of American men over sixty-five were not actively working. One hundred years later, three-quarters were unemployed.[37]

---

conception of "adolescence" rapidly caught on; "senescence" fell dead from the press. Hall, *Senescence, The Last Half of Life* (New York, 1922).

[37] The following statistics show the growth of retirement in America from 1870 to 1970:

Year	% Males 65 or Over Gainfully Employed (Gagliardo)	Labor Force Participation Rates, Males 65 and Over (Census)
1870	80.6	
1880	76.7	
1890	73.8	68.3
1900	68.4	63.1
1910	63.7	
1920	60.2	55.6
1930	58.3	54.0
1940	41.5	44.2
1950	48.4	45.8
1960		33.1
1970		26.8

Dominic Gagliardo, *American Social Insurance* (New York, 1955); U.S. Bureau of Economic Analysis, *Long Term Economic Growth* (Washington, D.C., 1973), pp. 212-14.

Most business firms in the nineteenth and early twentieth centuries did not impose a fixed retirement age upon their workers. Numerous studies made during the 1930's showed that the majority of American corporations did not have a policy of mandatory retirement. But most of them operated under informal policies which had the same effect.

The growth of the factory system unquestionably accelerated the process of retirement. The assembly line devoured its workers. As the lines moved faster, older men were thought to be unable to maintain the pace. The automotive industry became notorious for the speed with which it discarded old workers—often making them into lowly "sweepers." The workers themselves complained bitterly on that account: "You see the fellows who have been there for years who are now sweeping. That's why most of the fellows want to get out. Like you take Jim, he's been there for thirty years and now he's sweeping. When you aren't any good any more, they discard you like an old glove."[38]

But the growth of unemployment among elderly Americans was not the result of a capitalist conspiracy. The labor unions helped the process along. On the one hand, they fought for seniority rules, which kept middle-aged Americans from being laid off. But at the same time they struggled for stable retirement systems, which had the effect of further reducing employment of men in their sixties. The growth of retirement was the result of a complex set of causal circumstances which were beyond the control of capitalists or union leaders. It arose primarily from two great changes in demographic and social conditions of life—the rise in the average age of death and the fall of the age at which workers were thought to make their major contributions to society.

[38] Ely Chinoy, *Automobile Workers and the American Dream* (Boston, 1955), pp. 83-85.

Whatever the cause of the growth of retirement may have been, its consequences were clear. It brought a rapid increase in poverty among the aged. In the twentieth century, inequality of income between age groups grew steadily greater, even as race and sex discrimination were slowly being reduced.[39] In fact, the growth of retirement was full of pain and trouble not only for millions of individual Americans, but for the society as a whole.

Older women were not directly affected by that growth. So few women were in the work force during the nineteenth century that the proportion who were gainfully employed changed very little from 1870 to 1970.[40]

[39] Trends in inequality by race, sex, and age appear as follows:

Inequality	Income Inequality Index	Occupation Inequality Index	Education Inequality Index
Race: Non-white/white	+3.5	+11.7	+13.2
Sex: Female/male	+1.1	− 1.8	− 3.5
Age: 65 plus/25-65	−7.5	− 0.6	−16.6

Erdman B. Palmore and Kenneth Manton, "Ageism compared to Racism and Sexism," *Journal of Gerontology*, 28 (1973), 363-69. The equality index is a complement of the index of dissimilarity. It consists in the proportion of two distributions which overlap. It is calculated thus:

$$\sum_{i=1}^{N} (a \cdot x_i + b \cdot y_i)$$

where $x_i = \%$ of one group in i category
$y_i = \%$ of other group in 1 category
$a = 1$ when $x < y$
$a = 0$ when $x > y$
$b = 1$ when $y < x$
$b = 0$ when $y > x$

[40] From 1870 to 1970, employment of older women changed thus:

But in another way the lives of older women changed even more profoundly than those of men. The great fall in fertility and mortality rates made a radical change in the rhythm of life. Through the first two hundred years of American history, a typical woman continued to rear her children as long as she lived. But after 1800 a gap began to appear at the end of life. In 1850, a mother's last child married when she was fifty-nine, two years before the mean age at death.[41] In 1950, the youngest child married when its mother was forty-eight, with more than thirty years of life still before her.[42]

Year	% 65 and Over Gainfully Employed (Gagliardo)	Labor Force Participation, 65 and over (Census)
1870	5.8	
1880	5.8	
1890	7.7	7.6
1900	8.5	8.3
1910	8.6	
1920	7.9	7.3
1930	7.9	7.3
1940	5.8	7.2
1950	8.0	9.7
1960		10.8
1970		9.7

Dominic Gagliardo, *American Social Insurance* (New York, 1955), p. 32; U.S. Bureau of Economic Analysis, *Long Term Economic Growth* (Washington, D.C., 1973), pp. 212-14.

[41] Mortality calculated from age 20.

[42] Life expectancy at age 20 was 81 for American women in 1950. Today the end of child-rearing may also be dated from the moment when the last child leaves home, which occurs when the mother is approximately 45. One gerontologist, Leonard Cain, found that for people born in the 1880's, the death of the husband or wife occurred less than 1 year after the last child left home. But for the cohort of the 1890's the period jumped to more than 5 years, and for the 1900's cohort it grew to more than 10. Leonard D. Cain, "Aging and the Character of Our Times," *Gerontologist*, 8 (1968), 250-58. Our evidence suggests a slightly different pattern, with its beginning in the decade 1810-20, when intra-marital fertility began to decline in America. The pace of change was slow until the late 19th and early 20th centuries, when the decline in mortality added its effect. See Appendix Table VI.

Women began to experience a sort of maternal "retirement," and its effect was even more devastating upon them than that of work retirement upon their husbands, for the break came sooner in life and more suddenly. The impact was deepened by its tendency to coincide with the physiological changes of menopause. For many women, life after their children left home was desolate, dreary, and miserable. Most had been trained to do nothing other than their domestic tasks. The house became an empty cage. The consequences could be observed in physicians' offices, where general practitioners began to find that their most frequent visitors were women in middle age whose principal complaints consisted of a variety of minor ailments collectively diagnosed as the "empty-nest syndrome."[43]

At the same time that the change occurred in the life cycles of both women and men, patterns of residence and family interaction were also changing. During the nineteenth and twentieth centuries, solitary residence slowly increased among the elderly. In 1850, about one person in ten over the age of sixty-four was not the head of a household, or the spouse of a household's head. By 1880 that proportion had risen to one in eight; by 1953, one in six; by 1975, one in four.[44] A growing proportion of elderly people lived alone.

In this and other ways, the American family structure went through major changes during the nineteenth and twentieth centuries. We must be careful not to think of it as a shift from "extended" to "nuclear" families, or from nuclear families to isolated individuals. The process was much more complex. Throughout American history, most households have tended to consist of nuclear families. But early

---

[43] Information supplied by John Roper, M:D., Seattle, Wash., 1975.
[44] Tamara Hareven, "The Discovery of the Last Stage: Historical Discontinuities in Adulthood and Old Age," unpubl., p. 13.

American *neighborhoods* were made up of extended families. Related households were usually close to one another, often on adjacent plots. A regular pattern of interaction developed between related nuclear families within their neighborhoods.

That pattern slowly changed. By the mid-twentieth century it had become unusual for the members of an American household to be related to their neighbors.[45] Visiting between generations continued, but at increasing distance. Contacts were carefully maintained, but increasingly separated from the daily business of life; becoming instead "social," in the colloquial sense. Recent research has demonstrated that most older people in America never became totally isolated. The great majority lived near their children and grandchildren, and visited frequently.[46] Of old people with children, between 80 and 90 per cent lived less than an hour's journey from their nearest child. Approximately 40 per cent saw their children almost every day, and another 40 per cent did so every week.[47]

In 1962 between 70 and 80 per cent of older people said that they "rarely" or "never" felt lonely. Only about 20 per cent complained of feeling lonely even "sometimes." And only 9 per cent felt lonely "often." Loneliness was largely concentrated among older people who were widowed, or separated from a spouse. It was most intense among those who had been recently widowed, within five years. The agony of emptiness seemed to heal with time. Loneliness

[45] A test has been run on maps which show every household by name in the town of East Sudbury (now Wayland), Mass., in 1775, 1875, and 1975. In 1775, the predominant settlement pattern consisted of hamlet clusters composed of related nuclear households. That pattern was still visible in 1875, but much weaker. By 1975 it had vanished entirely; there was not a single known instance of one family having the same name as any of its neighbors.
[46] This is the conclusion of an excellent study. See Ethel Shanas *et al.*, *Old People In Three Industrial Societies* (New York, 1968).
[47] Ibid.

also existed among the very old—octogenarians—and among those who were frail and infirm. Nevertheless, elders were increasingly separated from the daily affairs of their children and grandchildren.[48]

In the twentieth century, the separation of the generations sometimes developed into the outright age segregation of "retirement villages" for older people. Communities of elderly Americans appeared in many different varieties. Some sprang up spontaneously; others were elaborately planned by private entrepreneurs and public agencies. A few were founded for the rich—with $200,000 houses and many amenities.

In Florida, Southern California, and on the East Coast, many retirement communities appeared for middle-class couples. In the cities, public housing projects were built for the elderly poor.[49] For people who had retired from blue collar jobs, trailer parks provided a popular solution. Communities of mobile homes sprang up on the outer fringes of American suburbs.[50] One of them even appeared in

[48] There were numerous exceptions—particularly among immigrant groups. Many Wisconsin Germans maintained a "stem family" pattern of residence long into the twentieth century. Oscar Hoffman, "Culture of the Centerville-Mosel Germans in Monitowoc and Sheboygan Counties, Wisconsin," unpubl. Ph.D. thesis, Univ. of North Carolina, 1940.

Other scholars have discovered the importance of "surrogate kin" networks in modern America—artificial families which tend to form among nuclear households that have moved away from their own relations. Geographic migration in America often does not impoverish association patterns, but enriches them. By moving, Americans do not break their extended family, and they often organize another. Even the family itself functioned as a voluntary association. "Surrogate kin" groups have been observed in the boardinghouses of Manchester, N.H., during the late 19th and early 20th centuries. They are discussed in an important forthcoming work by Tamara Hareven.

[49] For a study of one such project see Arlie R. Hochschild, *The Unexpected Community* (Englewood Cliffs, N.J., 1973), which finds an effective and viable community in that setting.

[50] See Sheila K. Johnson, *Idle Haven: Community Building Among the Working Class Retired* (Berkeley, 1971).

Concord, Massachusetts—a trailer park named "Walden Breezes," established, ironically, next to Thoreau's beloved pond.

Age segregated retirement communities were not imposed upon older people against their will, but rather adopted by their own free choice. One study asked older Americans, "Would you like to live in a village made up largely of retired people?" Nearly three-quarters (73 per cent) said "yes." Only 15 per cent said "no."[51]

There has also been a tendency toward a separation of the generations in patterns of association as well as residence. That trend appeared as early as 1842, when a New Yorker observed that in the town of Kinderhook a shoestore had become "the rendezvous of a coterie of venerable gentlemen, remarkable as survivors of an early epoch . . . ancients and . . . gentlemen of the old school."[52] Many towns had similar places which were specially reserved for the oldest inhabitants.

Those gatherings became more formal in the nineteenth and twentieth centuries. A great deal of research has been done by social gerontologists on patterns of association among elderly Americans in our time. Most of this work suggests that the elderly become not less active, but active

[51] R. W. Kleemeier, "Attitudes Toward Special Settings for the Aged," *Processes of Aging*, II, 101-21. The attitudes of the elderly toward age segregation are in striking contrast with the attitudes of sociologists who have sometimes written on the question in a mood of intense hostility toward retirement villages. See, e.g., Jerry Jacobs, *Fun City: An Ethnographic Study of A Retirement Community* (New York, 1974), in which the author takes an adversary position against his subjects on the merits of life in the community. "Notwithstanding the fact that different segments of the population are reasonably content with Fun City," Professor Jacobs is convinced that they *ought* to be unhappy with their "unnatural" lives of "bourgeois gentility." A similar attitude appears in Richard Garvin and Robert E. Burger, *Where They Go To Die: The Tragedy of America's Aged* (New York, 1968).

[52] Silas Wright Burt, "Memoir," MS, New-York Historical Society.

in a different way. They withdraw from a network of associations which are reserved mostly for younger people—professional groups, Parent-Teacher Associations, and others which are age related by their very nature. Instead elderly people join leisure groups, fraternal clubs, and generational associations of other kinds.

But all of these changes—in family structure, residence, and association patterns—have posed special difficulties for elderly people of great age who are unable to care for themselves. Increasingly, they have been placed in special institutions. Other arrangements were commonly made during the early nineteenth century. In America it was long the custom for one child, often the youngest daughter, to live at home, unmarried, caring for her parents until they died. It was a wretched life for the unfortunate young woman whose destiny it was to surrender her own marriage chances to the welfare of her aged parents. The classical example is Emily Dickinson, who stayed at home to care for her father. She finally became a melancholy recluse who ventured out of the house only at dusk, a lonely spinster who found freedom only in her poetry, which is full of sad pleasures and empty dreams.[53]

Early in the nineteenth century, "old age homes" began to be founded in America for the upper middle class. One example selected at random is St. Luke's Episcopal Home for Aged Women, established in 1852 to serve the parishes of New York City.[54] The managers of the home were instructed "to reserve the benefits of the home for those used to life's refinements." Only "needy gentlewomen" were admitted. They were given a great deal of autonomy within

[53] Richard Sewall, *The Life of Emily Dickinson* (2 vols., New York, 1975), II.

[54] Floyd Appleton, *Church Philanthropy in New York. A Study of the Philanthropic Institutions of the Protestant Episcopal Church in New York* (New York, 1906) p. 87.

the home—each individual had "entire control of her room," and there were no institutional rules regarding meals. But each woman was also required to sign over all her property to the home. There were many such homes. By 1900 the Episcopal Church was operating eight old age homes in New York City alone. Most other denominations were equally active.[55]

Fraternal organizations such as the Elks and Odd Fellows were also very active. The Loyal Order of the Moose built a famous establishment called "Moosehaven" in Orange Park, Florida, where the "guests," as they were carefully called, lived in "cottages" on a "campus" which bordered the St. John's River.[56]

For the poor, public old age homes were erected by state and local governments. In nineteenth-century America old

[55] A large literature has grown up on this subject. See e.g. Ethel McClure, *More Than A Roof; The Development of Minnesota Poor Farms and Homes for the Aged* (St. Paul, 1968); most of this writing is about specific institutions. See also Leon M. Bowes, *A History of the Norwegian Old People's Home* (Chicago, 1940); Judith Robinson, *Ensign on a Hill: The Story of Church Home and Hospital* (Baltimore, 1954); anon., *Brief History of the German Evangelical Aid Society, and Its Work in the Evangelicial Home for the Aged* (Brooklyn, 1893); Henry C. Bittner, *A History of the Lutheran Orphans and Old Folks' Home of Toledo, Ohio* (Toledo, 1933); Gustine Nancy Courson Weaver, *"Towed In," A Compilation of Stories about Certain Guests in Our Homes for the Aged* (St. Louis, 1930); Edith Mozorosky and Gertrude Viteles, "Care of Jewish Aged of Manhattan and the Bronx in New York," typescript, N.Y.P.L.; Julia A. Bangs, *An Historical Outline of the Methodist Episcopal Church Home in the City of New York* (New York, 1893); William S. Young, *A History of Hollenbeck Home* (Los Angeles, 1934); Presbyterian Home for Aged Women in the City of New York, *The First Hundred Years* (New York, 1969).

[56] R. W. Kleemeier, "Moosehaven: Congregate Living in a Community of the Retired," *American Journal of Sociology*, 59 (1954) 347-351. Still another institution was the Veterans' Old Age Home. A dissertation on its history is presently being written by Judy Cetina (Case-Western Reserve Univ.). Old age institutions were also occasionally established by business corporations for superannuated employees. J. C. Penney's "Penney Farms" are perhaps the most notable example. Many professional homes were also founded, such as "Pilgrim Place" in Claremont, California, for retired Congregational ministers and missionaries.

men and women who were forced to fall upon the public poor rolls felt deeply disgraced. In the town history of Easton, Massachusetts, for instance, we find the unhappy story of an elderly widow who had been the wife of one of the most influential men in the town. When he died at the age of eighty-seven, she had no relatives who would take her in, so she was forced to move into the town poorhouse. And there the old woman, herself eighty-seven, spent the last few months of her life braiding straw in order to pay for her own funeral. "She shrank with pain from the thought of being buried at the expense of the town."[57]

Each community did things a little differently. In Mobile, Alabama, during the nineteenth century a cluster of little cottages called "widow's row" was maintained for destitute old women.[58] More often, there was a poor farm or almshouse, which by the end of the nineteenth century had generally become an old age home no matter what it was called. It was filled with elderly people who were unable to care for themselves. Among those institutions there were some that were models of philanthropy, but most of them deserved their evil reputation. A few were horrible places where the elderly met with callous cruelty and endured suffering beyond description.

Even so, some of the aged poor counted themselves lucky to gain admission. The public records contain many accounts of individual misfortune of elderly Americans deepened even more by the difficulty of finding anyone to help them. In Brown County, Minnesota, during the late winter of 1868, a county officer presented a bill for "boarding a poor old man, . . . sick and unable to help himself . . . ; Oliver Mather, son of the old man, had driven him off, and

[57] Chaffin, *History of the Town of Easton, Massachusetts* (Cambridge, Mass., 1886), p. 449.

[58] William H. Brantley, "Henry Hitchcock of Mobile," *Alabama Review*, 5 (1952), 3-39.

did not want to support him." The Board of Commissioners concluded after a thorough investigation that Oliver Mather should be made to take care of his father, and the bill was disallowed. The outcome is unknown.[59]

That sort of misfortune was experienced by a minority of the elderly population. We must be careful not to generalize too broadly about old age on the basis of a few unlucky individuals. Only a small percentage of elderly Americans have lived in institutions at any given time—in 1960 less than 4 per cent did. But their misery was sometimes great.[60] The lot of the aged poor in nineteenth-century America was no better than it had been in early America. It may have been worse.

ₚₚ₋ₙₙ

The main lines of change in modern America were full of trial and trouble for the aged. With the growth of a cult of youth, the moral authority of old age was seriously eroded. The development of retirement impoverished large numbers of elderly Americans. At the same time, changes in the

[59] McClure, *More than a Roof*, Chapter III.

[60] The percentage of Americans 65 and over living in institutions was as follows:

Types of Institutions	U.S. 1960
Long-term Hospitals	1.3%
mental	1.1
chronic disease	0.2
Nursing Homes	1.0
private	0.9
public	0.1
Residential Homes	1.3
private	1.1
public	0.2
Other Institutions	less than 0.1
Total	3.7%

Shanas *et al.*, *Old People*, p. 21.

life cycle, family structure, residence patterns, and welfare institutions caused the generations to live apart more and more. Those three great tendencies interacted with one another. Gerontophobia and the cult of youth were deepened by the growing poverty of elderly Americans, the growth of poverty in turn was justified by gerontophobia. The separation of age groups reinforced both of those tendencies and was also reinforced by them.

But again, as in early America, there was a counter-tendency—an undercurrent which moved in the opposite direction. The social condition of the aged in the seventeenth century was strong at the same time that their psychic condition was weak. In modern America, as the social and economic condition of the aged worsened, their psychic condition may have grown a little better, in one way at least. As elders lost their authority within the society, they gained something important in return. Within the sphere of an individual family, ties of affection may have grown stronger as ties of obligation grew weak. Tocqueville was one of the first to notice this tendency in relations between parents and children in America. He came from a world of "aristocratic families," in which "every place is marked out before-hand. Not only does the father occupy a separate rank, in which he enjoys extensive privileges, but even the children are not equal among themselves. The age and sex of each irrevocably determine his rank and secure to him certain privileges." When Tocqueville visited America in 1831, he found a different set of domestic arrangements—a "democratic family," in his phrase. And the difference was nothing less than a revolution in the relation between the generations. The father's formal powers were much reduced, but there was also a countervailing tendency, which seemed to be especially visible in family manners and family correspondence. In "aristocratic ages," Tocqueville wrote, "the style is always correct, ceremonious, stiff, and so cold that the natural warmth of the heart can hardly be felt in the language. In democratic countries on the contrary, the language addressed by a son to his father is always marked by mingled freedom, familiarity and affection, which at once show that new relations have sprung up in the bosom of the family."[61] It appeared to Tocqueville that ". . . in proportion as manners and laws become more democratic, the relation of father and son becomes more intimate and more affectionate; rules and authority are less talked of, confidence and tenderness are often increased, and it would seem that the natural bond is drawn closer in proportion as the social bond is loosened."[62] Relations between parents and children became more affectionate as they became less authoritarian. Often the new relations were established on the childrens' terms, and in that respect parents were the losers. But the new relations enlarged the possibilities for sympathy and love which had been blocked in the rigidly hierarchical world, and in this way parents were the gainers.

As psychic relationships eased between parents and children, they became easier still between grandparents and grandchildren. Another manifestation of the change in age relationships was the growth of that modern American institution, the indulgent grandparent, who showers upon the third generation presents which were denied to the second, smiles benevolently upon infractions of the strictest rules, and astonishes the righteous parent with an invincible determination to "spoil" the grandchildren at every chance.

That phenomenon is so close and ordinary to us that we

---

[61] Tocqueville, *Democracy in America* (2 vols., New York, 1959, Bradley ed.), II, p. 206.
[62] Ibid. II, p. 205.

have difficulty seeing its importance. One anthropological study of indulgent grandparents has concluded after a learned "cross-cultural" analysis that "indulgent grandparents are associated with societies . . . where grandparents are disassociated from authority."[63] Here is another irony in the history of age relations. As the economic and social condition of many elderly people grew worse in modern America, psychic conditions grew a little better.

[63] Dorian Apple, "The Social Structure of Grandparenthood," *American Anthropologist,* 58 (1956), pp. 656-63. The author also has written a doctoral dissertation on this subject—"Grandparents and Grandchildren: A Sociological and Psychological Study of Their Relationship" (Radcliffe, 1954).

IV. OLD AGE BECOMES A SOCIAL PROBLEM
1909-1970

> *There is no experience in an industrial neighborhood more poignant and heartbreaking than those connected with old age.*
>
> Jane Addams (1860-1935)

EARLY in the twentieth century, Americans learned to think of old age in a new way. That stage of life began to be seen as a problem to be solved by the intervention of "society." The dawn of that discovery may be dated to the year 1910 or thereabouts. It simultaneously appeared in the appointment of the first public commission on aging (Massachusetts, 1909), and the first major survey of the economic condition of the aged (Massachusetts again, 1910); in the first federal old age pension bill (1909), and the first state old age pension system (Arizona, 1915); in the invention of a new science named geriatrics (1909), and the first published textbook in that field (1914).

In a general sense, of course, old age had always been a social problem, for which institutional remedies were invented as early as the fifth century. But there was something new in the modern world—an instrumental attitude which lay at the center of modernity itself, a Promethean spirit which was first successfully applied to the physical universe and then to social relations as well. It was a style of thought which made an artifact of society itself, and government a tool for its improvement.

In America, there had not been much of this activity during the nineteenth century. Social conditions seemed not to require it, and the prevailing social ethic did not encourage it. The political thought of Jefferson and the economic thought of Adam Smith both rested upon the assumption that, as a remedy for the ills of the world, Nature was more to be trusted than Man. Social evils were thought to be temporary impediments to the moral progress of mankind which would, inevitably, be overcome. No modern nation had less government than the United States in the nineteenth century. And none was more secure in its blind and stubborn optimism, which was so strong that not even the sufferings of the Civil War could shake it.

But after the turn of the century, a new spirit was abroad in America, a nascent sense that government was necessary; planning was good; and regulation was a requirement for order, justice, and even freedom in the modern world. The cause of that new attitude has been variously attributed by historians: to the "closing" of the frontier; to the rising wave of immigration, which reached its height in the first decade of the twentieth century; to the deep economic depression of the 1890's; to the growth of the great American cities; to the steady expansion of a new industrial order. For all of those reasons, and more, Americans were forced to think about their society in a new way.

Old age was merely one social problem among many which were "discovered" at the same time. The first signs of its discovery actually began to appear before 1908. One of the earliest was an article called "Old Age Pensions," published by *Cosmopolitan* magazine in June 1903. The author was Edward Everett Hale. He presented a simple but startling truth—that "there is now no place in our working order for older men."

Hale himself was something of an exception to his own

rule. An octogenarian in 1903, he was still gainfully employed as Chaplain to the United States Senate. But he was deeply sensitive to the plight of others less fortunate than himself. Hale proposed an old age pension plan to which every worker would contribute $2.00 a year until he was sixty-nine, and from which he would thereafter receive an annuity of $100 for the rest of his life.[1]

In Hale's home state of Massachusetts, an old age pension bill was first proposed in the same year—1903—but without effect; 114 old age pension bills were introduced in Massachusetts between 1903 and 1929, and not one of them was passed. The legislature preferred to deal with the problem by passing a law which made it a criminal offense for a child with means to fail to support an aged parent.

There was continual argument for old age pensions. A largely academic group called the American Association for Labor Legislation was founded in 1906 by social scientists, including John R. Commons and Richard Ely of Wisconsin and Henry Farnam of Yale. But nothing much was accomplished until after 1908. Then the movement suddenly began to have an effect.

In 1908 the American economy went through a recession which was short, but very severe.[2] Recovery was achieved by 1909, but not before unemployment had risen from less

[1] Edward Everett Hale, "Old Age Pensions," *Cosmopolitan*, 35 (1903), 168-69.

[2] The major economic indicators measure its magnitude as follows:

Year	Industrial Production (*1913 = 100*)	GNP (billions, *1958 $*)	Total Unemployment Rate (%)
1906	78.9	108.9	1.7
1907	80.6	110.6	2.8
1908	68.0	101.5	8.0
1909	80.2	113.6	5.1
1910	85.3	115.1	5.9

U.S. Bureau of Economic Analysis, *Long Term Economic Growth, 1860-1970* (Washington, D.C., 1973), series A1, A15, B1.

than 2 per cent to more than 8 per cent. In the larger context of American history, the recession of 1908 was not a great event. By comparison with the depressions of the 1890's and 1930's, when 25 per cent of American workers lost their jobs, it was not a major disturbance. But it left its mark upon the history of social thought in America, less by its depth and duration than by its speed and timing. For a very long period before 1908, the relative number of the elderly in America had grown at the same time that their social and economic status had declined. Length of life had increased far beyond its ancient level, but length of employment had moved in the opposite direction. Forced retirement had become common, but pensions remained rare. And loss of work meant loss of wages at the same time that the shift of so many workers from farms to factories had caused an increasing dependency upon wage income. The major trends were full of danger for elderly Americans and the recession of 1908 suddenly dramatized their difficulties.[3]

Still, the extraordinary thing about the American discovery of old age as a social problem was not that it came so suddenly, but that it came so late. France had established a national system of old age support as early as 1850; in Great Britain the question had become a political issue in the 1870's. Most European nations enacted compulsory old age insurance decades before America did—Germany in 1889, Austria in 1906, England in 1908, France in 1910, Romania in 1912, Sweden in 1913. The United States was very much the laggard nation.

In 1908, Theodore Roosevelt sent a message to Congress which helped to draw attention to the problem. He called

[3] Of course, this is not to argue that a new consciousness sprang full blown into being within the span of a single year. There was movement before 1909, and a long process of sustained development thereafter. But an extraordinary surge of social concern for the problem of old age suddenly occurred in the wake of the recession of 1908 as part of a general awakening of social thought, one which has been overlooked by most American historians.

the situation an "outrage" to the American conscience. "It is a reproach to us as a nation," he declared, "that in both Federal and State legislation we have afforded less protection to public and private employees than any other industrial country in the world." President Roosevelt's humanity was offended by the suffering of so many of his countrymen. And his racial pride was appalled by the thought that "even the Ottoman Turks" were more enlightened in their social legislation than the United States of America was.[4]

If America was slow to discover the problem of old age, it was not because that problem was small. In fact, it was great, and growing rapidly. In 1910, when the first serious attempt was made to determine the economic status of elderly people in Massachusetts, the findings were grim. Nearly one out of four were on the dole. Twenty-three per cent were public paupers, or inmates of asylums and almshouses, or otherwise dependent upon institutional support. That estimate took no account of informal charity from families, friends, and neighbors.[5]

[4] Hace Sarel Tishler, *Self-Reliance and Social Security, 1870-1917* (Port Washington, N.Y., 1971), p. 98.

[5] The results of the Massachusetts survey of 1910 were published by Lee Welling Squier, *Old Age Dependency in the United States* (New York, 1912), p. 6. They were as follows:

Status of Citizens 65 and Older, Massachusetts, 1910	*No.*	*%*
Not dependent	135,788	76.7
Dependent	41,212	23.3
prisons	556	0.3
asylums and hospitals	1961	1.1
almshouses	3480	2.0
benevolent homes	2598	1.5
public outdoor relief	3075	1.7
private outdoor relief	2312	1.3
U.S. Pensions	27,230	15.4
Total	177,000	100.0

The compilers explained that "occasional aid from relatives, friends or neighbors, or even from a church, society, or settlement, has not been con-

At the same time that a large portion of the elderly population were paupers, an even larger proportion of institutionalized paupers were elderly. Of all the people who lived in state pauper institutions in 1910, the vast majority were sixty-five or older—60 per cent in Ohio, 62 per cent in Pennsylvania, 87 per cent in Wisconsin, and 92 per cent in Massachusetts.[6]

Many other aged Americans had to struggle to maintain their independence, and did so only at a heavy cost. Settlement workers, who knew at first hand the condition of elderly people who were not on relief, described a world of misery and want which made a dramatic contrast to the hopes and expectations of so many young Americans. Worse than the want was the fear. A woman who visited elderly New Yorkers in Greenwich Village found them consumed by fear—fear of poverty, fear of illness, fear of becoming a burden to their children, fear of being left alone, fear of having to go on relief, most of all fear of being sent to an institution on Blackwell's Island.[7]

The problem of old age was primarily a problem of poverty. In this, the world's wealthiest nation, its solution presented no serious material difficulties. But an ideological obstacle lay squarely in the way. Most Americans who expressed themselves on the subject in 1910 imagined that the only proper remedy for poverty among the old was thrift among the young. The gospel of thrift has been central to the system of secular morality in America since the Puritans. But like most other gospels, it was more easily preached than

---

sidered to constitute dependency in the proper sense. Only assistance received through the regular channels of charity, public and private, has been taken into account." Even within those limits, other scholars who examined the data judged them to be conservative. See Abraham Epstein, *Facing Old Age; A Study of Old Age Dependency in the United States and Old Age Pensions* (New York, 1922), pp. 22-25.

6 Epstein, *Facing Old Age*, p. 30. "Elderly" and "old" in statistical statements means 65 and over in this chapter, unless otherwise stated.

7 Mabel Nassau, *Old Age Poverty in Greenwich Village* (New York, 1915).

practiced. Though thrift has always been an American ideal, it has never been an American habit. For most Americans in the past, saving was simply impossible. The price of labor closely shadowed the cost of living, and employment was unstable, even for men in the prime of life. In 1878 the Massachusetts Bureau of Labor Statistics discovered that two-thirds of the workers in that state had been out of work for an average of ninety-four days during the previous year. And nearly half had lost another twenty days to illness. Most complained of being underpaid; many (one out of five) complained of not being paid at all. When those Massachusetts workers were asked if they had been able to put anything away for their old age, only 19 per cent replied in the affirmative. One worker added that he hoped never to reach old age. "With present conditions of business," he wrote in 1878, "I don't want to live to sixty-five."[8]

Business conditions were bad in 1878; America was caught in the trough of a deep depression. In periods of prosperity, of course, unemployment was not so severe. But between 1780 and 1950 most American workers lived through recurrent panics and economic depressions which wiped out the few savings they had scraped together in good times. When they finally reached old age, pathetically little was left to show for a lifetime of unremitting toil. Savings, in any form, have always been highly concentrated among the largest wealth-holders in America. During the past one hundred and thirty years, the net savings of the lower two-thirds of the population has commonly approached zero.[9]

Even middle class Americans who might have managed to save at least part of their income for their old age were

8 Massachusetts Bureau of Labor Statistics, *Tenth Annual Report, January, 1879* (Boston, 1879), pp. 100-116; quoted in Tishler, *Self-Reliance and Social Security*, p. 19.

9 Gabriel Kolko, *Wealth and Power in America* (New York, 1962), 48-49; Lee Soltow, *Men and Wealth in the United States, 1850-1870* (New Haven, 1975), p. 120. The Gini coefficient of saving in 1870 was .83.

not likely to do so. Voluntary savings were not common; compulsory savings plans were intensely unpopular. In 1908, a poll of government clerks in Washington, D.C., found that only 186 out of 10,494 were in favor of a pension plan supported by compulsory savings. Three-quarters of them opposed such an arrangement, even if it were paid for entirely by the government.[10]

The vast majority of Americans lived only for the economic moment. That national attitude which H. G. Wells called our "optimistic fatalism" kept even affluent Americans from making prudent provision for their own old age. The clergy preached the gospel of savings; teachers taught the lessons of thrift. But Americans borrowed and bought beyond the limit of their means, secure in a stubborn faith that things would somehow work out.

Insurance companies offered old age annuity plans to the public in 1910, but few people purchased them. In that year a vice president of the Metropolitan Life Insurance Company observed that "Insurance companies in this country have hitherto failed to find any considerable demand on the part of the insuring public for annuities."[11] The cost of the plans was sometimes very low—one required a

---

[10] The poll asked government clerks to choose one of five plans, with the following results:

		No. for
1. An immediate increase in salaries without any retirement or pension plan		7479
2. A retirement pension plan paid for entirely by the government		317
3. A retirement annuities plan paid for by compulsory savings		186
4. An increase in salary, and retirement on annuities from a compulsory savings plan		1067
5. An increase in salary plus a pension plan paid for by the government		1465
Total		10,494

Source: Squier, *Old Age Dependency in the United States,* p. 256.
[11] Squier, *Old Age Dependency in the U.S.,* p. 266 *passim.*

premium payment of only thirteen cents a week. But benefits were even lower, and few workers could hope to gain much from them. The ratio of premiums to payments offered small inducement to prospective investors. The private insurance industry of the United States has always been grossly inefficient as a supplier of "a social service"—far worse than the clumsiest bureaucracy. Some American insurance companies drew off as much as two-thirds of annuity premiums for administrative costs and corporate profits. The heavy expenses of high executive salaries, lavish headquarters, and corporate overhead made annuity insurance a bad bargain for prospective buyers.[12]

But there were not many prospective buyers in any case. Two states, Massachusetts in 1907 and Wisconsin in 1911, sponsored their own voluntary annuity plans, with premiums much lower than those of private companies and payment ratios substantially higher.[13] Even so, public interest was not very great. By 1919, after twelve years of operation, only about three hundred people had actually drawn annuities under the Massachusetts plan.

Many private companies pensioned a few loyal employees; in the nineteenth century, the word "pensioner" carried a connotation of special favor. But until the twentieth century few companies established comprehensive retirement systems. The first large private corporation to do so was the American Express Company, in 1875.[14] The railroads came close behind. The Baltimore & Ohio led the way with a retirement plan in 1884. Other railroads followed at a distance. Only twelve private pension plans are

12 Ibid.

13 The first was the Massachusetts Savings Bank Insurance System, begun in 1907, which allowed savings banks to sell annuities. A leading proponent was Louis Brandeis. The model was England's Postal Savings Bank Act of 1864, which had not been widely successful.

14 American Express retired its employees on half-pay after 60—a very generous arrangement by the measure of other early pensions.

known to have existed in the United States as late as 1900. But many railroads acted early in the twentieth century. The basis of their arrangements was the so-called "railroad formula," which paid a pension equal to 1 per cent of a worker's wage multiplied by the number of his years in service. It was not a lavish arrangement; a man who had worked for twenty years received 20 per cent of his income after retirement.[15]

Industrial corporations were slower to act, perhaps because of the larger numbers of employees and dollars involved.[16] United States Steel established one of the first industrial plans, based upon the railroad formula, with an endowment from Andrew Carnegie. Many other corporations created plans between 1905 and 1915.[17] Standard Oil did so in 1909, Armour in 1911, Du Pont in 1908, John Deere in 1908, International Harvester in 1908, Proctor &

[15] The age of retirement varied from one plan to another. The B. & O. made retirement compulsory at 65; the Pennsylvania, voluntary at the same age, and compulsory at 70. Normally, retirement seems to have been voluntary at 60 and compulsory at 70.

[16] Old age pensions were also established by craft unions—among them the German-American Typographia and the United Brotherhood of Carpenters and Joiners.

[17] Private pension plans in the United States grew as follows:

Year	No. Plans	No. Workers Covered (millions)
1875	1	n.a.
1900	12	n.a.
1920	270	n.a.
1930	720	2.4
1935	1090	2.6
1940	1965	3.7
1945	7425	5.6
1950	12,330	9.8
1955	23,000	15.4
1960	n.a.	21.2
1965	n.a.	25.3
1970	n.a.	29.7

n.a. = not available.

Nathan W. Shock, *Trends in Gerontology* (Stanford, 1951); *Statistical Abstract of the U.S., 1975,* Table 468.

Gamble in 1904, Wells Fargo in 1903, Western Electric in 1906, Westinghouse in 1908. But only a small minority of workers were protected by the plans, and the size of their pensions was pathetically small. Everything was weighted on the side of the companies. A worker could not win a pension without long and loyal service, but he could lose it in an instant, whenever the company chose to take it away. Most private pensions existed not as a right, but a favor. A worker had no contractual rights to his benefits. Moreover, the plans were carelessly set up, with no sound actuarial studies of their cost. And many collapsed during business recessions, when they were needed most.

Government workers were in even worse straits than those in private industry. The federal government had no regular retirement or pension system for its employees. Those in the Civil Service worked as long as they were able— sometimes longer. Superannuated employees became a serious problem in Washington, D.C. Retirement bills were presented to the Congress in almost every session after 1900, but Congressmen feared the wrath of their constituents. No action was taken before 1920.

The United States government treated its animals better than its human work force. Four-legged federal workers retired on full rations, much to the fury of many employees. John W. Perry, a postal worker, was astonished to read in his union newspaper that an artillery horse named Rodney was retired from active duty with full support to the end of his days. "For the purpose of drawing a pension," Perry wrote, "it would have been better had I been born a horse than a human being. I have been a 'wheel horse' for the Government for the past fifty years and can not get a pension."[18]

In the early twentieth century most state and municipal workers received no pensions. It was discovered in 1910 that

[18] Quoted in Epstein, *Facing Old Age*, pp. 169-70.

only nine of the fifty-six largest American cities had pension plans for their policemen, firemen, and teachers. Over-all, government workers were probably worse off than even the employees of private corporations. The problem was endemic in America.

The remedy which most European nations had adopted by 1910 was a system of compulsory old age insurance. But that idea was anathema to Americans.[19] The national hostility to a compulsory pension plan was rooted in the deepest political and moral principles of the Republic. Even the Massachusetts Commission on Old Age regarded compulsory pensions as a repudiation of the American way of life. "If such a scheme be defensible or excusable," it declared, "then the whole economic and social system is a failure. The adoption of such a policy would be a confession of its breakdown."[20]

Compulsory old age pension plans were denounced by clergymen as hostile to the morals of the Republic. They were condemned by economists as destructive to the spirit of enterprise. They were attacked by politicians as dangerous to American liberty. Capitalists called them a corrupt form of socialism. Labor leaders denounced them as "deferred wages."[21]

[19] Not because it was a new idea. As early as 1796, a national pension plan was proposed by Thomas Paine in one of his greatest pamphlets, *Agrarian Justice*. See *The Complete Writings of Thomas Paine,* ed. by Philip S. Foner (2 vols., New York, 1945), I, 605-23. Paine's idea began as a response to an Anglican bishop who had published a sermon entitled "The Wisdom and Goodness of God, in having made both Rich and Poor." Paine was infuriated by that blasphemy. "It is wrong to say that God made *rich* and *poor,*" he wrote, He made only male and female; and He gave them the earth for their inheritance." *Agrarian Justice* was Paine's reply. He proposed to raise a "national fund" from a ground rent on cultivated lands. Everyone at the age of 50 was to receive an annual pension of £10. The money was to be paid as "a right and not a charity" to "every person, rich or poor . . . to prevent invidious distinctions."

[20] *Report of the Massachusetts Commission on Old Age Pensions, Annuities and Insurance* (Boston, 1910).

[21] Businessmen, of course, were not of one mind on the subject. Gerard Swope, the president of General Electric, actively promoted them, and Al-

But ironically, at the same time that compulsory old age pensions were condemned as un-American, the United States maintained much the largest public pension system in the world. From the Civil War until World War I, the federal government spent more than $5 billion dollars in veterans' benefits—an enormous sum in an era when its total expenditures were only about $300 million a year.[22]

The number of federal military pensions rose from 127,000 immediately after the Civil War to nearly a million in 1905.[23] That vast army of veterans—a good deal

fred I. du Pont headed the pension movement in Delaware. See Thomas R. Cole, "An Essay on Aging in Modern American History," Master's thesis, Wesleyan Univ., 1975, p. 90; Irving Bernstein, *The Lean Years* (Boston, 1972), p. 138. By 1927 a survey by the Pennsylvania Old Age Pensions found that a majority of business leaders had come to favor some sort of state action. But compulsory pensions or insurance systems were generally condemned. Labor leaders did not oppose all pension plans. The A. F. of L. began to support voluntary state pensions in 1909, and had expressed favorable interest as early as 1902. But it staunchly opposed compulsory insurance systems. See letter, Alan B. Heppel to author, Aug. 13, 1976.

[22] That was the budget in 1890.

[23] It is perhaps of some causal significance that the discovery of old age as a social problem in America coincided with a decline in the proportion of Americans receiving military pensions. The support of Civil War veterans in such large numbers may have explained the lag between America and Europe, in part at least. The number and size of pensions changed as follows:

Year	A Veterans on rolls	B Average Payment	C Expenditures (millions)
1866	127,000	$118	15
1870	199,000	146	29
1880	251,000	227	57
1890	538,000	197	106
1900	994,000	139	138
1910	921,000	174	160
1920	770,000	410	316
1930	841,000	503	418
1940	849,000	517	429
1950	3,026,000	664	2009
1960	3,959,737	836	2907
1970	4,721,952	1108	5232
1974	3,868,745	1330	6475

Note: "veterans on the rolls" include both living veterans receiving pen-

larger than the Army of the Potomac had ever been—did not include Confederate soldiers. The Southern states maintained their own military pensions, which swelled the rolls to still larger proportions. From the 1880's to nearly World War I, veterans' pensions were by far the biggest single item in the federal budget. In some years they accounted for more than 40 per cent of the whole.

By 1900, most Civil War veterans were in their late fifties, sixties, and seventies. Military pensions in America had become primarily a system of old age assistance. A large proportion of the nation's elderly citizens benefited by them—perhaps as many as two-thirds.[24] But old people who stood most in need of pensions were least able to qualify for them. Blacks, immigrants, and paupers who had not served in the Union army gained little from the enormous program. Social reformers were driven to fury by the absurdity of it all.

"After all," one of them wrote, "it is idle to speak of a popular system of old age pensions as a radical departure from American traditions, when our pension roll numbers several hundred thousand more names than that of Great Britain. It is preposterous to claim that the cost of such a pension would be excessive, when the cost of our pensions is . . . more than three times as great as that of the British system."[25]

Americans studied the pension question as if it were a branch of theology. Military pensions were defended as necessary to maintain the honor of the Republic, but old age pensions were condemned as an unholy amalgam of sin

sions and deceased veterans whose dependents receive support. Calculated from data in *Historical Statistics of the U.S.*, series Y 826, and *Statistical Abstract of the U.S., 1976*, table 550. Average and total payments are in current dollars. From 1866 to 1955, column B was calculated from data in A and C. From 1960 to 1974, column C was calculated from data in A and B.

24 Tishler, *Self-Reliance and Social Security*, p. 89.

25 I. N. Rubinow, *Social Insurance, with Special Reference to American Conditions* (New York, 1913), pp. 404-5.

and socialism. The distinction was baffling to outsiders not indoctrinated in the national faith. But to true believers, the line between military and old age pensions was as clear as that between transubstantiation and consubstantiation had been for Christians during the Reformation. When the pension problem was wrapped in Old Glory, the veteran's bread and wine was miraculously changed into the flesh and blood of patriot soldiers. But when it came in other forms the sacred change did not take place.

Leaders of the growing pension movement in the United States found themselves stymied by that way of thinking, which seemed all the more astonishing in a nation which boasted of its pragmatic genius. On the major social question of pensions, Americans found themselves entangled in a web of moral absolutes.

The first attempt to establish a national system of old age pensions recognized the prevailing system of political morality in an appropriately bizarre fashion. Representative William B. Wilson, a coalminer and union leader who later became the Secretary of Labor in Wilson's Cabinet, introduced the first national pension plan in 1909.[26] He proposed to create an "Old-Age Home Guard of the United States Army," in which all Americans sixty-five and over were invited to "enlist" as privates, if their property was less than $1500, or if their income was under $20 a month. Their duty was to report once a year to the War Department on the state of patriotism in their neighborhoods. For that service, their "pay" was to be $120 a year. The bill was referred to the House Committee on Military Affairs, and never reported out.

Other proposals quickly followed. The first outright old age pension bill was introduced in Congress in 1911 by Vic-

[26] The first, at least, that I have found. Questions of priority are always doubtful.

tor Berger, a Socialist Representative from Milwaukee. It, too, was lost, as Wilson's had been, but not before it seriously raised the issue of social insurance for the aged in national politics. The movement for old age pensions steadily gathered strength in America before World War I. Its leaders were often immigrants or the children of immigrants, who were disproportionately eastern European in origin, urban in residence, Jewish in religion, and socialist in politics. They were often denounced by their enemies as "un-American," and so they were, in a society which had been predominantly Protestant and Anglo-Saxon. The American past had belonged to others. But the future belonged to themselves.

Among the most important was Isaac Max Rubinow (1875-1936), born in Grodno, Russia, the youngest son of a cloth merchant who came to America in 1892, when Isaac was seventeen. Young Rubinow had already gained the rudiments of an education at the Moscow Gymnasium, and continued his studies in New York, winning his A.B. from Columbia and M.D. from New York University. He began to practice medicine among the poor in New York, but was persuaded by his experience in the slums that the major problem was social rather than medical, and returned to Columbia as a graduate student in social science. In 1903 Rubinow sent an article to the *Political Science Quarterly,* proposing a system of unemployment insurance. It was rejected by the editor—his old teacher, E. R. A. Seligman—on the grounds that it was "un-American and revolutionary." Undaunted, Rubinow abandoned medicine altogether and became a specialist in social statistics for both the government and private industry. From 1910 to 1934, he published major works on social insurance which won him a reputation as the leading expert in that field.[27] His stocky figure

---

[27] Rubinow's major works included *Social Insurance* (1913) and *The Quest for Security* (1934).

and Van Dyke beard were familiar sights at meetings on social welfare, where he doggedly attacked the "voluntarism"
of American society and fought for a system of compulsory
social insurance in the United States.

Equally important was Abraham Epstein, whose back-
ground was similar in many ways. Born in Russia in 1892,
Epstein came to New York City in 1910 and then moved on
to Pittsburgh, where he managed to pursue an education at
the University of Pittsburgh despite his poverty. After a
year of graduate study, which produced a published thesis
in 1918, Epstein was hired as director of research by the
Pennsylvania old age pension commission. He worked in
that job until 1927, when he founded the American Association of Old Age Security.

In the decade after 1910 men such as Isaac Rubinow and
Abraham Epstein published tirelessly on the subject of "social" insurance. Learned journals and little magazines were
filled with their proposals for old age pensions, unemployment insurance, and other welfare schemes. But very little
was accomplished. Arizona enacted the first state pension
plan in 1915 (maximum payment, $15 a month), but a con-
servative judge declared it unconstitutional. As late as 1922,
no state had succeeded in enacting a workable old age pension system. Only the Territory of Alaska had one, for
needy "pioneer residents" who had reached the age of sixty-
five.[28]

An old age assistance law was passed by the Pennsylvania
legislature in 1923. The act was quite weak, but any act at
all was too much for the Pennsylvania Chamber of Commerce. It brought an action in the state court and won a

[28] Alaska had opened a "Pioneer's Home" at Sitka in 1913. It was quickly
filled. Two years later a pension was provided for "any pioneer of Alaska,
regardless of sex," who was at least 65 years old, a resident for 10 years, and
in need of assistance. See Cole, "Essay on Aging," p. 60; Alaska Territory
Reporting of the Alaska Pioneer's Home (Sitka, 1915), p. 6.

decision which condemned any sort of individual assistance except poor relief as unconstitutional. When a constitutional amendment was proposed, the Chamber of Commerce called it "un-American and socialistic, . . . an entering wedge of communistic propaganda in Pennsylvania."[29]

In the 1920's the floodgates suddenly opened, and a torrent of pension legislation poured forth. Two things had happened. First, resistance had begun to collapse before the plain fact that poverty was growing rapidly among the aged. By roughly comparable measures, dependency of elderly Americans was 23 per cent in 1910, 33 per cent in 1922, and 40 per cent in 1930—before the Great Depression began to take effect. When the Depression struck, the situation grew even worse. Old age dependency rose nearly to 50 per cent in 1935, and to two-thirds in 1940.[30] But the "prosperity" decade of the 1920's was almost as cruel in its effect upon the elderly as the Depression of the 1930's.

In 1930, the American Federation of Labor finally changed its mind and supported a compulsory old age insurance system. The major political parties—both Democratic and Republican—began to endorse the same idea. In New York, Governor Franklin Roosevelt appointed a commission to draft an old age pension bill and to abolish the almshouses.[31] At the same time, politicians began to be prodded into action by one of the most improbable pressure groups in American history. As long as social welfare plans were proposed by socialists, scholars, and immigrants from eastern Europe, American political leaders could look the other way. But in the 1920's a social insurance movement began to grow from the grassroots of the Republic. Even

[29] Cole, "Essay on Aging," p. 88.
[30] Jackson K. Putnam, *Old Age Politics in California, from Richardson to Reagan* (Stanford, 1970), p. 5.
[31] See F. D. Roosevelt, *Public Papers and Addresses* (New York, 1938), I, 43.

while men such as Epstein and Rubinow denounced the "voluntarism" of American society as the root of the problem, it was a voluntary association which found a remedy.

One of the many social organizations which flourished in America among the fraternal menagerie of Elks, Lions, and Moose was an association called the Fraternal Order of Eagles. The Eagles were a national association with "Aeries" in every state and a national convention called a "Grand Aerie," which convened every summer. In 1921, all of that fraternal machinery was cranked up and set in motion for the purpose of securing old age pensions in America. The leader was Frank Hering, a "Past Grand Worthy President" of the society, who drafted a resolution on the subject of old age pensions and persuaded his own Aerie in Indiana to adopt it in May 1921. In August of the same year, the Grand Aerie approved the plan and established an Old Age Pension with Hering as president.

The Eagles cooperated freely with almost anyone interested in the question; they hired Abraham Epstein as Hering's assistant, and worked closely with labor unions and other groups. It was said that in Indiana a pension club was formed in every town which had an Aerie. The Eagles founded community pension clubs, sponsored mass meetings, organized publicity campaigns, and lobbied incessantly in state capitols. All the instruments of an American pressure group were skillfully orchestrated in a concerted effort, and it quickly began to obtain results.

Conservative opponents of pensions—Chambers of Commerce and Associations of Manufacturers—began to apply counterpressure. But the Eagles were not to be resisted. In 1923, Pennsylvania, Montana, and Nevada all enacted state old age pension laws. Ten years later most other states had done so. Those bills were often actually drafted by the Eagles. The pensions which resulted were often very small, and qualifications were very strict. Opponents were unable to defeat the principle of old age support, but often succeeded in diminishing its effect. Conservative judges and governors also fought stubbornly against it. Pennsylvania's plan was declared unconstitutional; pension laws in California, Washington, and Wyoming were vetoed. But by 1933, most American states had established an old age insurance program, at least in some rudimentary form.[32]

Despite the enactment of state old age pensions during the 1920's, the economic condition of the elderly continued to grow worse. As the Depression of the 1930's grew more severe, dependency rapidly increased. In 1937, less than 5 per cent of elderly Americans had pensions; more than 50 per cent were unemployed.[33] Agitation began to increase

[32] Roy Lubove, *The Struggle for Social Security, 1900-1935* (Cambridge, Mass., 1968), provides a good survey of this subject. See also Cole, "An Essay on Aging," p. 61. He observes that progress was made more rapidly in rural, agricultural states and with territories with comparatively young populations—Alaska, Arizona, Colorado, Kentucky, Montana. The urban, industrial states moved more slowly, partly because of the greater magnitude of the problem.

[33] In 1937 the economic status of elderly Americans (65 and over) was as follows:

Status	Number	%
I. Self-supporting	2,746,000	35.1
A. By income from wages, savings and investments	2,172,000	27.8
B. Federal pensions	104,000	1.4
C. State and local pensions	66,000	0.8
D. Private Pensions	175,000	2.2
E. Union Pensions	10,000	0.1
F. Insurance Annuities	204,000	2.6
G. Other resources	15,000	0.2
II. Wholly or party dependent upon others	5,070,000	64.9
A. Federal programs	1,374,000	17.7
B. Organized Private Charity	10,000	0.1
C. Public Homes and Institutions	141,000	1.7
D. Private Homes	55,000	0.7
E. Friends and Relatives	3,480,000	44.6
F. Other	10,000	0.1
Total	7,816,000	100.0

Gagliardo, *American Social Insurance*, p. 45; Marjorie Shearon, "Economic Status of the Aged," *Social Security Bulletin*, Mar. 1938, p. 6; Aug. 1938; p. 7.

among the elderly themselves, and spread throughout the nation. Until the 1920's the lead had been taken by Eastern states such as Massachusetts and Progressive Midwestern states such as Wisconsin, with the South and West bringing up the rear. Now things began to happen in California.[34] A great tide of migration had brought large numbers of elderly people to the Pacific coast. By 1930 the proportion of people sixty-five and over was twice the national average in many California cities and towns. Unemployment of older workers in the state was more severe than in the nation at large.[35] In 1929, California had passed the first mandatory pension system in the nation, after intense lobbying by the Fraternal Order of Eagles. It was one of the more generous programs in the nation, but still very restrictive. The minimum age was high—seventy. And maximum benefits were low—less than $23 a month. Elaborate red tape and stringent requirements made qualification very difficult. The state pension helped very little to diminish the proportions of the problem.

In California, the elderly were organized in a way which promoted the possibility of political action. Many belonged to "state societies" which brought together people from a single place of origin to share both their memories of the past and their fears for the future. Other organizations, such as C. H. Parsons's *Old Folks Picnic Association* in the 1920's, had a similar function. In the warm sun of Southern California, pension schemes grew in great abundance. By 1937 one observer counted more than eighty different plans in public discussion—ideas that reached all the way from a modest proposal to solve the social problem of old age by distributing free fishing licenses to the elderly, to schemes for full financial support of everyone over sixty-five. It was

[34] The following account is based upon Jackson K. Putnam's excellent study, *Old Age Politics in California.*

[35] In 1940, when 58 per cent of elderly Americans were unemployed, the comparable figure for California was 69 per cent.

an age of panaceas—the time of Pyramid Clubs and the Chain Letter Mania, which promised a bonanza for everybody by increasing the circulation of wealth. In a world whose economic ills were diagnosed by the academic doctors as a problem of "excess capacity" and sluggish circulation, people were prepared to try almost any sort of experiment. Many old age schemes were taken up in that spirit.

One of the first, in 1933-34, was Upton Sinclair's "EPIC" movement, which proposed to "end poverty in California" by a variety of measures, including an old age pension of $50 a month. Sinclair, a radical novelist, won the Democratic nomination for Governor, but he frightened moderates of his own party, who joined the Republicans to defeat him after an hysterical campaign in which his opponents insisted that EPIC actually meant "end property, introduce communism" in California.[36]

More bizarre was the so-called "Ham and Eggs movement," which was appropriately based in Hollywood. It was founded by an unemployed radio announcer named Robert Noble, who had endorsed Upton Sinclair's EPIC plan and lost his job because of it. Noble had sold California real estate without much success in the 1920's. During the 1930's he began to peddle pension plans instead. He founded an organization called the California State Pension movement, with the slogan "Twenty-five dollars every Tuesday," which more or less summarized its central idea. The money was to be given to everyone who was fifty and out of work, in the form of stamped scrip which would expire at a given date. The plan was a modification of Yale economist Irving Fisher's "dated money" scheme, which proposed to invigorate the economy by accelerating the circulation of money.

[36] The EPIC plan is described in Upton Sinclair's tract, *I, Governor of California and How I Ended Poverty: A True Story of the Future* (Los Angeles, 1933). His defeat is the subject of *I, Candidate for Governor: and How I Got Licked* (Pasadena, 1935).

Noble no sooner founded the movement than he lost control of it to a hair tonic salesman named Willis Allen, who (with his brother Lawrence) improved the slogan from "Twenty-five dollars every Tuesday" to "Thirty dollars every Thursday." The idea swept California. Soon the Allens claimed a following of 300,000 dues-paying members (at a penny a day) who bought Ham and Eggs badges and Ham and Eggs books, and abundantly provided for the old age of the Allen brothers, at least. The organization was ostensibly non-profit, but the money was paid to promotional organizations run by the Allens and their friends. The accounting was looked after by a former shellac salesman named Ray Fritz, who, as the golden stream began to flow, would walk about the office saying, "Is she sweet or is she sweet? Wowie!"[37]

The Ham and Eggs movement made the most of its chances for publicity. When a pauper named Archie Price committed suicide in a San Diego park and allegedly left a note reading, "Too young to receive an old age pension and too old to work," Ham-and-Eggers exhumed his body from Potter's Field and reburied it in an expensive cemetery. He had 7000 emotional mourners, and Sheridan Downey, Democratic candidate for Senator, delivered an oration. The Democratic nominee for Governor, Culbert Olson, endorsed the Ham and Eggs idea, and was elected with the Ham and Eggs vote.[38] A little later, the movement collapsed in a cloud of scandal. But its mass marches on Sacramento, its rallies, radio programs, and populist rhetoric left a mark on California politics.

The most popular old age panacea was not Ham and Eggs, but the Townsend Plan, which grew to the propor-

[37] Winston and Marian Moore, *Out of the Frying Pan* (Los Angeles, 1939), pp. 67-99.
[38] Governor Olson had his own old age plan, called the Sixty-Sixty movement, which promised to lower the minimum age for social security to sixty, and to raise the benefits to $60 a month. Nothing came of it.

tions of a national crusade in the 1930's. Its founder, Dr. Francis Townsend, made a most unlikely Messiah. He was sixty-seven years old when the movement began—tall, gaunt, and austere, with white hair, steel-rimmed glasses, and a stiff, white celluloid collar. Townsend was born in an Illinois log cabin, raised on the middle border of America, schooled in a country classroom, and converted at a camp meeting. He tried his hand—and failed—as a hay merchant in California, a teamster in Spokane, a homesteader in Kansas, and a country doctor in the Black Hills of South Dakota. After a stint as an army doctor in World War I, he moved to Long Beach, California, where he dabbled in real estate during the boom years of the 1920's. Then the Depression came. Townsend was no stranger to misfortune, but the great California collapse was beyond anything in his economic experience. He took a job as physician for the Long Beach Health Department, and, in his own words, "stepped into such distress, pain, and horror; such sobbing loyalties under the worst possible circumstances as to shake me even today with their memory."[39]

Then, in 1933, at the age of sixty-seven, Dr. Townsend lost his own job too. "I had little else to do," he later remembered, and so he filled the empty hours by writing letters to the editor of a local newspaper. One of them, which appeared in the "vox-pop" column of the Long Beach *Press Telegram* on September 30, 1933, argued that the cause of the Depression was primarily excess production, and the cure was an old age pension plan (supported by a sales tax) of $150 a month for everyone over sixty, "on condition that they spend the money as they get it." That single sentence summarized the main lines of the Townsend Plan. A few changes were later made—the pension was raised to

[39] Francis Townsend, *New Horizons: An Autobiography* (Chicago, 1943), p. 131.

$200 and the regressive sales tax was replaced first by a levy on incomes and finally by a transaction tax.[40] But the outlines were intact in the first version of the plan.[41]

The Townsend Plan was meant to provide a remedy for both the general economic problems of the 1930's and the problem of old age as well. The elderly, whom Townsend called "civil veterans of the Republic" were given the happy responsibility of becoming "circulators of money"—"distributor custodians" of the nation's wealth—which it was their patriotic duty to spend as swiftly as possible.

Townsend immediately won a favorable response from elderly friends and neighbors. His problem was how to mobilize his support. "My solution lay in advertising," he later wrote. He skillfully exploited the techniques of mass journalism to spread the word. Townsend began humbly, by placing a one-inch advertisement in the local Long Beach paper, asking for elderly volunteers to help in a petition campaign. To his surprise, a dozen people showed up the next day, ready to work. Within two weeks they had collected four thousand signatures. In late 1933 the plan began to spread like wildfire, and "Father Townsend's" modest proposal took on the proportions of a national crusade. In San Diego, for example, there were about 35,000 people sixty and over in a population of 180,000. By early 1935, 30,000 people in that city alone had become dues-paying Townsendites, and 105,000 had signed Townsend petitions. Thousands of clubs sprang up in every state—by 1936, there were 1200 in California alone. Their members were heavily

---

[40] Townsend candidly explained that the pension should be raised to $200 "so that nobody could come along and offer more. The country couldn't stand more." But he reckoned without Upton Sinclair, who proposed a pension of $400 a month—a figure so absurd in the 1930's as to contribute to the collapse of Sinclair's EPIC campaign.

[41] Numerous antecedents existed—among them a plan by Seattle's Stuart McCord, inspired by Bellamy's *Looking Backward*, and an idea of Bruce Barton's in *Vanity Fair*.

middle class, Anglo-Saxon, Republican, Protestant, and white. In the summer of 1934, the Townsendites decided that their Long Beach Congressman was not sufficiently sympathetic to their plan, and at the next election defeated him—an early lesson in the voting power of elderly Americans, when they chose to exercise it. Their new Congressman was John S. McGroarty, seventy-two years old, a pleasant old gentleman who styled himself the "poet laureate of California." Congressman McGroarty promptly introduced a bill in the House of Representatives proposing to enact the Townsend Plan in federal law. It failed by a margin of four to one. But in 1936 Townsend claimed a following of 3.5 million followers, and probably had them.

Politicians sat up and took notice. Through all of this incredible cacophony, the California legislature slowly and steadily enlarged and strengthened the state's old age pension system. By 1940 the California pension had risen to nearly $500 a year—highest in the nation.

At the same time, panaceas like the Townsend Plan slowly yielded to a new generation of California old age movements. Most important was the California League of Senior Citizens, founded in 1941 by a former Ham-and-Egger named George McLain, who organized a continuing "old folks lobby" in the state capitol, and sought programs by piecemeal reform. As a result, pensions continued to rise from about $40 a month in 1940 to $80 in 1952, to $160 in 1961, and to more than $194 in 1970. More people were allowed to qualify, and with less humiliation.

The American social insurance movement was, in short, a mixed bag of American progressives and Russian socialists, serious scholars and California cranks, union leaders and enlightened capitalist, Ham and Eggers and the Fraternal Order of Eagles. In 1935, all of those groups came together to produce the most important single piece of old age legislation in American history—the Social Security Act. The prime movers were yet another group—the conservative liberals and liberal conservatives who were the major architects of the New Deal. Their primary purpose was to preserve the traditional fabric of America's capitalist and democratic institutions. They were highly successful.

In June 1934, President Franklin Roosevelt sent a special message to Congress, reporting that his Administration was seeking a "sound means" of promoting the economic security of ordinary Americans by old age support and unemployment insurance. Roosevelt, in his accustomed way, appointed a multiplicity of commissions, committees, and boards to study the problem. But control remained in conservative hands. The founders of the social insurance movement were deliberately kept at arm's length. The Democratic Administration prevented such men as Isaac Rubinow from having a major role in the drafting of the bill. And Abraham Epstein bitterly complained that "the administration has refused to listen to anyone who knew anything about the problem."[42]

As the Social Security bill slowly took form, Rubinow and Epstein criticized its many deficiencies—its omission of health insurance, its regressive tax base, the absence of contributions from general revenues, the large fund reserves, and the clumsy and inefficient administrative apparatus. Townsend attacked it, too, as generally insufficient to meet the real needs of the elderly. His period of greatest popularity came *after* the passage of the Social Security Act, as a reaction to its limitations.

In truth, the Social Security program, as it was enacted in 1935,[43] was extraordinarily weak and ineffectual by the

[42] Lubove, *The Struggle for Social Security*, p. 175.

[43] The Social Security Act included three major parts. First, it provided unemployment relief, administered through the states and supported by a payroll tax. Second, it created a system of old age insurance with pensions ranging from $10 to $85 a month. Third, it established federal subsidies for state old age pension programs and other systems of social welfare.

standards of welfare legislation in other western nations.[44]

The Social Security system was deliberately designed to make no major change in the distribution of wealth. The rhetoric with which it was launched promised a great uplifting for oppressed humanity, but the Act was carefully restricted in both its methods and its effects. Social Security taxes were so highly regressive in their structure that the net effect of the program may actually have been to increase the inequality of wealth distribution a little. The fundamental conservatism of the New Deal is nowhere more apparent than in its most important single piece of social legislation.[45]

But the most astonishing fact about Social Security was not that it was passed in so conservative a form, but rather that it was passed at all in so conservative a nation. With its enactment the American Republic collectively acknowledged that survival was a basic human right, and that the supply of the minimal means of subsistence to every needy individual was a social obligation. Once that principle was established, the practice was progressively enlarged. The Congress has tended to broaden the Social Security Act biennially—mostly in election years—1939, 1950, 1952, 1954, 1956, 1958, 1960, 1961, 1965, 1967, 1969, and on into the 1970's.

---

[44] The leading historian of that era writes: "In many respects, the law was an astonishingly inept and conservative piece of legislation. In no other welfare system in the world did the state shirk all responsibility for old age indigency and insist that funds be taken out of the current earnings of workers. By relying on regressive taxation and withdrawing vast sums to build up reserves, the act did untold economic mischief. The law denied coverage to numerous classes of workers, including those who needed security most: notably farm laborers and domestics. Sickness, in normal times the main cause of joblessness, was disregarded. The act not only failed to set up a national system of unemployment compensation but did not even provide adequate national standards." W. B. Leuchtenburg, *Franklin D. Roosevelt and the New Deal, 1932-40.* (New York, 1963), p. 132.

[45] See e.g. Frances Perkins in *New York Times*, Jan. 27, 1935.

Right wing Republicans and Southern Democrats did their best to destroy the Social Security system: passage of the Act was followed quickly by litigation in which the Supreme Court sustained its constitutionality by the strength of a single vote.[46] But though a certain muted hostility continued to be heard from reactionary politicians even in the 1970's, it was clear to the most rock-ribbed conservatives in the Republic that a headlong assault on Social Security was a sure form of political suicide. Forty years after the Act was passed, most Democrats and Republicans eagerly competed for the credit of expanding the system.

Once the first solid commitment was made by the Social Security Act, the federal government became increasingly active in many ways. The growing interest of political leaders in old age as a social problem was promoted by the increasing political influence of the elderly themselves. The American electorate has grown steadily older during the twentieth century.[47] Yet elderly Americans have not com-

[46] The constitutional standing of Social Security was settled in a series of 5 to 4 decisions: *Steward Machine Company v. Davis* (301 U.S. 548) and *Helvering v. Davis* (301 U.S. 619). The outcome was determined in 1937 by the retirement of conservative Justice Willis Van Devanter and the "conversion" of Justice Owen Roberts to a moderate position on social legislation. The Supreme Court in 1935 had been hostile to old age pensions. In the case of *Retirement Board v. Alton Railroad Co.* (1935), the Court had voted 5 to 4 to invalidate the Railroad Retirement Pension Act. Ironically, it was a "retirement" which rescued a system of protection against the economic costs of retirement.

[47] The tendency appears in the following statistics of age composition in the American electorate:

Age Group	Percentage							
	1900	*1910*	*1920*	*1930*	*1940*	*1950*	*1960*	*1970*
20-44	67.6	67.1	64.6	62.4	59.4	56.9	52.4	51.0
45-64	24.5	25.1	27.3	28.5	30.2	30.7	32.7	33.1
65-up	7.9	7.8	8.1	9.1	10.4	12.4	14.9	15.9

The trend was reinforced by the fact that older Americans voted more regularly than younger ones. And American electors tended to be older than the electorate. See D. Cowgill, "The Aging of Populations and Societies," *Annals of the American Academy of Political and Social Science*, 415 (1974), 7.

monly behaved as a voting bloc. The reluctance of many Americans to think of themselves as old has reinforced this tendency; most of them have been inclined to consider themselves in other terms when they have gone to the polls —except in critical moments, as during the 1930's, when they elected Congressman McGroarty.

Nevertheless, elderly people began to organize pressure groups to work their will upon the polity. It was as an interest group rather than as a voting bloc that the power of elderly people was most clearly felt in American politics.[48] Many lobbying associations were organized—the National Association of Retired Federal Employees (1921), the National Retired Teachers Association (1947), the American Association of Retired Persons (1958), the National Council of Senior Citizens (1961), and the National Caucus of the Black Aged (1970). In 1971 no less than four hundred interest groups were invited to attend a White House Conference on Aging.[49]

Those groups became highly effective as lobbying organizations, and helped to secure a broad variety of legislation on old age. But it was not merely a question of organization. An ideology was also created which persuaded politicians as well as pushing them. One early statement was issued in 1942 by a Harvard philosopher, Ralph Barton Perry, in his gentle "plea for an age movement."[50] The arguments became more strident in the 1970's with groups such as the "Gray Panthers," who undertook "consciousness-raising"

[48] Robert H. Binstock, "Interest Group Liberalism and the Politics of Aging," *Gerontologist* 12 (1972), 265-80.

[49] Ibid. p. 269. A vast literature has been published by political scientists on this subject. In addition to Binstock, see F. A. Pinner *et al.*, *Old Age and Political Behavior* (Berkeley, 1959); W. Donahue and C. Tibbits (eds.): *Politics of Age* (Ann Arbor, 1962); John C. Henretta, "Political Protest Among the Elderly: An Organizational Study," unpubl. Ph.D. thesis, Harvard, 1973. Also important is Angus Campbell, "Politics through the Life Cycle," *Gerontologist*, II (1971), 112-17.

[50] Ralph Barton Perry, *Plea for An Age Movement* (New York, 1942).

on questions of age. The combined effect of organization and ideology was considerable. A broad variety of service programs proliferated for the elderly—far beyond anything that Epstein or Rubinow could have envisioned.

The most important single piece of legislation was the Older Americans Act of 1965. We might observe its effects upon a single city. In Boston, a Commission on the Affairs of the Elderly served to coordinate the federal funds which suddenly became available under many different programs. A citizen over sixty had only to call the "Elderly Hotline" (funded by the federal government) to tap an astonishing range of social services. He could summon a "Home Care Corporation" which supplied health aid, homemaking assistance, transportation and escort service, and help with errands, chores, and emergencies of every kind. There was a "Nutrition Program," which furnished hot meals at thirty halls around the city, or, if none of them were convenient, in the home itself. A "Consortium on Elder Opportunities" helped elderly people to find paying jobs, and a "Retired Senior Volunteer Program" placed them in volunteer work. A "Visiting Aides" Program provided companions to those who needed them, a "Supplemental Security Income Program" addressed itself to problems of poverty, and a "Senior Shuttle" offered a free ride anywhere in town.[51]

To conservative critics, it all seemed a free ride, funded by the federal government, controlled by a vast bureaucracy, and generally destructive of the "American way of life." But a new way of life was developing in which private purposes were becoming closely wedded to public means.

⚬⚬

[51] Commission on Affairs of the Elderly, "Service Programs for Older Bostonians," (n.d., c. 1976), mimeographed pamphlet.

At the same time that the social insurance movement grew from small beginnings into a potent political force, other people were attacking the problem of old age from different directions. Not least important was a parallel movement among American physicians, who made old age into a special branch of medical science. Physicians had long been interested in old age, primarily as part of a perennial search for ways to prolong youth. In every scientific generation, there have always been a few investigators who have dreamed of discovering the secret of eternal life, and many more who have hoped merely to make death wait a little longer. In America, one of the first was Doctor Benjamin Rush (1745-1812), an eccentric Philadelphia polymath who published promiscuously on many subjects, among them old age.[52] For a long life he recommended temperance, equanimity—and matrimony. "In the course of my inquiries," Dr. Rush reported, "I met only one person beyond eighty years of age who had never been married."[53] For the diseases of old age he prescribed heat, cleanliness, exercise, the company of the young, and his sovereign remedy—bleeding. Many other works of the same sort were published in America—works of much interest to social historians, for the prescriptions for long life embody the moral precepts of the culture in which they appear. A long life was commonly thought to be a good life.[54]

[52] Benjamin Rush, "An Account of the State of the Body and Mind in Old Age," *Medical Inquiries and Observations*, II (1793), 293-321. For a general survey of the history of this subject, see G. L. Gruman, "A History of Ideas about the Prolongation of Life," *Transactions of the American Philosophical Society*, 56 (1966), 1-102.

[53] He was probably correct about matrimony, by the way. Recent studies show that married people live longer than those who are single or separated.

[54] see e.g. Anthony Carlisle, *An Essay on the Disorders of Old Age* (Philadelphia, 1819); Charles Caldwell, *Thoughts on the Effects of Age on the Human Constitution* (Louisville, Ky., 1846); G. E. Day, *A Practical Treatise on the Domestic Management and Most Important Diseases of Advanced Life* (Philadelphia, 1849). And, generally, see William D. Postell, "Some

In the nineteenth century, other physicians began to study old age in a new spirit—not so much to keep it from happening as to understand its effects. European scientists broke the first ground. Major treatises were published in the nineteenth century by Charcot (1816), Prus (1840), Pennock (1847), Geist (1857-60), and others. That was the work of individuals. But early in the twentieth century, the scattered work of individuals began to be brought together to form a new medical discipline called "geriatrics." Its birthplace was New York City, and its father was an Austrian immigrant, I. N. Nascher. Born in Vienna and brought to America as a child, Nascher began to study medicine in New York City. Once, as a student, he was making his hospital rounds when he came upon an elderly woman with many symptoms of serious illness. The teacher diagnosed her disease with terrible finality as "old age."

"What can be done about it?" Nascher asked.

"Nothing," he was told.

Afterward, Nascher devoted himself primarily to making the problem of old age a special branch of medicine, which he appears to have been the first to call "geriatrics." In 1912 he founded a professional group called the "Society of Geriatry" in New York City. From Nascher's time to our own era, geriatrics has grown steadily as a science. No epic discoveries have been made. No revolution has been wrought in either diagnosis or therapy. The process of aging still remains not merely an unknown, but a mystery. Its cause continues to be elusive. But it has been studied with more rigor than before, and many of its operations are understood with increasing clarity. As a therapeutic discipline,

American Contributions to the Literature of Geriatrics," *Geriatrics,* I (1946), 41-45; Postell, "Some Comments on the Early Literature of Geriatrics in America," *New Orleans Medical and Surgical Journal,* 98 (1945-46), 49-51; J. T. Freeman, "The History of Geriatrics," *Annals of Medical History,* n.s., X (1938), 324-25.

geriatrics, broadly conceived, has had many successes. If aging cannot be "cured," it can be eased and made more comfortable. The physical pain of growing old, which was so intense in early America, has been much reduced. The invention and improvement of eyeglasses, false teeth, hearing aids, and other prosthetic devices have made a major difference in the physical experience of growing old.

At the same time, the practitioners of geriatric medicine have labored to change the attitudes of physicians toward their elderly patients. American doctors have tended to share the general prejudices of their society, and added a few of their own. Aesculapius proposed as a principle of medical ethics that physicians should seek to cure only those patients who can be restored to active life. In a more moderate form, that attitude is still widespread. The very old have often found it difficult to obtain a physician's attention, unless they are also very rich. Geriatric medicine has struggled against those attitudes. If it has not succeeded in reversing them, perhaps it has made some difference.

Surrounding the science of geriatrics, as a circle of darkness surrounds the light, is a twilight zone inhabited by hucksters and healers of every shape and hue. Always, men have hunted the fountain of youth with a determination equal to their distance from the object. In the twentieth century many panaceas have been peddled to the elderly as remedies for aging. For the very rich, society doctors have prescribed all manner of injections, ointments, and potions. In the 1920's, a popular geriatric fad was monkey glands; in the 1940's, Fletcherizing; in the 1950's, cortisone injections; in the 1960's, estrogen. In the 1970's, vitamin E was prescribed by country-club physicians in kidney-killing doses. Some of those fads (even the most scientifically respectable) may actually have shortened life. The rapid rise of cancer among affluent, middle-aged American women in the 1970's was due in part to the use of estrogen by physicians who were treating the symptoms of menopause.

For Americans too poor to afford those expensive nostrums, antidotes to aging were bottled and sold across the drugstore counter. Patent medicines have had a long and fascinating history in America.[55] By the 1970's they had become a billion-dollar business. In Massachusetts in October 1975, twelve ounces of a concoction named Geritol cost nearly $4.00—more than the best bonded Bourbon. One popular tonic, Serutan ("nature's spelled backward") cost $2.00 for seven ounces.

The vast health industry in America has exploited the elderly in an ingenious variety of ways. One example is what might be called the arthritis racket—a huge business all in itself. More than twenty million Americans are thought to suffer from some form of arthritis. They spend perhaps $400 million a year in hope of finding relief from its painful and crippling symptoms. The health hucksters have offered them arthritis clinics, vibrating devices, exotic diets of alfalfa and pokeberries, and many drugs and liniments. According to Consumer's Union, most of what Americans buy for arthritis has no helpful effect upon that condition, and may actually make it worse. Regulatory agencies and private critics have become more active in policing this vast industry, but the problem always outruns the remedy.

Government has also taken a hand in dealing with the medical problem of old age in a more direct and important way. The National Health Surveys, which were first taken in 1935-36, showed for the first time the full extent of disability among the elderly. Nothing much was done on the

---

[55] James H. Young, *The Toadstool Millionaires; A Social History of Patent Medicines in America Before Federal Regulation* (Princeton, 1961), tells the story.

national level to diminish it for thirty years. In the 1930's the health care which was available to the elderly was what they could buy from their physicians, or beg from a charity.

The major change came in 1965, with the passage of the Medicare and Medicaid programs. Medicare provided federal money for most of the health needs of people over sixty-five; Medicaid paid the bills of the poor. Those large programs have made medical care more fully accessible to the elderly and poor than ever before in American history.[56]

But in our modern world of social engineering, every solution becomes another problem. So it has been with Medicare and Medicaid. Those programs brought a revolution in the "health care industry," as it was coming to be called. They had been bitterly opposed by conservatives as a form of "socialized medicine." But the result has not been socialism at all—rather, a corrupt medical form of state capitalism, which has combined the vices of both ideological worlds without the virtues of either. The American health system has encouraged physicians to become medical entrepreneurs—except that it is the patient who assumes the risk and the physician who takes the profit. Proprietary hospitals and nursing homes have become business corporations more profitable than Exxon or United States Steel. Drug companies have driven up the prices of medicines by conspiracy and collusion. No other society in the world has tolerated a system of medical care which was so expensive and so corrupt. If medical care has been supplied to the elderly by these means, the social costs have been considerable.[57]

---

56 Peter Corning, *The Evolution of Medicare from Idea to Law* (Washington, D.C., 1969); Max Skidmore, *Medicare and the American Rhetoric of Reconciliation* (University, Ala., 1970).

57 A responsible critique of some of the abuses and scandals in the nursing home industry is Mary Adelaide Mendelson, *Tender Loving Greed; How the Incredibly Lucrative Nursing Home Industry Is Exploiting America's Old People and Defrauding Us All* (New York, 1974).

In the mid-twentieth century, as geriatrics has expanded as a field of medicine, social scientists have developed their own discipline for the study of old age—social gerontology. The first American scholar to show a sustained and serious interest in it was G. Stanley Hall, a psychologist at Clark University, who published a treatise called Senescence in 1922.[58] But social gerontology was not a popular subject in the universities until the late 1940's, when it suddenly began to grow very rapidly.[59] The first important professional organization was the Gerontological Society, organized in 1945 with 80 members; by 1950 it had grown to 300; by 1960, to nearly 2000. Others quickly followed.[60] The major journals of gerontology were started, for the most part, between 1946 and 1970.[61] International Congresses began to be held in Europe—the first at Liège in 1950.

[58] Granville Stanley Hall, Senescence, The Last Half of Life (New York, 1922).

[59] One measure of the expansion of social gerontology is the growth of the number of doctoral dissertations in the field. Statistics are available from 1934 to 1968:

| | | Number of Dissertations on Aging in: | | | | | |
Period	Biology	Medicine	Psychology	Soc. Sci.	Total	All Dis.	%
1934-38	10	4	6	9	29	2640	0.22
1939-43	5	0	7	13	25	15,474	0.16
1944-48	4	0	8	10	22	11,597	0.19
1949-53	10	5	41	26	82	35,105	0.23
1954-58	17	6	58	47	128	43,673	0.29
1959-63	19	3	80	52	154	54,500	0.28
1964-68	58	6	84	78	226	88,373	0.26

Julie L. Moore and James E. Birren, "Doctoral Training in Gerontology," Journal of Gerontology, 26 (1971), 249-57.

[60] The American Geriatric Society was founded in 1950; the National Geriatric Society in 1952; the Committee of Geriatrics in 1956. In 1946, the American Psychological Association established a division on maturity and old age.

[61] The earliest that I can find was a German journal—Zeitschrift für

Every discipline had its own pioneer. In psychology she was Bernice Neugarten, who began to teach the psychology of aging at the University of Chicago during the early 1940's under the auspices of the Committee of Human Development. When she first offered a course, which she modestly described as "something of a pioneer effort," she found very little reading material to assign on the subject. But over the next twenty years, the literature expanded swiftly—much of it written by her own students. Bernice Neugarten was primarily a social psychologist. Developmental psychology also expanded rapidly, particularly with the work of J. E. Birren and K. W. Schaie. Every discipline of the social sciences has made a contribution—every discipline but history, unhappily. Outstanding work was produced in sociology by Ethel Shanas and Irving Rosow, in anthropology by Margaret Clark, in economics by Juanita Kreps and Theodore Schulze, in psychiatry by Carl Eisdorfer, in health services by Elaine and Stephen Brody. Strong institutional centers have developed at Duke, Brandeis, Berkeley, and Chicago.

One might ask what all this activity has accomplished. Social gerontology in its first thirty years has succeeded in one thing, at least. It has managed to institutionalize itself. It has not succeeded in creating a body of theory. For a time there was much discussion of "activity theory" and "disengagement theory," but those controversies seem to be fading. Probably, gerontology will never be a theoretical discipline in its own right, but rather a consumer of theory from

---

Altersforschung. Many others followed quickly: the *Journal of Gerontology* (1946), *Newsletter of the Gerontological Society* (1952), *Geriatrics* (1946), *Aging and Human Development* (1970), *Gerontologia* (1956), *Experimental Gerontology* (1966), *Age and Aging* (1972), *Industrial Gerontology* (1971), *Journal of Geriatric Psychiatry* (1967), and many more. *A Classified Bibliography of Gerontology* was first published by the Forest Park Foundation in 1951, with supplements for more recent publications.

other sciences. Its major function seems to be that of an applied social science. Within that realm, it has begun to play an important and constructive part. Its major role, perhaps, has been to destroy the myths which so thickly encrust the subject of aging, to oppose the age prejudice which has grown so strong in America, and to sharpen our sense of old age as a social problem.

The first generation of social gerontologists attacked myths of weakness in old age—sexuality myths, senility myths, alienation myths, incompetence myths. In the 1960's and 1970's, a second generation of social gerontologists has begun to appear, and their objects are a little different. The arguments which the first generation developed against the myths of aging have in some instances become myths in their own turn. A countercurrent is developing—a new departure in social gerontology which seeks not merely to improve the condition of elderly people in American society, but to balance the requirements of the old against those of the young. How these things might be done is the business of the next chapter.

V.   A THOUGHT FOR THE FUTURE

Better to go down dignified
With boughten friendship at your side
Than none at all. Provide, provide!
                    Robert Frost (1874-1963)

WHAT will old age be like in the future? What lies
ahead for us? If an historian's subject is change
through time, then the future, no less than the past, is a
part of history; both are parts of the great world process in
which we live. We do not commonly think in that manner
today; as a consequence, the future always takes us by surprise.[1] Of course, there is no way of knowing what will hap-

[1] As Robert L. Heilbroner wisely observes, "At bottom our troubled state
of mind reflects an inability to see the future in an *historic* context. If current events strike us as all surprise and shock it is because we cannot see
these events in a meaningful framework. If the future seems to us a kind of
limbo, a repository of endless surprises, it is because we no longer see it as
the expected culmination of the past, as the growing edge of the present.
More than anything else, our disorientation before the future reveals a loss
of our historic identity." Heilbroner, *The Future as History* (New York,
1960), p. 15.
There are, of course, many ways of talking nonsense about "the future
as history." One way is to imagine that we can predict the future on the
basis of our knowledge of the past. This ancient dream is the basis of a
modern fad called "futurology"—an academic humbug. Another form of
nonsense is that which seeks to model the future upon the past, which is
tendency to seek in past cultures a guide for the improvement of our own.
Peter Laslett warns us that it is easy to be "unrealistic as to accessibility of
the experience of such communities or cultures when it comes to creating
models of our own behavior." Further, he writes that "we must be on our
guard against using our historical experience too much in a *compensatory
way*, that is, to see in it only those qualities which would make up for the

pen next. An historical volume can never hope to end with a Book of Revelation.

Nevertheless, to study history is to discover that there are at least two enduring certainties in the world. First, what will happen in the future is always determined in some degree by what has happened in the past. The future is always different from the past, but also derived from it and linked with it by the continuum of historical events. If the study of history never allows us to know the future in advance, it helps us to be ready when it comes, by providing a sense of context which gives pattern to what would otherwise be a swirling chaos of meaningless events.

Second, what happens in the future is also determined by what we wish to happen. We are not merely witnesses to our history, but its agents and even its authors. Not that we can ever hope to have our way. History is a rubble heap of shattered hopes—it is the record of our disappointments. But though we rarely get the things we most desire in the world, our desires make a difference in the things we get. The study of history is valuable not least because it helps us to clarify our own intentions. It teaches us to recognize our opportunities, and exposes the obstacles that lie in the way.

What ought our intentions to be for the future history of age relations? What are our opportunities? What are the obstacles in the path? We have traced the American history of old age through a long process of complex change. If we stand back and study the larger configurations of that process, we find that its complexity may be reduced to a single

deficiencies and dissatisfactions which are painfully obvious in the present. An excessively legitimatory use of the past has also to be avoided, that is, drawing upon it in order to justify a proposed change in our contemporary world by appeal to a vanished situation, which may in fact be entirely irrelevant to ourselves." Laslett, "The Traditional English Family and the Aged in Our Society," unpubl., Case-Western Reserve Univ. 1975.

dialectical unity. First, in early America (1607-1820), we discovered an era of growing *gerontophilia,* in which old age was exalted and venerated, sometimes hated and feared, but more often honored and obeyed. Then we found a period of deep change (1780-1820), during the era of the American and French revolutions. Attitudes toward old age suddenly began to change, as did the life experiences of the aged. After the transition, we found an era of growing *gerontophobia*—a protracted period (1780-1970) during which Americans increasingly glorified youth instead of age, and the elderly often became victims (self-victims as well as social victims) of prevailing attitudes and social arrangements. During the first two-thirds of the twentieth century (1910-70) there was another period of deep change, when old age began to be perceived as a social problem, and an elaborate system of social welfare was created to deal with it.

Now, in the late twentieth century, a fifth period may be beginning in the history of age relations. Many people are working to make it so. Scholars, politicians, social planners, and elderly Americans themselves are actively seeking to create better conditions for old age. They are often experts on their chosen subject, but they have not studied its history, and the absence of historical perspective on any problem makes a major difference in the way it is understood. Commonly, specialists in the social problem of old age seek to reverse the errors of the recent past, which so often made social victims of the aged. But if we take a longer view, we discover that that reversal is not perhaps the best of remedies. If modern America made a cult of youth and victims of the aged, early America made a cult of age and victims of the young. Before we try to turn the recent past upon its head, we might take a more extended view of our historical experience.

To do so is to discover a different sort of purpose. If we

wish to work toward a new model of age relationships, then surely it should be a world without *gerontophobia* on the one hand or *gerontophilia* on the other. It might be built upon an ideal of *gerontophratria* instead—a fraternity of age and youth, a brotherhood of generations. It should be a world in which the deep eternal differences between age and youth are recognized and respected without being organized into a system of social inequality.

It is in our power to create such a synthesis of our own historical experience—a system of age relations in which youth is not oppressed by age, as often it was in early America; and age is not oppressed by youth, as sometimes it is in the modern world. Such an opportunity has come to us today. But if we wish to make the most of it, it is necessary for us to make three major changes in our economic, social, and cultural institutions. All of these changes are difficult, but each of them is possible—for the momentum of modern history is moving powerfully in the right direction. We must add only an act of our collective will.

First, we must deal with a serious economic problem. If age and youth are to coexist without oppression, then neither youth nor age must be economically dependent upon the other. In early America, youth was kept in a condition of prolonged economic dependency upon age; in the nineteenth and early twentieth centuries, age often became economically dependent upon youth. Prevailing attitudes toward age and youth were anchored in those material realities, without being caused by them.

During the past fifty years, an elaborate system of social welfare has been enacted for elderly Americans—a complex web of private pensions, public assistance, and, most important, Social Security. The system has worked, after a fashion. By and large, the economic condition of people over sixty-five has dramatically improved. It was infinitely better in 1975 than in 1935 or 1925 or 1910. The income of elderly Americans has risen remarkably during the past fifty years, both in absolute and relative terms, in dollar values and purchasing power. Poverty has diminished. There is more security and economic stability for the elderly in America today than at any earlier time in the twentieth century.

But this system of social welfare is coming under heavy strain: Its fiscal structure is fundamentally unsound; legislators have been quicker to raise Social Security benefits than to raise the taxes on which they are based. The result is a great and growing imbalance between Social Security revenues and expenditures. At the time of this writing, the Social Security system is still barely in the black. But in the foreseeable future more money will be due to elderly Americans under existing law than is paid in by younger workers. At its present rate of depletion, the Social Security trust fund will be gone by the mid-1980's.[2]

Social Security is only one example of such a problem. Another is the pension system of New York City, where strong municipal unions have succeeded in winning pension contracts which are beyond the fiscal power of the city to keep. The full crisis is a few years ahead. But sooner or later the pension system in New York City must be radically changed, or it will collapse under its own weight. And New York is not alone; many other American cities and states differ only in degree.

In 1975, Republicans in Washington—notably, President Gerald Ford—professed to be outraged by the "profligacy" of New York City. But the most extravagant pension sys-

2 *New York Times,* Mar. 1, 1976.

tem of all is the federal plan, passed with President Ford's support. Many federal employees have pensions today which include an automatic annual increase equal to the rise in the cost of living plus 1 per cent. Former Congressman Hastings Keith of Massachusetts has attempted to call attention to the problem by advertising his own pension. Having "retired" from his seat in Congress after about a decade's service, he received in November 1975 a pension of $2095 a month! If inflation were to continue at its 1976 rate, Congressman Keith's pension would rise by the end of his normal life span to $16,000 a month! Clearly, something must change.[3]

The growing fiscal problem of pensions in America—public and private—is further compounded by changes in the age structure of the American population. In 1976, for every 100 workers who were paying Social Security taxes, 30 people were collecting social benefits. By the year 2050, for every 100 people in the work force, 45 will be receiving support. In a nation with a growing population and a dynamic economy more workers enter the labor force than leave it during any given year. As a consequence, more people pay Social Security taxes than receive Social Security benefits. The result is what has been called the "Social Security Paradox"—everyone can hope to get more than he gives, as long as more and more people are giving. That happy arrangement prevailed in the 1950's and 1960's, when the American population was growing rapidly and the economy was strong. But in late 1975, rates of population growth fell close to zero and the economy became very soft. If present trends continue, the Social Security paradox will begin to run in reverse. Everyone must get *less* than he gives when fewer people are giving, unless some extra source of income is discovered.

[3] *New York Times,* Nov. 2, 1975.

On top of everything else, inflation is rapidly eroding the value of pensions for many Americans. Congressman Keith was a happy exception in the size of his monthly check. Americans on Social Security today receive a maximum of $3300 a year—barely enough to sustain life. Cost of living increases have been built into Social Security (as in Congressman Keith's pension), but at enormous and perhaps ruinous expense.

Our present system of social welfare for the elderly simply cannot continue in its present form. One of three changes must inevitably take place. Either a larger source of income must be found, or smaller benefits must be distributed, or some new system must be invented. The first remedy would necessarily require an increase in taxes, which is not impossible. Taxes can—and probably will—be raised above their present levels. But not far enough to solve the problem. Given the increasingly regressive tax system in America, the relative decline in the nation's tax base, the increase in the relative proportions of the elderly, and the growth of inflation, it is improbable that Social Security taxes can be enlarged sufficiently to maintain present levels of support far into the future.

In short, it is unlikely that the present system can be saved by small improvements. Its collapse may be postponed for a few decades by piecemeal reform. But it is unsound at its very core—unsound in its tax structure, unsound in its fiscal organization, unsound in its demographic assumptions, unsound in its level of payments, unsound in its limitations and exclusions. Social Security is unfair to the elderly and expensive to the young. And it can only be corrected by root-and-branch reform. We must find some new way of providing collectively for our old age. And it should be a way in which the elderly receive more than a minimal subsistence payment.

But at the same time it should not exploit the young. That is another serious danger in our old age security system. As the number of the elderly increases—as the economic cost of old age security rises in a relative sense, and as the political power of elderly Americans also grows— there is a danger that the young could become victims once again. Not as they did in early America, but in a new way, with heavy social welfare taxes oppressing them in the early years of adulthood—a time of life in America today when the economic margin is often very thin. We should try to design a new set of social welfare institutions which does not make one generation the economic servant of another. With a little ingenuity and a great deal of thought about the future, it might be possible for us to find a way. One idea comes to mind which is more nearly in keeping with the libertarian spirit of American politics, and with the individualist spirit of American society than our present arrangements are.

Let us begin by granting one collectivist assumption. Every organized society has a public responsibility for the welfare of its individual members. Every civilized nation in the world today, including the United States of America, has asknowledged that commitment. The question is how that responsibility can best be met. We attempted to do so in the 1930's primarily by building a system of social welfare upon a model which was borrowed from the nations of central Europe and shaped by a cultural history which was more highly collectivized than our own. It worked after a fashion. But the free institutions of our open society are capable of something better. We could create an entirely different American system of social welfare which would be stronger, more equitable, more generous, more libertarian, less bureaucratic, and more nearly in keeping with the special genius of American society. With a little imagination, the voluntary institutions of an open society might be converted into more efficient instruments of social welfare than all the clumsy and dangerous weapons of collectivism.

Instead of supporting elderly people by grants of income at the end of life, it would be cheaper, easier, and less disagreeable in many ways to give each American a grant of capital at the beginning of life instead. Small capital payments would be more effective than large payments in the form of income.

Many American banks offer seven-year savings certificates which pay an interest of 9 per cent a year. It is doubtful that interest rates will remain that high, but given the record of the Federal Reserve Board they are not likely to fall very far.[4] Let us assume that on long term investments interest of 8 per cent will be generally available. Suppose that every American received at birth a sort of "national inheritance"—a gift of capital in the amount of $1400.[5] The gift would be surrounded with many restrictions. It could never be spent, loaned, borrowed, alienated, expended, or employed as collateral in any way. This capital sum would be invested—perhaps in a savings account, or in government securities. The money would not be taxable. It would be

[4] Interest rates have risen more or less continuously in America since the Federal Reserve Board acquired effective power to regulate them.

[5] Thomas Paine proposed a somewhat similar plan his last great pamphlet, *Agrarian Justice*, which he wrote in the winter of 1795-96. He suggested that everyone should be given a capital of £15 at the age of tewnty-one, "as a compensation in part, for the loss of his or her natural inheritance, by the introduction of a system of landed property." Also, Paine suggested an old age pension of £10 a year for everyone who was fifty or older. See p. 168, n.19 *supra*.

The western world followed the route of annuities rather than capital grants. Annuities were more simple to enact, but ruinously expensive in the long run.

left to earn compound interest until the infant who originally received it reached the age of sixty-five. At 8 per cent, over sixty-five years, the original $1400 would grow to $225,000![6]

At the age of sixty-five, the income from the $225,000 would provide an old age pension. At 7 per cent the pension would be more than $15,000 for each American—far more than Social Security provides today. A husband and wife together would have a non-taxable household income of more than $31,000 a year. Upon their death, the money would return to the Treasury.

Yet the cost to the public would consist only of the initial payment of the original capital sum to each American child. In 1975, approximately three million children were born in the United States. If each child had received a "national inheritance" of $1400, the total annual expense of the plan would have been $4.2 billion—a small fraction of present expenditure for social insurance. In 1974 alone the American government spent roughly $100 billion for that purpose —nearly $60 billion for Social Security alone—and costs were rising at a rate of more than 16 per cent a year. At such a

6 An original investment of $1400 at 8 per cent interest compounded over sixty-five years would increase as follows:

Age	Accumulated wealth
Birth	$ 1400.
5	2200.
10	3200.
15	4700.
20	6900.
25	10,000.
30	15,000.
35	22,000.
40	33,000.
45	48,000.
50	71,000.
55	104,000.
60	153,000.
65	225,000.

speed social insurance expenditures will double in less than five years!

The administrative cost of a "national inheritance" system would also be cheaper than present arrangements. The huge Social Security Administration could be dismantled. No new bureaucracy would be required; the Treasury Department would simply deposit a check for $1400 in a long-term sevings account at a federally insured bank, or issue government securities in a suitable form. No supervision would be necessary beyond the existing machinery for bank inspection. The banks themselves could be required to meet the minimal administrative requirements of the system—which would be no greater than that for any other savings account. The returns to the banks could be very great. Certainly, the old age of bankers would be most plentifully provided for. But rates and payments could be fixed at levels sufficient to guard against excess profits—enough to allow banks a fair return for their services, but nothing more.

The effect of this new plan upon the entire society would be as salutary as its effect upon the individual. The capital stock of the nation would be enormously invigorated—and a growing economic problem resolved. The national economy faces the prospect of a serious shortage of capital—a "capital gap," which is not entirely a fiction invented by the banking industry. A capital gap would make it difficult for new factories, houses, schools, and hospitals to be constructed. Many major reforms, such as urban renewal and environmental improvement, require heavy capital investment. But in America today capital is becoming scarce. The national inheritance plan would provide a powerful remedy.

Inflation, of course, could destroy the plan. But if it were set up properly, the plan could destroy inflation. The "national inheritance" system would itself serve as a more

powerful weapon against inflation than any economic instrument we presently command. Inflation today has many
causes—increased demand, administered prices, the growth
of oligopoly. But probably most powerful are the repeated
deficits which American government has run in the past
forty years, and the debt it has accumulated. In the single
month of October 1975 alone, the Treasury Department
reported an operating deficit of $13 billion.

The national inheritance plan would create something
new in public finance—a major program which was funded
before the money is spent! The effect on prices would be the
opposite of deficit spending. The accumulation of a surplus
in the form of a national inheritance, rather than a deficit
in the form of a national debt, would tend to reduce inflation—possibly even to reverse it.

Moreover, each person's capital would return to the
Treasury, where it could be used to reduce the national
debt, which is now rising out of control. The national inheritance plan could thus become an enormous sinking
fund, such as Alexander Hamilton proposed in 1790, to restore the public credit of the Republic.

There will be many major difficulties in the enactment
of the plan. The first and greatest—so great that many practical social planners will regard it as laughable—is the fact
that the plan would not take effect for sixty-five years after
its first enactment. We would have to maintain our present
system, or something like it, for a very long time. That will
be extremely expensive for us to do—not so much because
of added cost of the national inheritance plan, which is a
very modest addition to existing expenditures, but rather
because of the weaknesses inherent in our present system
of social insurance. But this is not an argument against the
plan; rather, it is still another indictment of the present
system. We must hope to purchase time (at ruinous ex-

pense) by piecemeal reform, at the same time that we design a more fundamental and lasting solution.

A very long period—nearly a lifetime—would separate the enactment of the national inheritance plan from its first operation as a system of old age insurance. This presents a problem of politics. If the plan would not produce results for sixty-five years, virtually everyone in the electorate would be dead before it begins to work. Its passage would therefore be an altruistic act, of a sort which the history of American politics has taught us not to expect.

The plan will succeed only if the electorate is given a stake in the outcome. That could be done by enlarging it to include other measures—themselves equally important to our society. There is, among many other things, a growing economic problem in the American system of higher education. The demand for college education is increasing at a rapid rate, but the costs are already near or at a level which most American families cannot afford to pay.

The educational problem could be eased by an extension of the national inheritance plan. In addition to the $1400 granted for old age support, another sum of $1400 could be granted under similar restrictions to every newborn child. In twenty years, it would grow to $6900, which might be used to pay part of the cost of college education. That would require another investment of $4 billion a year—a very large sum, but less than the cost of most other proposals for aid to higher education and a small fraction (about 4 per cent) of present educational expenditures in America.

This addition (and others like it) will give at least part of the present generation a motive for supporting the plan, from which otherwise they would have nothing to gain. It would bind their interest to the future of the Republic. But even so, the enactment of the plan would require Americans to tax themselves for the sake of their posterity. Most people who voted on the question would gain from it less than they would be asked to give. If American politics is merely a calculus of private interests, then the plan has small chance of success. To that difficulty is added another —the tendency on the part of many Americans to live entirely in the present, without thought for either the past or the future. The spirit of pragmatism in American thought is, among other things, a way of separating today from yesterday and tomorrow. Americans can no longer allow themselves to remain secure in the comfortable illusion that the future will take care of itself. We must plan for it, work for it, study it as part of the long continuum of events in which we live.

The enactment of the national inheritance plan is highly problematical. Many people will actively oppose it. Doctrinaire capitalists will resist another federal "giveaway," even though it could help to sustain capitalism for many generations. Socialist intellectuals will condemn a form of welfare which is associated with private capital, though it could create an instrument of social welfare more powerful than any collectivist alternative. Labor leaders will see in it a threat to their own pension plans. Social scientists will discover a dozen technical ways of proving that it could not possibly work. Practical politicians will waffle and delay until the existing welfare system collapses upon their heads, and if the plan is enacted they will undertake to destroy its fiscal integrity in every election year.

Those difficulties are compounded by the fact that the plan must be enacted in the form of a Constitutional Amendment—to protect it from future changes which could easily destroy it. In any election year some political leaders will be tempted to remove restrictions on the use of the capital, and thus ruin the integrity of the plan. Obviously, therefore, the plan presents many practical difficulties—but fewer than any other arrangement. The American government is presently committed to an expensive program of social welfare, but it cannot pay the bills. If it continues to operate with heavy deficits, sooner or later the Treasury will be unable to find purchasers for its notes. When that happens, the American government—not New York City or New York State, but the United States of America—will fall into bankruptcy. Many nation-states have done so in the past. Our own government actually came close to bankruptcy in the Revolutionary era, and again in 1860. The government of England approached insolvency in 1639; the government of France was virtually bankrupt in 1787; the government of Russia was nearly so in 1916, as was the government of China in the 1940's. We might profit by their example. Deficit spending was not invented in the twentieth century. It was often tried in the past, and when the experiment was prolonged, the results were always and inevitably the same. We *must* find an alternative to our present system of social welfare. Though the national inheritance plan is difficult, our present arrangements are impossible. Those who scoff at the practicability of the national inheritance plan may be invited to think of a better way.

Economic reform—perhaps the national inheritance plan—is necessary to progress in age relations, but it is not sufficient to produce that effect. Other changes must also be made in our social institutions. We must learn to think of elderly people as individuals, rather than as a homogeneous group. We should seek to enlarge their autonomy and independence. If autonomy means anything, it must refer to the right and power to choose freely for oneself the sort of life one wishes to lead. We must try to enlarge freedom of choice for elderly Americans.

In the United States today, the elderly are often victims of an elaborate system of age prejudice. Racism is in retreat; sexism is everywhere on the defensive. But "ageism" is still growing stronger.[7] Elderly Americans increasingly find themselves discriminated against solely because they are elderly. Age discrimination is most serious today in opportunities for employment. Compulsory retirement now comes to many people at the age of sixty-five, if not sooner. When a worker reaches a fixed age he is forced to retire without regard to his own wishes, and it does not matter whether or not he can still perform the job.

Forced retirement at a fixed age rests upon a fallacy: it assumes that senescence is the same as senility. It begins with the presumption that a person's ability may be measured by the number of his years. But that presumption is false. Chronological age is not an accurate measure of competence. We all grow older in different ways, and the range of difference is very great. Moreover, if some forms of intelligence decline with age, others generally increase. In many jobs (except those requiring heavy physical labor), performance improves with age. Workers over sixty, even over seventy, are absent from work less often, have fewer accidents, work more harmoniously with others, are judged by their supervisors to be more dependable, show better judgment, and are generally superior to younger workers both in the quality and the quantity of their output. That has been found by social scientists to be generally the case in both Europe and America.[8]

---

[7] Erdman B. Palmore and Kenneth Manton, "Ageism Compared to Racism and Sexism," *Journal of Gerontology*, 28 (1973), 363-69.

[8] R. L. Peterson, "Effectiveness of Older Workers in a Sample of American Firms"; J. Daric, "Employment of Elderly Workers in France," *Report of the Third Congress of the International Association of Gerontology* (Edinburgh, 1955), Chapters VIII, IX.

There are, of course, many jobs which older people can no longer accomplish. Some jobs require youth as a defining characteristic. Others necessarily require the characteristics of youthfulness—those which call for heavy physical labor or for extraordinarily good physical coordination. But the requirements even for those jobs should be specified in functional terms rather than in a fixed number of years. Each person should be free to work as long as he or she can meet the functional requirements. A judgment of incompetence cannot be made on the basis of chronological age, not without inaccuracy and gross injustice. The range of aptitude and aspiration is as broad for people above the age of sixty-five as it is for those below it. To pass a judgment upon *everyone* of a certain age is wrong—no matter what the age might be.[9]

And forced retirement at a fixed age runs against the interest of society as well as that of the individual. Anyone who has worked in a university knows of many cases in which faculty members were forced out of the classroom at the moment in their careers when they were actually more effective as teachers and scholars than ever before. University presidents have often insisted upon the retirement of a distinguished faculty member against the anguished protests of faculty, students, and alumni, primarily for economic reasons. It saves money to discharge a senior professor earning $35,000 a year and replace him with a young

[9] Jobs involving power and authority (judicial posts, for example) present a special problem. But once again the problem should not be solved by imposing chronological age limits upon officeholders. The eighteenth-century American idea of a "rotation in office" (before it was corrupted by Jacksonians into a partisan device) was surely a constructive and useful idea. It is dangerous for a society to award power without limit. Time limits are particularly important to the maintenance of a free republic. But those limits should take the form of terms of office, for the young as well as the old. The limits should be narrowly defined, and rigorously observed. But they should be tenure limits, not age limits.

instructor who is paid $15,000. However, the results are very damaging not merely for the individual, but for the community as well.

It has been argued in defense of mandatory retirement that the economy cannot survive without it, that massive unemployment of younger workers would result if older workers were allowed to hold their jobs as long as they wished. That is simply not so. It is increasingly the case today that many Americans are retiring earlier than they have to. A majority of Americans dislike their jobs—and stop working as soon as possible. Retirement is for many people a release from the misery of unremitting toil, from the tedium of the task system, from the slavery of fixed routine for forty years, from the tyranny of clock and calendar. Retirement, for most workers, is liberation.

But for others the right to work is central to life itself. Those people are probably a minority today, but for them retirement is not liberation, but confinement. It is a source of agony, degradation, pain, and despair, and it is often inflicted upon them not because they are unable to do their work, but because they have suddenly reached their sixty-fifth birthday and are forced to stop working.

Of course, a fixed retirement age is an administrative convenience in many ways. Some argue that it brings an equity of sorts to employment. If everyone retires at a certain age, then there are no difficult distinctions to be drawn. But imagine another kind of equity—one in which anyone is free to work as long as he wishes, unless incompetence, incapacity, or senility can be demonstrated. The burden of proof would not rest upon an individual, but rather upon his employer.

Age prejudice is, in its nature, no different from prejudice of any other kind. A person is judged not on the basis of his individual merit, but on the basis of the age group to which he happens to belong. If it is unfair to take away the right to work because of a person's color, creed, or gender, then surely it is also wrong to deny it on the ground of age alone. It might be argued that age discrimination is different from race or sex or religious discrimination, in that it applies to everyone. But it does not apply to everyone equally. For some people, age discrimination in employment is far more severe than it is for others. It makes no difference in the lives of people who do not *have* to be employed. In that way it is like Voltaire's comment that equality before the law means that the rich and poor are equally forbidden to sleep under a bridge at night. And just as some people must work more than others for economic reasons, so also must they do so for other compulsions as well. A free society must recognize the individuality of its members; it must respect their differences as well as their similarities. It must attempt to enlarge their autonomy by promoting freedom of choice—freedom to choose work or retirement.

There is already a law in the United States called the "Age Discrimination in Employment Act," which forbids prejudice on the ground of age in hiring and firing. But the provisions of the Act are limited to workers under sixty-five! Thus the people most in need of such a statute are denied its protection.[10] The principle which that law recognizes should be enlarged to protect *all* Americans.

Freedom of choice for the elderly should be also extended in other areas as well as employment. We should attempt to increase the freedom of elderly Americans to

[10] That is an old theme in American social welfare. Abraham Lincoln's Emancipation Proclamation was largely limited to slaves over whom Lincoln had no control, slaves in areas under Confederate rule. It did not apply to most of the slaves who might have actually benefitted by it. So also Social Security was originally passed in a form which omitted those elderly Americans who most desperately needed it. But once the principle was enacted, it slowly expanded.

choose their places of residence. Many Americans prefer to live in the house they purchased when they were young. Others would rather live elsewhere, in "retirement communities," inhabited exclusively by the elderly. Many surveys on the subject show, surprisingly, that most Americans over sixty-five prefer to live in retirement communities, despite the common opinion of social scientists that such environments are "unnatural" and, in some sense, wrong. But other elderly Americans prefer to remain where they have always lived. A variety of pressures makes any free decision in this matter very difficult. The rise in real estate taxes is increasingly forcing elderly Americans to move away from the home which they struggled and saved for many years to acquire. Once away from it, too often they become dependent upon public support greater than the taxes which they are no longer able to pay. In 1975, Congress extended the "Older Americans Act" of 1965, in an effort to assist the elderly to maintain independent lives in their own homes by helping with housing, food, and transportation. That was a move in the right direction, but it is too slow. Local governments, perhaps with federal assistance, should liberalize their tax laws for elderly citizens. The loss of tax revenue would be balanced in a large degree by savings in welfare costs.

As people grow old, their range of choices tends to grow more narrow. All of us must live with the consequences of the choices we made when we were young, and we must also learn to live within the physiological limits of old age itself. But at the same time, there are social and cultural limits upon the aged which can be removed. They exist only because we have put them there. In every area of life, we must learn to think of the elderly as autonomous individuals. Again, gerontologists have demonstrated that we have a strong tendency to think of the elderly in terms of stereotypes. We too often imagine that all old people are the same. And when that happens, America becomes for the aged not an open society, but a closed one. We must abandon that habit of thought which encourages the growth of fixed and rigid social policy for older Americans. We must work, in employment, in housing, in association, in other areas, to enlarge freedom of choice for the elderly. The promotion of individual autonomy in all its many meanings—security, welfare, integrity, independence, privacy—should be the major object of social policy in an open society.

Finally, there is a third change which must be made—not economic, or social, but cultural in its nature. It is a question of ethics—of our deepest social values. Nothing is more stubbornly resistant to purposeful reform than an ethical system. Values and attitudes may seem to be impermanent in their very nature, but they are extremely difficult to change. Physical structures may be rebuilt and institutional structures may be reformed, but values may be revised only with the greatest difficulty. Nevertheless, a powerful change is already under way in American ethics. It is a salutary change, and we should try to help it along. During the past century American society has been dominated by what is commonly called the "work ethic." It is an idea which makes work the major business of life and productivity its major end. It is an activist ethic—an ethic of doing rather than being, of action rather than existence.

In America, the work ethic has played a role of great and vital importance. It was indispensable to the growth of the economy, and important also to maintenance of the stability of our society. The work ethic, Max Weber taught us, was important primarily as a form of discipline in a system which rested upon "the rational organization of formally free labor." A society without external restraints required a strong inner discipline, and that is what the work ethic provided.

Today, the work ethic is still widely defended and deeply believed. For many people it is a good and healthy discipline—a useful and happy way of organizing their lives. It probably remains meaningful for more Americans today than any single ethical alternative. But today it is no longer necessary, as it was in the past, to secure both growth and stability in American society. In fact, it might be argued that in a nation which has the power to produce more than it consumes, in a society which is constantly plagued by problems of excess production, in an economy which is beginning to run up against its environmental limits, the work ethic becomes a source of weakness rather than strength. Any ethic which drives people endlessly to produce more goods and more services, to increase productivity, is increasingly dysfunctional to the maintenance of social cohesion in an America which has begun to face the problem of "overgrowth," as it is called.

The work ethic will always remain important in the lives of individual Americans, but as a way of organizing American society itself, its time has surely passed. There are many other life ethics in the world. In a free society, a person should be able to choose from a broad variety of ethical beliefs. Cultural pluralism requires a plurality of ethical structures which might coexist in an open system.

There are, of course, some ethics for which our society can have no place. A civilized society cannot tolerate the warrior ethic, which holds that fighting is the highest form of human action and military courage is its highest virtue. Many societies and social classes in the past have lived by that ideal. It still retains its power in parts of America, but is rapidly in retreat today. In the same way, the fascist ethic cannot exist within a free society. We can have no room for totalitarian beliefs which regard individual human beings as the interchangeable parts of a great machine of state. In its classical form fascism is nearly gone from the western world, but in a more general sense it has always existed, still exists, and must be opposed.

The ethics of aristocracy are also incompatible with an egalitarian society: elitism in its classical form is dangerous to the great organizing ideas of our culture. And the tribal ethic is also inconsistent with the third great revolutionary ideal—that of fraternity among people. If peace, freedom, equality, and brotherhood are to flourish in the world, the ethics of militarism, fascism, elitism, and tribalism cannot be tolerated. But other ethics can and must be encouraged to coexist. The ethic of productivity is not the only sort of work ethic people have lived by. There is an ethic of creativity, which stresses not the productivity of labor, but rather its craftsmanship. A carpenter or mason or even an automobile assembly crew could live and work according to an ethic of creativity, seeking primarily to produce a product which is beautiful and good.

There are other ethical structures which are not work ethics at all. They are ethics of being, not doing. We can imagine a life organized around an ethic of experience, or an ethic of perception, or an ethic of participation, or an ethic of feeling, or an ethic of sharing, or an ethic of enduring, or an ethic of simply surviving. Our world should have room for ethical beliefs of those sorts too. A society which rests only upon an ethic of productivity is one in which the "best" people are those in the prime of their productive powers. This means that people in the middle years of life will have a moral advantage over the very young and the very old.

Here is a project for American humanists. We might attempt to study in an empirical way the immense ethical variety of life—to understand the astonishing range of ethics which actually exist in the world. We might learn from that study that the ethical possibilities of life are broader than any social scientist has known, deeper than any philosopher has guessed, stronger than any psychologist has suspected. And when that lesson is learned it might be taught to Americans, so that people of every age and generation could live together in a common spirit of respect for their mutual differences. It is only on that basis that a just and free and open society can be built.

APPENDIX

Table I

The Changing Age Composition of the American Population: Elderly Americans as a Proportion of Total Population

| | | | % Pop. Aged at Least | | | | | |
Place	Year	Pop.	45	50	55	60	65	70
Virginia	1625			1.1				
Bedford & New Rochelle, N.Y.	1698	tp	14.8	12.2	8.3	5.7	1.8	0.8
New York	1746	wm				5.2		
	1749	wm				4.8		
	1756	wm				6.4		
	1771	wm				5.6		
	1786	wm				4.2		
New Hampshire	1767	tm				4.4		
	1773	tm				4.2		
	1774	tm				4.2		
	1775	tm		8.4				
Concord, Mass.	1771	tm		16.3		8.4		1.3-2.4
Connecticut	1774	wp						2.2
New Haven, Conn.	1774	tp						2.1
	1787	tp	11.8	10.6	7.1	5.2	2.0	0.8
Maryland	1776	wm	13.3	10.3	6.5	4.4	2.2	1.6
		wf	12.2	8.4	5.2	3.4	1.9	1.0
		bm	10.2	7.7	4.1	1.7	1.5	1.0
		bf	9.3	7.2	3.5	3.3	1.6	1.1
		tp	11.6	8.6	5.0	3.5	1.8	1.2
United States	1790	wm	11.9					
	1800	wm	11.9					
	1810	wp	12.2					
	1820	wp	12.4					
	1830	wp		8.3		4.0		1.5
	1840	wp		8.3		3.9		1.5
	1850	wp		9.2		4.3		1.5
	1860	wp						
	1870	tp	14.9	10.8	7.3	5.0	3.0	
	1880	tp	16.0				3.4	
	1890	tp	17.3	12.9	9.2		4.2	
	1900	tp	18.1	13.6	9.7	6.8	4.4	
	1910	tp	19.1	14.2	10.0	7.0	4.5	
	1920	tp	21.0	15.5	11.0	7.6	4.8	
	1930	tp	23.1	17.4	12.5	8.7	5.6	
	1940	tp	26.8	20.3	14.8	10.4	6.8	
	1950	tp	28.5	22.5	17.0	12.2	8.2	
	1960	tp	29.4	23.3	17.9	13.2	9.2	
	1970	tp	30.5	24.5	19.0	14.1	9.9	
	1974	tp	30.7		19.5		10.3	

Abbreviations:
t = total   m = male   f = female   p = population   w = white   b = black

Table II

The Changing Age Composition of the American Population
Median Age, 1710-1790

Colony	Pop.	Year	% Under 16	Median Age
New Hampshire	tm	1767	49.2	16.3
		1773	49.9	16.0
		1774	49.9	16.0
		1775	50.9	15.6
Massachusetts	tp	1764	47.9	16.8
Rhode Island	wp	1755	49.4	16.2
		1774	46.0	17.6
New York	tp	1712	49.1	16.3
		1723	48.1	16.8
		1746	49.1	16.3
		1749	47.9	16.8
		1756	47.6	17.0
		1771	46.2	17.5
New Jersey	wp	1726	48.6	16.6
		1737	47.6	17.0
West Jersey	wp	1745	49.3	16.3
		1772	49.3	16.3
Maryland	wp	1704	40.2	n.a.
		1708	37.8	n.a.
		1710	44.3	n.a.
		1712	46.7	17.3
		1755	49.3	16.3

Note: For years before 1790, median age was calculated analogically from census data which report the proportion of the population under 16. The bases of the calculations were detailed age distributions in the Maryland census of 1776 and the New Haven census of 1787.

Sources: See Table I.

Sources: U.S., 1790-1970: census data, 1974, *Statistical Abstract of the U.S., 1976*, p. 6; New Haven, 1787: Timothy Dwight; New York, 1746-1786: Greene and Harrington, *American Population before the Federal Census of 1790* (New York, 1932), pp. 95-104; New Hampshire: Robert V. Wells, *The Population of the British Colonies in North America before 1776* (Princeton, 1975), pp. 72-73; Bedford & New Rochelle, 1698: ibid., pp. 92, 116-17; Concord, Mass.: unpublished family reconstitution data, kindness of Robert Gross and the Brandeis Concord Group; Maryland, 1776: Brumbaugh, *Maryland Records* I, 1-89; Connecticut, 1787: Dwight; Virginia, 1625: Robert V. Wells, *The Population of the British Colonies in North America before 1776* (Princeton, 1975), p. 163.

APPENDIX

Table III

The Changing Age Composition of the American Population
Median Age, 1790-1974

		Total			White			Non-white	
	Male	Female	Total	Male	Female	Total	Male	Female	Total
U.S. 1790				15.9					
1800				15.7	16.3	16.0			
1810				15.9	16.1	16.0			
1820	16.6	16.7	16.7	16.5	16.6	16.5	16.9	17.4	17.2
1830	17.1	17.3	17.2	17.2	17.3	17.2	16.7	17.1	16.9
1840	17.8	17.7	17.8	17.9	17.8	17.9	17.0	17.5	17.3
1850	19.2	18.6	18.9	19.5	18.8	19.2	17.3	17.4	17.4
1860	19.8	19.1	19.4	20.2	19.3	19.7	17.5	17.5	17.5
1870	20.2	20.1	20.2	20.6	20.3	20.4	18.2	18.9	18.5
1880	21.2	20.7	20.9	21.6	21.1	21.4	17.9	18.0	18.0
1890	22.3	21.6	22.0	22.9	22.1	22.5	18.5	18.3	18.4
1900	23.3	22.4	22.9	23.8	22.9	23.4	20.0	19.5	19.7
1910	24.6	23.5	24.1	24.9	23.9	24.5	21.5	20.6	21.1
1920	25.8	24.7	25.3	26.1	25.1	25.6	23.1	21.9	22.4
1930	26.7	26.2	26.5	27.1	26.6	26.9	23.9	23.1	23.5
1940	29.1	29.0	29.0	29.5	29.5	29.5	25.4	25.1	25.2
1950	29.9	30.5	30.2	30.4	31.1	30.8	25.9	26.2	26.1
1960	28.7	30.3	29.5	29.4	31.1	30.3	22.7	24.3	23.5
1970	26.8	29.3	28.1	27.6	30.2	28.9	21.5	23.8	22.7
1974			28.7			29.5			23.2

Sources: Historical Statistics of the United States, Series A 86-94; Statistical Abstract of the U.S., Chart 26, p. 26.

Table IV

Length of Life in America, 1652-1960
Survival from Age Twenty to Old Age

Place	Year	Pop.	% Surviving from Age 20 to Age				
			50	55	60	65	70
Charles Co., Md.	1652-1699	wm	39.9		20.3		6.6
Somerset Co., Md.	1650-1711	wm	45.6		28.1		7.6
Philadelphia, Pa.	1768-1790	tp	38.3		24.5		11.2
Salem, Mass.	1782-1790	tp	35.9		27.4		20.0
Surrey Co., Va.	1650-1680	wm	52.5		29.8		13.8
Middlesex Co., Mass.	1661-1675	tm	74.2		54.9		34.6
American colonies	1650-1700		58.5		39.5		20.8
United States	1840	wm	73.0		59.6	50.0	38.8
	1850	wm	73.5		59.4	50.2	39.9
	1860	wm	73.6		60.5	52.3	41.2
	1870	wm	75.7		63.6	54.5	43.1
	1880	wm	78.8		66.1	56.8	45.8
	1890	wm	81.1		60.8	59.8	48.4
	1900	wm	85.5		73.7	64.3	53.5
	1910	wm	88.4		77.6	69.3	59.5
	1920	wm	89.5		80.7	73.9	65.4
	1930	wm	92.7		85.3	79.7	71.5
	1940	wm	94.3		87.8	82.4	74.9
	1950	wm	95.0		89.1	84.8	78.6
	1960	wm	95.4		90.0	86.9	82.5

Note: Demographic historians are beginning to agree on mortality rates and survivorship in the southern colonies, but the pattern is still doubtful for New England. The first generation of family reconstitution projects for New England towns obtained results different from those in this table. Studies of mortality in Plymouth by John Demos and Ipswich by Susan Norton reached conclusions which might be compared with our data (Shuchman); with U.S. whites, 1959-61; and early Europe:

Age	Proportion of Population Surviving to Exact Ages from Age 21				
	Ipswich (Norton) 17c	Plymouth (Demos) 17c	Middlesex Co. (Shuchman) 17c	United States (Keyfitz) 1959-61	Sweden (Keyfitz) 1778-82
20/21	1000	1000	1000	1000	1000
40	900	948	862	954	821
60	687	768	549	775	557
70	525	688	346	688	320

Demos's results indicate a pattern of survivorship after age 20 which was nearly as high in Plymouth during the 17th century as in the United States during the late 20th. Further, he argued that infant mortality was roughly 100 per thousand—a level not attained in modern America until the 1920's. Miss Norton obtained roughly the same result. The inherent implausibility of those estimates should lead us to examine carefully the method by which they were obtained. Both Mr. Demos and Miss Norton worked from genealogies and vital records in which deaths were heavily under-registered. Neither attempted to assess the magnitude of error in their sources. More important, neither had any way of estimating accurately the size of the population at risk—the critical denominator of any mortality calculation.

A better method was used by Carol Shuchman, "Examining Life Expectancies in Seventeenth Century Massachusetts," (unpubl., Brandeis, 1976). Miss Shuchman, following the work of Russell Menard and Lorena Walsh, calculated mortality rates and survivorship on the basis of the ages of men reported in legal deposition given in the court of Middlesex County, Mass. She established the age at death wherever possible (and was able to find the deaths of 80% of deponents). Then she calculated the population at risk by assuming that deponents were present in her statistical universe only from the year in which they gave their depositions to the year of their death. Her sources for death dates were the same as those of family reconstitution studies. But by carefully controlling the population at risk, she obtained different results. Still, even by her measure, mortality rates were low in 17th-century New England, and survivorship was high—higher than Europe and much higher than the southern colonies, but substantially lower than 19th- and 20th-century America.

Miss Shuchman's results may themselves be erroneous in several ways. First, 20% of death rates are missing. Second, one may doubt whether her deponents were representative of the general population. Third, there is the question of accuracy in reported ages at deposition and death. She was unable to make estimates for women, few of whom made depositions. It is known that life expectancy for New England women was lower than for men in the 17th century. The restriction of her study to men therefore biases her survivorship estimates upward. Errors in age reporting, however, biased her results downward, for people reported themselves to be older than they actually were. But the magnitude of this error is less than 0.3%. The direction of error from missing deaths is indeterminate; probably deaths at a great age were more likely to be noticed, which would bias results upward. Also it is probable that deponents tended to have a social status that was higher than average, which would also bias the results upward. In short, Miss Shuchman's results may be understood as a lower bound. Mortality was at least as high as her estimates tell us, and probably higher. If so, the results which were obtained from the first-generation family reconstitution studies for New England are certainly too low.

Sources: Statistics for Sweden (1778-1782) and the United States (1959-61) are calculated from data in Nathan Keyfitz and William Flieger, *World Population* (Chicago, 1968). The Ipswich and Plymouth data are from John Demos, *A Little Commonwealth* (New York, 1970), and Susan L. Norton, "Population Growth in Colonial America: A Study of Ipswich, Mass.," *Population Studies*, 25 (1971), 441. Other sources are listed in Table V.

Table V

Length of Life in America, 1652-1960
Survival from Birth to Old Age

Place	Year	% Surviving from Birth to Age		
		60	65	70
Charles Co., Md.	1652-1699	11.1		3.6
Somerset Co., Md.	1650-1711	15.2		4.1
American Colonies	1650-1700	33.8	23.1	12.3
Middlesex Co., Mass.	1661-1675	44.5	32.9	20.8
Philadelphia, Pa.	1770-1790	11.4-14.0		5.2-6.2
Salem, Mass.	1782-1790	12.9-17.8		9.4-12.6
Massachusetts	1830	37.5	32.0	n.a.
United States	1840	36.4	30.7	23.8
	1850	39.2	33.1	26.3
	1860	42.3	36.6	38.8
	1870	43.2	37.0	29.2
	1880	46.3	39.3	32.1
	1890	49.2	42.8	24.6
	1900	56.5	49.3	41.0
	1910	62.8	56.1	48.2
	1920	70.0	64.1	56.7
	1930	76.9	71.9	64.5
	1940	81.6	76.6	69.6
	1950	85.0	80.1	75.0
	1960	86.6	83.6	79.3

Note: Dates refer to birth cohorts except for Philadelphia, Salem and Middlesex Co. Sources are as follows: Charles County from Allan Kulikoff, "Tobacco and Slaves," unpubl. dissertation, Brandeis University, 1975. Somerset County from Russell R. Menard, "The Demography of Somerset County, Maryland," unpubl. paper presented at Stony Brook Conference on Social History, June 1975. Middlesex County, Mass., from Carol Shuchman, "Examining Life Expectancies in Seventeenth Century Massachusetts," unpubl. paper, Brandeis University, 1976. U.S., 1840-1960, from Paul H. Jacobsen, "Cohort Survival for Generations since 1840," *Milbank Memorial Quarterly,* 42 (1964), 44-45. Philadelphia and Salem from Barton, *op. cit.*

Table VI

The Demographic Life Cycle in America, 1650-1950

Men

Mean Age at:	1650	1700	1750	1800	1850	1890	1950
First marriage	24	25	26	25	26	26	23
Last birth	42	42	43	42	37	37	29
Last child comes of age	63	63	64	63	58	57	50
Last child marries	65	64	66	67	61	59	50
Death	52	52	c.52	c.56	62	66	77

Women

	1650	1700	1750	1800	1850	1890	1950
Menarche	n.a.	n.a.	n.a.	15.2	14.6	14.2	12.8
First marriage	20	21	23	22	24	23	20
Last birth	38	38	39	39	35	32	26
Last child comes of age	59	59	60	60	56	53	47
Last child marries	60	61	63	64	59	56	48
Death	c.50	c.50	c.50	c.56	61	71	81

Note: These data refer not to age cohorts, but to a cross-section of the entire population at a given moment. It represents the mean age at which each stage in the life cycle is reached at a single point in time. The result is a demographic fiction of the same sort as a total fertility rate or a standard life table, which describes everyone's average experience according to rates prevailing in a single year, rather than experience through an actual life span. But the estimates are probably very close to the actual experiences of marriage cohorts, centered on the indicated years. The reader should be warned that this is the first attempt to describe the life cycle throughout the full span of American history, from limited data. The result is only a rough approximation.

Sources: Age at first marriage from 1850 to 1950 is from Patrick Festy, "Canada, United States, Australia and New Zealand: Nuptiality Trends," *Population Studies,* 27 (1973), 479-92. Marriage age before 1850 is an arithmetical mean of Kulikoff's Maryland marriages and Daniel Scott Smith's Massachusetts marriages. Age at last birth is drawn from Paul Glick, "The Life Cycle of the Family," *Marriage and Family Living,* XVII (1953), 4, and from data in Smith and Kulikoff. The age of parents at the coming of age of their last child is the date of last birth plus or minus a correction for childhood mortality drawn from data in Shuchman, Walsh, and Menard. The marriage date of the last child is drawn from Glick, p. 4, for 1890 and 1950. Estimates before 1890 are the sum of age at last birth plus age at first marriage minus a mortality correction. Age at death is from NIH standard mortality tables, Jacobsen, Walsh and Menard, Kulikoff, and Smith. Values before 1800 are the mean of Maryland and Massachusetts estimates in these works—a procedure identical to that used by Jacobsen in 1850. It is assumed that sex specific mortality was proportionately equal in Maryland and Massachusetts. Mortality in 1750 was assumed to be the same as 1700. 1800 is a linear interpolation between 1750 and 1850. In fact, mortality rates were falling in the southern colonies and rising in New England during the early 18th century. Menarche 1850-1950 is from Tanner's work; 1800 is from estimates in midwifery manuals, American Antiquarian Society.

Table VII

The Economic Life Cycle in America, 1680-1959
Mean Wealth-holding by Age in Current Dollars
(Age 50-59 = 100)

Age Group	Hingham Taxables 1680	Hingham Artisans 1749	Hingham Farmers 1749	American Males 1850	American Males 1870	American Males 1963
20-29	22	23	54	13	20	19
30-39	44	46	52	43	55	49
40-49	84	84	56	84	91	69
50-59	100	100	100	100	100	100
60-69	91	102	72	116	112	93
70-up	76	128	70	125	125	

Note: Periodization for 1963 data is 20-34, 35-44, 45-54, 55-64, 65-up. Hingham data refers to wealth-holders only; U.S. data refers to all males. Sources include Daniel Scott Smith, "Old Age and the 'Great Transformation': A New England Case Study," unpubl. paper, 1976; Lee Soltow, *Men and Wealth in the United States, 1850-1870* (New Haven, 1975), pp. 70, 85; and *Statistical Abstract of the United States, 1962*, p. 342.

ACKNOWLEDGMENTS

This book began in 1975 as the Bland-Lee Lectures at Clark University—an occasion my wife and I will long remember. As we made ready to drive west to Worcester, a blizzard struck New England, and an easy trip of twenty miles became an arctic adventure on the Boston Post Road. We arrived late in the afternoon, expecting to find an empty room and a cancellation notice chalked up on the blackboard. But to our astonishment, we were welcomed with a warmth that was more than equal to the cold of that February day. It is a pleasure to acknowledge the hospitality of both the faculty and students of Clark University, and the kindness of our host, George Billias.

Professor Billias also read and criticized an early draft of the book, as did Andrew Achenbaum, Linda Auwers, Thomas Cole, John Demos, Robert Gross, Tamara Hareven, Peter Laslett, and Daniel Scott Smith, all of whom generously shared their own research with me. I am grateful for their help. Bertram Wyatt-Brown and David Van Tassell invited me to attend a seminal conference on "human values and aging" at Case-Western Reserve University in October 1975, and Prof. Van Tassell allowed me to draw freely upon much unpublished material from the conference. I have also had the benefit of criticism from the Brandeis and Boston University Colloquia, and from sessions at Temple University, the University of Calgary, and the University of Edinburgh, where portions of the work were presented during the past academic year.

Many scholars helped in other ways. Rudolph Binion, Herbert Moller, and Nancy Roelker all offered constructive criticism from the perspective of European social history. John Schrecker helped me to find materials on aging in Asian history; Ramsay Macmullen answered my questions about old age in the ancient world; Robert Binstock introduced me to the literature of social gerontology; and Robert Kohn helped with a problem about the physiology of aging. Erik Erikson gave advice on the life cycle; Peter Swiggart and Leslie Fiedler offered suggestions about old age in modern America; and Maris Vinovskis, Alan Heppel, and Morton Keller helped me deal with the history of old age in modern America.

Among my students, Helena Wall, Lewis Kachur, and Yosef Riemer helped with the research, Scott Richards and Amy Lerner typed the manuscript, John Mahoney did the xeroxing, and Jeff Adler did the photography. Many librarians and curators have contributed in major ways—especially Mary Brown and Georgia Baumgartner at the American Antiquarian Society, and Edna Dolber and Mrs. Ivon Mills at the Brandeis Library.

It is a pleasure to be associated with the Oxford University Press, where Sheldon Meyer presided over the publication of the book with his remarkable combination of efficiency and understanding; and Caroline Taylor edited the book with more industry and attention to detail than I have ever received. Brandeis University provided a grant-in-aid which covered the costs of research and typing.

My father, John Henry Fischer, read the manuscript and improved it in many ways. And my brother, Miles Pennington Fischer, studied the book with an historian's understanding and a lawyer's attention to detail. The next generation of Fischers contributed nothing at all, but like to see their names in print: Susan Frederick Fischer, Anne Whitmore Fischer, John Anderson Fischer, and William Pennington Fischer. My largest debt, always, is to Judith.

Wayland, Mass.   D.H.F.
December 1976

INDEX